THIS IS YOUR **PASSBOOK**® FOR ...

SUBSTATION ELECTRICIAN

NATIONAL LEARNING CORPORATION®
passbooks.com

COPYRIGHT NOTICE

Copyright © 2020 by

NLC®

National Learning Corporation

212 Michael Drive, Syosset, NY 11791
(516) 921-8888 • www.passbooks.com
E-mail: info@passbooks.com

PUBLISHED IN THE UNITED STATES OF AMERICA

PASSBOOK® SERIES

THE *PASSBOOK® SERIES* has been created to prepare applicants and candidates for the ultimate academic battlefield – the examination room.

At some time in our lives, each and every one of us may be required to take an examination – for validation, matriculation, admission, qualification, registration, certification, or licensure.

Based on the assumption that every applicant or candidate has met the basic formal educational standards, has taken the required number of courses, and read the necessary texts, the *PASSBOOK® SERIES* furnishes the one special preparation which may assure passing with confidence, instead of failing with insecurity. Examination questions – together with answers – are furnished as the basic vehicle for study so that the mysteries of the examination and its compounding difficulties may be eliminated or diminished by a sure method.

This book is meant to help you pass your examination provided that you qualify and are serious in your objective.

The entire field is reviewed through the huge store of content information which is succinctly presented through a provocative and challenging approach – the question-and-answer method.

A climate of success is established by furnishing the correct answers at the end of each test.

You soon learn to recognize types of questions, forms of questions, and patterns of questioning. You may even begin to anticipate expected outcomes.

You perceive that many questions are repeated or adapted so that you can gain acute insights, which may enable you to score many sure points.

You learn how to confront new questions, or types of questions, and to attack them confidently and work out the correct answers.

You note objectives and emphases, and recognize pitfalls and dangers, so that you may make positive educational adjustments.

Moreover, you are kept fully informed in relation to new concepts, methods, practices, and directions in the field.

You discover that you arre actually taking the examination all the time: you are preparing for the examination by "taking" an examination, not by reading extraneous and/or supererogatory textbooks.

In short, this PASSBOOK®, used directedly, should be an important factor in helping you to pass your test.

SUBSTATION ELECTRICIAN

DUTIES

Substation electricians inspect, test, repair, and maintain both high and medium voltage electrical equipment related to power transmission and distribution, with a specialization of substations. Tasks include: oversight of construction and commissioning new equipment; routine maintenance and testing and analyzing test results; troubleshooting faulty equipment and monitoring the operation of substations. Performs related duties as required.

SCOPE OF THE EXAMINATION

The written test is designed to test for knowledge, skills, and/or abilities in such areas as:
AC theory; DC theory; Ohm's Law; transformers; rectifiers; switchgear; relay logic; basic electrical theory; and other related areas.

HOW TO TAKE A TEST

I. YOU MUST PASS AN EXAMINATION

A. *WHAT EVERY CANDIDATE SHOULD KNOW*

Examination applicants often ask us for help in preparing for the written test. What can I study in advance? What kinds of questions will be asked? How will the test be given? How will the papers be graded?

As an applicant for a civil service examination, you may be wondering about some of these things. Our purpose here is to suggest effective methods of advance study and to describe civil service examinations.

Your chances for success on this examination can be increased if you know how to prepare. Those "pre-examination jitters" can be reduced if you know what to expect. You can even experience an adventure in good citizenship if you know why civil service exams are given.

B. *WHY ARE CIVIL SERVICE EXAMINATIONS GIVEN?*

Civil service examinations are important to you in two ways. As a citizen, you want public jobs filled by employees who know how to do their work. As a job seeker, you want a fair chance to compete for that job on an equal footing with other candidates. The best-known means of accomplishing this two-fold goal is the competitive examination.

Exams are widely publicized throughout the nation. They may be administered for jobs in federal, state, city, municipal, town or village governments or agencies.

Any citizen may apply, with some limitations, such as the age or residence of applicants. Your experience and education may be reviewed to see whether you meet the requirements for the particular examination. When these requirements exist, they are reasonable and applied consistently to all applicants. Thus, a competitive examination may cause you some uneasiness now, but it is your privilege and safeguard.

C. *HOW ARE CIVIL SERVICE EXAMS DEVELOPED?*

Examinations are carefully written by trained technicians who are specialists in the field known as "psychological measurement," in consultation with recognized authorities in the field of work that the test will cover. These experts recommend the subject matter areas or skills to be tested; only those knowledges or skills important to your success on the job are included. The most reliable books and source materials available are used as references. Together, the experts and technicians judge the difficulty level of the questions.

Test technicians know how to phrase questions so that the problem is clearly stated. Their ethics do not permit "trick" or "catch" questions. Questions may have been tried out on sample groups, or subjected to statistical analysis, to determine their usefulness.

Written tests are often used in combination with performance tests, ratings of training and experience, and oral interviews. All of these measures combine to form the best-known means of finding the right person for the right job.

II. HOW TO PASS THE WRITTEN TEST

A. NATURE OF THE EXAMINATION

To prepare intelligently for civil service examinations, you should know how they differ from school examinations you have taken. In school you were assigned certain definite pages to read or subjects to cover. The examination questions were quite detailed and usually emphasized memory. Civil service exams, on the other hand, try to discover your present ability to perform the duties of a position, plus your potentiality to learn these duties. In other words, a civil service exam attempts to predict how successful you will be. Questions cover such a broad area that they cannot be as minute and detailed as school exam questions.

In the public service similar kinds of work, or positions, are grouped together in one "class." This process is known as *position-classification*. All the positions in a class are paid according to the salary range for that class. One class title covers all of these positions, and they are all tested by the same examination.

B. FOUR BASIC STEPS

1) Study the announcement

How, then, can you know what subjects to study? Our best answer is: "Learn as much as possible about the class of positions for which you've applied." The exam will test the knowledge, skills and abilities needed to do the work.

Your most valuable source of information about the position you want is the official exam announcement. This announcement lists the training and experience qualifications. Check these standards and apply only if you come reasonably close to meeting them.

The brief description of the position in the examination announcement offers some clues to the subjects which will be tested. Think about the job itself. Review the duties in your mind. Can you perform them, or are there some in which you are rusty? Fill in the blank spots in your preparation.

Many jurisdictions preview the written test in the exam announcement by including a section called "Knowledge and Abilities Required," "Scope of the Examination," or some similar heading. Here you will find out specifically what fields will be tested.

2) Review your own background

Once you learn in general what the position is all about, and what you need to know to do the work, ask yourself which subjects you already know fairly well and which need improvement. You may wonder whether to concentrate on improving your strong areas or on building some background in your fields of weakness. When the announcement has specified "some knowledge" or "considerable knowledge," or has used adjectives like "beginning principles of..." or "advanced ... methods," you can get a clue as to the number and difficulty of questions to be asked in any given field. More questions, and hence broader coverage, would be included for those subjects which are more important in the work. Now weigh your strengths and weaknesses against the job requirements and prepare accordingly.

3) Determine the level of the position

Another way to tell how intensively you should prepare is to understand the level of the job for which you are applying. Is it the entering level? In other words, is this the position in which beginners in a field of work are hired? Or is it an intermediate or advanced level? Sometimes this is indicated by such words as "Junior" or "Senior" in the class title. Other jurisdictions use Roman numerals to designate the level – Clerk I, Clerk II, for example. The word "Supervisor" sometimes appears in the title. If the level is not indicated by the title, check the description of duties. Will you be working under very close supervision, or will you have responsibility for independent decisions in this work?

4) Choose appropriate study materials

Now that you know the subjects to be examined and the relative amount of each subject to be covered, you can choose suitable study materials. For beginning level jobs, or even advanced ones, if you have a pronounced weakness in some aspect of your training, read a modern, standard textbook in that field. Be sure it is up to date and has general coverage. Such books are normally available at your library, and the librarian will be glad to help you locate one. For entry-level positions, questions of appropriate difficulty are chosen – neither highly advanced questions, nor those too simple. Such questions require careful thought but not advanced training.

If the position for which you are applying is technical or advanced, you will read more advanced, specialized material. If you are already familiar with the basic principles of your field, elementary textbooks would waste your time. Concentrate on advanced textbooks and technical periodicals. Think through the concepts and review difficult problems in your field.

These are all general sources. You can get more ideas on your own initiative, following these leads. For example, training manuals and publications of the government agency which employs workers in your field can be useful, particularly for technical and professional positions. A letter or visit to the government department involved may result in more specific study suggestions, and certainly will provide you with a more definite idea of the exact nature of the position you are seeking.

III. KINDS OF TESTS

Tests are used for purposes other than measuring knowledge and ability to perform specified duties. For some positions, it is equally important to test ability to make adjustments to new situations or to profit from training. In others, basic mental abilities not dependent on information are essential. Questions which test these things may not appear as pertinent to the duties of the position as those which test for knowledge and information. Yet they are often highly important parts of a fair examination. For very general questions, it is almost impossible to help you direct your study efforts. What we can do is to point out some of the more common of these general abilities needed in public service positions and describe some typical questions.

1) General information

Broad, general information has been found useful for predicting job success in some kinds of work. This is tested in a variety of ways, from vocabulary lists to questions about current events. Basic background in some field of work, such as sociology or economics, may be sampled in a group of questions. Often these are principles which have become familiar to most persons through exposure rather than through formal training. It is difficult to advise you how to study for these questions; being alert to the world around you is our best suggestion.

2) Verbal ability

An example of an ability needed in many positions is verbal or language ability. Verbal ability is, in brief, the ability to use and understand words. Vocabulary and grammar tests are typical measures of this ability. Reading comprehension or paragraph interpretation questions are common in many kinds of civil service tests. You are given a paragraph of written material and asked to find its central meaning.

3) Numerical ability

Number skills can be tested by the familiar arithmetic problem, by checking paired lists of numbers to see which are alike and which are different, or by interpreting charts and graphs. In the latter test, a graph may be printed in the test booklet which you are asked to use as the basis for answering questions.

4) Observation

A popular test for law-enforcement positions is the observation test. A picture is shown to you for several minutes, then taken away. Questions about the picture test your ability to observe both details and larger elements.

5) Following directions

In many positions in the public service, the employee must be able to carry out written instructions dependably and accurately. You may be given a chart with several columns, each column listing a variety of information. The questions require you to carry out directions involving the information given in the chart.

6) Skills and aptitudes

Performance tests effectively measure some manual skills and aptitudes. When the skill is one in which you are trained, such as typing or shorthand, you can practice. These tests are often very much like those given in business school or high school courses. For many of the other skills and aptitudes, however, no short-time preparation can be made. Skills and abilities natural to you or that you have developed throughout your lifetime are being tested.

Many of the general questions just described provide all the data needed to answer the questions and ask you to use your reasoning ability to find the answers. Your best preparation for these tests, as well as for tests of facts and ideas, is to be at your physical and mental best. You, no doubt, have your own methods of getting into an exam-taking mood and keeping "in shape." The next section lists some ideas on this subject.

IV. KINDS OF QUESTIONS

Only rarely is the "essay" question, which you answer in narrative form, used in civil service tests. Civil service tests are usually of the short-answer type. Full instructions for answering these questions will be given to you at the examination. But in case this is your first experience with short-answer questions and separate answer sheets, here is what you need to know:

1) Multiple-choice Questions

Most popular of the short-answer questions is the "multiple choice" or "best answer" question. It can be used, for example, to test for factual knowledge, ability to solve problems or judgment in meeting situations found at work.

A multiple-choice question is normally one of three types —

- It can begin with an incomplete statement followed by several possible endings. You are to find the one ending which *best* completes the statement, although some of the others may not be entirely wrong.
- It can also be a complete statement in the form of a question which is answered by choosing one of the statements listed.
- It can be in the form of a problem – again you select the best answer.

Here is an example of a multiple-choice question with a discussion which should give you some clues as to the method for choosing the right answer:

When an employee has a complaint about his assignment, the action which will *best* help him overcome his difficulty is to
- A. discuss his difficulty with his coworkers
- B. take the problem to the head of the organization
- C. take the problem to the person who gave him the assignment
- D. say nothing to anyone about his complaint

In answering this question, you should study each of the choices to find which is best. Consider choice "A" – Certainly an employee may discuss his complaint with fellow employees, but no change or improvement can result, and the complaint remains unresolved. Choice "B" is a poor choice since the head of the organization probably does not know what assignment you have been given, and taking your problem to him is known as "going over the head" of the supervisor. The supervisor, or person who made the assignment, is the person who can clarify it or correct any injustice. Choice "C" is, therefore, correct. To say nothing, as in choice "D," is unwise. Supervisors have and interest in knowing the problems employees are facing, and the employee is seeking a solution to his problem.

2) True/False Questions

The "true/false" or "right/wrong" form of question is sometimes used. Here a complete statement is given. Your job is to decide whether the statement is right or wrong.

SAMPLE: A roaming cell-phone call to a nearby city costs less than a non-roaming call to a distant city.

This statement is wrong, or false, since roaming calls are more expensive.

This is not a complete list of all possible question forms, although most of the others are variations of these common types. You will always get complete directions for answering questions. Be sure you understand *how* to mark your answers – ask questions until you do.

V. RECORDING YOUR ANSWERS

Computer terminals are used more and more today for many different kinds of exams.

For an examination with very few applicants, you may be told to record your answers in the test booklet itself. Separate answer sheets are much more common. If this separate answer sheet is to be scored by machine – and this is often the case – it is highly important that you mark your answers correctly in order to get credit.

An electronic scoring machine is often used in civil service offices because of the speed with which papers can be scored. Machine-scored answer sheets must be marked with a pencil, which will be given to you. This pencil has a high graphite content which responds to the electronic scoring machine. As a matter of fact, stray dots may register as answers, so do not let your pencil rest on the answer sheet while you are pondering the correct answer. Also, if your pencil lead breaks or is otherwise defective, ask for another.

Since the answer sheet will be dropped in a slot in the scoring machine, be careful not to bend the corners or get the paper crumpled.

The answer sheet normally has five vertical columns of numbers, with 30 numbers to a column. These numbers correspond to the question numbers in your test booklet. After each number, going across the page are four or five pairs of dotted lines. These short dotted lines have small letters or numbers above them. The first two pairs may also have a "T" or "F" above the letters. This indicates that the first two pairs only are to be used if the questions are of the true-false type. If the questions are multiple choice, disregard the "T" and "F" and pay attention only to the small letters or numbers.

Answer your questions in the manner of the sample that follows:

32. The largest city in the United States is
A. Washington, D.C.
B. New York City
C. Chicago
D. Detroit
E. San Francisco

1) Choose the answer you think is best. (New York City is the largest, so "B" is correct.)
2) Find the row of dotted lines numbered the same as the question you are answering. (Find row number 32)
3) Find the pair of dotted lines corresponding to the answer. (Find the pair of lines under the mark "B.")
4) Make a solid black mark between the dotted lines.

VI. BEFORE THE TEST

Common sense will help you find procedures to follow to get ready for an examination. Too many of us, however, overlook these sensible measures. Indeed, nervousness and fatigue have been found to be the most serious reasons why applicants fail to do their best on civil service tests. Here is a list of reminders:

- Begin your preparation early – Don't wait until the last minute to go scurrying around for books and materials or to find out what the position is all about.
- Prepare continuously – An hour a night for a week is better than an all-night cram session. This has been definitely established. What is more, a night a week for a month will return better dividends than crowding your study into a shorter period of time.
- Locate the place of the exam – You have been sent a notice telling you when and where to report for the examination. If the location is in a different town or otherwise unfamiliar to you, it would be well to inquire the best route and learn something about the building.
- Relax the night before the test – Allow your mind to rest. Do not study at all that night. Plan some mild recreation or diversion; then go to bed early and get a good night's sleep.
- Get up early enough to make a leisurely trip to the place for the test – This way unforeseen events, traffic snarls, unfamiliar buildings, etc. will not upset you.
- Dress comfortably – A written test is not a fashion show. You will be known by number and not by name, so wear something comfortable.
- Leave excess paraphernalia at home – Shopping bags and odd bundles will get in your way. You need bring only the items mentioned in the official notice you received; usually everything you need is provided. Do not bring reference books to the exam. They will only confuse those last minutes and be taken away from you when in the test room.
- Arrive somewhat ahead of time – If because of transportation schedules you must get there very early, bring a newspaper or magazine to take your mind off yourself while waiting.
- Locate the examination room – When you have found the proper room, you will be directed to the seat or part of the room where you will sit. Sometimes you are given a sheet of instructions to read while you are waiting. Do not fill out any forms until you are told to do so; just read them and be prepared.
- Relax and prepare to listen to the instructions
- If you have any physical problem that may keep you from doing your best, be sure to tell the test administrator. If you are sick or in poor health, you really cannot do your best on the exam. You can come back and take the test some other time.

VII. AT THE TEST

The day of the test is here and you have the test booklet in your hand. The temptation to get going is very strong. Caution! There is more to success than knowing the right answers. You must know how to identify your papers and understand variations in the type of short-answer question used in this particular examination. Follow these suggestions for maximum results from your efforts:

1) Cooperate with the monitor

The test administrator has a duty to create a situation in which you can be as much at ease as possible. He will give instructions, tell you when to begin, check to see that you are marking your answer sheet correctly, and so on. He is not there to guard you, although he will see that your competitors do not take unfair advantage. He wants to help you do your best.

2) Listen to all instructions

Don't jump the gun! Wait until you understand all directions. In most civil service tests you get more time than you need to answer the questions. So don't be in a hurry. Read each word of instructions until you clearly understand the meaning. Study the examples, listen to all announcements and follow directions. Ask questions if you do not understand what to do.

3) Identify your papers

Civil service exams are usually identified by number only. You will be assigned a number; you must not put your name on your test papers. Be sure to copy your number correctly. Since more than one exam may be given, copy your exact examination title.

4) Plan your time

Unless you are told that a test is a "speed" or "rate of work" test, speed itself is usually not important. Time enough to answer all the questions will be provided, but this does not mean that you have all day. An overall time limit has been set. Divide the total time (in minutes) by the number of questions to determine the approximate time you have for each question.

5) Do not linger over difficult questions

If you come across a difficult question, mark it with a paper clip (useful to have along) and come back to it when you have been through the booklet. One caution if you do this – be sure to skip a number on your answer sheet as well. Check often to be sure that you have not lost your place and that you are marking in the row numbered the same as the question you are answering.

6) Read the questions

Be sure you know what the question asks! Many capable people are unsuccessful because they failed to *read* the questions correctly.

7) Answer all questions

Unless you have been instructed that a penalty will be deducted for incorrect answers, it is better to guess than to omit a question.

8) Speed tests

It is often better NOT to guess on speed tests. It has been found that on timed tests people are tempted to spend the last few seconds before time is called in marking answers at random – without even reading them – in the hope of picking up a few extra points. To discourage this practice, the instructions may warn you that your score will be "corrected" for guessing. That is, a penalty will be applied. The incorrect answers will be deducted from the correct ones, or some other penalty formula will be used.

9) Review your answers

If you finish before time is called, go back to the questions you guessed or omitted to give them further thought. Review other answers if you have time.

10) Return your test materials

If you are ready to leave before others have finished or time is called, take ALL your materials to the monitor and leave quietly. Never take any test material with you. The monitor can discover whose papers are not complete, and taking a test booklet may be grounds for disqualification.

VIII. EXAMINATION TECHNIQUES

1) Read the general instructions carefully. These are usually printed on the first page of the exam booklet. As a rule, these instructions refer to the timing of the examination; the fact that you should not start work until the signal and must stop work at a signal, etc. If there are any *special* instructions, such as a choice of questions to be answered, make sure that you note this instruction carefully.

2) When you are ready to start work on the examination, that is as soon as the signal has been given, read the instructions to each question booklet, underline any key words or phrases, such as *least, best, outline, describe* and the like. In this way you will tend to answer as requested rather than discover on reviewing your paper that you *listed without describing*, that you selected the *worst* choice rather than the *best* choice, etc.

3) If the examination is of the objective or multiple-choice type – that is, each question will also give a series of possible answers: A, B, C or D, and you are called upon to select the best answer and write the letter next to that answer on your answer paper – it is advisable to start answering each question in turn. There may be anywhere from 50 to 100 such questions in the three or four hours allotted and you can see how much time would be taken if you read through all the questions before beginning to answer any. Furthermore, if you come across a question or group of questions which you know would be difficult to answer, it would undoubtedly affect your handling of all the other questions.

4) If the examination is of the essay type and contains but a few questions, it is a moot point as to whether you should read all the questions before starting to answer any one. Of course, if you are given a choice – say five out of seven and the like – then it is essential to read all the questions so you can eliminate the two that are most difficult. If, however, you are asked to answer all the questions, there may be danger in trying to answer the easiest one first because you may find that you will spend too much time on it. The best technique is to answer the first question, then proceed to the second, etc.

5) Time your answers. Before the exam begins, write down the time it started, then add the time allowed for the examination and write down the time it must be completed, then divide the time available somewhat as follows:

- If 3-1/2 hours are allowed, that would be 210 minutes. If you have 80 objective-type questions, that would be an average of 2-1/2 minutes per question. Allow yourself no more than 2 minutes per question, or a total of 160 minutes, which will permit about 50 minutes to review.
- If for the time allotment of 210 minutes there are 7 essay questions to answer, that would average about 30 minutes a question. Give yourself only 25 minutes per question so that you have about 35 minutes to review.

6) The most important instruction is to *read each question* and make sure you know what is wanted. The second most important instruction is to *time yourself properly* so that you answer every question. The third most important instruction is to *answer every question*. Guess if you have to but include something for each question. Remember that you will receive no credit for a blank and will probably receive some credit if you write something in answer to an essay question. If you guess a letter – say "B" for a multiple-choice question – you may have guessed right. If you leave a blank as an answer to a multiple-choice question, the examiners may respect your feelings but it will not add a point to your score. Some exams may penalize you for wrong answers, so in such cases *only*, you may not want to guess unless you have some basis for your answer.

7) Suggestions
   a. Objective-type questions
      1. Examine the question booklet for proper sequence of pages and questions
      2. Read all instructions carefully
      3. Skip any question which seems too difficult; return to it after all other questions have been answered
      4. Apportion your time properly; do not spend too much time on any single question or group of questions
      5. Note and underline key words – *all, most, fewest, least, best, worst, same, opposite,* etc.
      6. Pay particular attention to negatives
      7. Note unusual option, e.g., unduly long, short, complex, different or similar in content to the body of the question
      8. Observe the use of "hedging" words – *probably, may, most likely,* etc.
      9. Make sure that your answer is put next to the same number as the question
      10. Do not second-guess unless you have good reason to believe the second answer is definitely more correct
      11. Cross out original answer if you decide another answer is more accurate; do not erase until you are ready to hand your paper in
      12. Answer all questions; guess unless instructed otherwise
      13. Leave time for review

   b. Essay questions
      1. Read each question carefully
      2. Determine exactly what is wanted. Underline key words or phrases.
      3. Decide on outline or paragraph answer

4. Include many different points and elements unless asked to develop any one or two points or elements
5. Show impartiality by giving pros and cons unless directed to select one side only
6. Make and write down any assumptions you find necessary to answer the questions
7. Watch your English, grammar, punctuation and choice of words
8. Time your answers; don't crowd material

8) Answering the essay question

Most essay questions can be answered by framing the specific response around several key words or ideas. Here are a few such key words or ideas:

M's: manpower, materials, methods, money, management
P's: purpose, program, policy, plan, procedure, practice, problems, pitfalls, personnel, public relations
   a. Six basic steps in handling problems:
      1. Preliminary plan and background development
      2. Collect information, data and facts
      3. Analyze and interpret information, data and facts
      4. Analyze and develop solutions as well as make recommendations
      5. Prepare report and sell recommendations
      6. Install recommendations and follow up effectiveness

   b. Pitfalls to avoid
      1. *Taking things for granted* – A statement of the situation does not necessarily imply that each of the elements is necessarily true; for example, a complaint may be invalid and biased so that all that can be taken for granted is that a complaint has been registered
      2. *Considering only one side of a situation* – Wherever possible, indicate several alternatives and then point out the reasons you selected the best one
      3. *Failing to indicate follow up* – Whenever your answer indicates action on your part, make certain that you will take proper follow-up action to see how successful your recommendations, procedures or actions turn out to be
      4. *Taking too long in answering any single question* – Remember to time your answers properly

IX. AFTER THE TEST

Scoring procedures differ in detail among civil service jurisdictions although the general principles are the same. Whether the papers are hand-scored or graded by machine we have described, they are nearly always graded by number. That is, the person who marks the paper knows only the number – never the name – of the applicant. Not until all the papers have been graded will they be matched with names. If other tests, such as training and experience or oral interview ratings have been given, scores will be combined. Different parts of the examination usually have different weights. For example, the written test might count 60 percent of the final grade, and a rating of training and experience 40 percent. In many jurisdictions, veterans will have a certain number of points added to their grades.

After the final grade has been determined, the names are placed in grade order and an eligible list is established. There are various methods for resolving ties between those who get the same final grade – probably the most common is to place first the name of the person whose application was received first. Job offers are made from the eligible list in the order the names appear on it. You will be notified of your grade and your rank as soon as all these computations have been made. This will be done as rapidly as possible.

People who are found to meet the requirements in the announcement are called "eligibles." Their names are put on a list of eligible candidates. An eligible's chances of getting a job depend on how high he stands on this list and how fast agencies are filling jobs from the list.

When a job is to be filled from a list of eligibles, the agency asks for the names of people on the list of eligibles for that job. When the civil service commission receives this request, it sends to the agency the names of the three people highest on this list. Or, if the job to be filled has specialized requirements, the office sends the agency the names of the top three persons who meet these requirements from the general list.

The appointing officer makes a choice from among the three people whose names were sent to him. If the selected person accepts the appointment, the names of the others are put back on the list to be considered for future openings.

That is the rule in hiring from all kinds of eligible lists, whether they are for typist, carpenter, chemist, or something else. For every vacancy, the appointing officer has his choice of any one of the top three eligibles on the list. This explains why the person whose name is on top of the list sometimes does not get an appointment when some of the persons lower on the list do. If the appointing officer chooses the second or third eligible, the No. 1 eligible does not get a job at once, but stays on the list until he is appointed or the list is terminated.

X. HOW TO PASS THE INTERVIEW TEST

The examination for which you applied requires an oral interview test. You have already taken the written test and you are now being called for the interview test – the final part of the formal examination.

You may think that it is not possible to prepare for an interview test and that there are no procedures to follow during an interview. Our purpose is to point out some things you can do in advance that will help you and some good rules to follow and pitfalls to avoid while you are being interviewed.

What is an interview supposed to test?
The written examination is designed to test the technical knowledge and competence of the candidate; the oral is designed to evaluate intangible qualities, not readily measured otherwise, and to establish a list showing the relative fitness of each candidate – as measured against his competitors – for the position sought. Scoring is not on the basis of "right" and "wrong," but on a sliding scale of values ranging from "not passable" to "outstanding." As a matter of fact, it is possible to achieve a relatively low score without a single "incorrect" answer because of evident weakness in the qualities being measured.

Occasionally, an examination may consist entirely of an oral test – either an individual or a group oral. In such cases, information is sought concerning the technical knowledges and abilities of the candidate, since there has been no written examination for this purpose. More commonly, however, an oral test is used to supplement a written examination.

Who conducts interviews?

The composition of oral boards varies among different jurisdictions. In nearly all, a representative of the personnel department serves as chairman. One of the members of the board may be a representative of the department in which the candidate would work. In some cases, "outside experts" are used, and, frequently, a businessman or some other representative of the general public is asked to serve. Labor and management or other special groups may be represented. The aim is to secure the services of experts in the appropriate field.

However the board is composed, it is a good idea (and not at all improper or unethical) to ascertain in advance of the interview who the members are and what groups they represent. When you are introduced to them, you will have some idea of their backgrounds and interests, and at least you will not stutter and stammer over their names.

What should be done before the interview?

While knowledge about the board members is useful and takes some of the surprise element out of the interview, there is other preparation which is more substantive. It *is* possible to prepare for an oral interview – in several ways:

1) Keep a copy of your application and review it carefully before the interview

This may be the only document before the oral board, and the starting point of the interview. Know what education and experience you have listed there, and the sequence and dates of all of it. Sometimes the board will ask you to review the highlights of your experience for them; you should not have to hem and haw doing it.

2) Study the class specification and the examination announcement

Usually, the oral board has one or both of these to guide them. The qualities, characteristics or knowledges required by the position sought are stated in these documents. They offer valuable clues as to the nature of the oral interview. For example, if the job involves supervisory responsibilities, the announcement will usually indicate that knowledge of modern supervisory methods and the qualifications of the candidate as a supervisor will be tested. If so, you can expect such questions, frequently in the form of a hypothetical situation which you are expected to solve. NEVER go into an oral without knowledge of the duties and responsibilities of the job you seek.

3) Think through each qualification required

Try to visualize the kind of questions you would ask if you were a board member. How well could you answer them? Try especially to appraise your own knowledge and background in each area, *measured against the job sought*, and identify any areas in which you are weak. Be critical and realistic – do not flatter yourself.

4) Do some general reading in areas in which you feel you may be weak

For example, if the job involves supervision and your past experience has NOT, some general reading in supervisory methods and practices, particularly in the field of human relations, might be useful. Do NOT study agency procedures or detailed manuals. The oral board will be testing your understanding and capacity, not your memory.

5) Get a good night's sleep and watch your general health and mental attitude

You will want a clear head at the interview. Take care of a cold or any other minor ailment, and of course, no hangovers.

What should be done on the day of the interview?

Now comes the day of the interview itself. Give yourself plenty of time to get there. Plan to arrive somewhat ahead of the scheduled time, particularly if your appointment is in the fore part of the day. If a previous candidate fails to appear, the board might be ready for you a bit early. By early afternoon an oral board is almost invariably behind schedule if there are many candidates, and you may have to wait. Take along a book or magazine to read, or your application to review, but leave any extraneous material in the waiting room when you go in for your interview. In any event, relax and compose yourself.

The matter of dress is important. The board is forming impressions about you – from your experience, your manners, your attitude, and your appearance. Give your personal appearance careful attention. Dress your best, but not your flashiest. Choose conservative, appropriate clothing, and be sure it is immaculate. This is a business interview, and your appearance should indicate that you regard it as such. Besides, being well groomed and properly dressed will help boost your confidence.

Sooner or later, someone will call your name and escort you into the interview room. *This is it.* From here on you are on your own. It is too late for any more preparation. But remember, you asked for this opportunity to prove your fitness, and you are here because your request was granted.

What happens when you go in?

The usual sequence of events will be as follows: The clerk (who is often the board stenographer) will introduce you to the chairman of the oral board, who will introduce you to the other members of the board. Acknowledge the introductions before you sit down. Do not be surprised if you find a microphone facing you or a stenotypist sitting by. Oral interviews are usually recorded in the event of an appeal or other review.

Usually the chairman of the board will open the interview by reviewing the highlights of your education and work experience from your application – primarily for the benefit of the other members of the board, as well as to get the material into the record. Do not interrupt or comment unless there is an error or significant misinterpretation; if that is the case, do not hesitate. But do not quibble about insignificant matters. Also, he will usually ask you some question about your education, experience or your present job – partly to get you to start talking and to establish the interviewing "rapport." He may start the actual questioning, or turn it over to one of the other members. Frequently, each member undertakes the questioning on a particular area, one in which he is perhaps most competent, so you can expect each member to participate in the examination. Because time is limited, you may also expect some rather abrupt switches in the direction the questioning takes, so do not be upset by it. Normally, a board member will not pursue a single line of questioning unless he discovers a particular strength or weakness.

After each member has participated, the chairman will usually ask whether any member has any further questions, then will ask you if you have anything you wish to add. Unless you are expecting this question, it may floor you. Worse, it may start you off on an extended, extemporaneous speech. The board is not usually seeking more information. The question is principally to offer you a last opportunity to present further qualifications or to indicate that you have nothing to add. So, if you feel that a significant qualification or characteristic has been overlooked, it is proper to point it out in a sentence or so. Do not compliment the board on the thoroughness of their examination – they have been sketchy, and you know it. If you wish, merely say, "No thank you, I have nothing further to add." This is a point where you can "talk yourself out" of a good impression or fail to present an important bit of information. Remember, *you close the interview yourself.*

The chairman will then say, "That is all, Mr. _____, thank you." Do not be startled; the interview is over, and quicker than you think. Thank him, gather your belongings and take your leave. Save your sigh of relief for the other side of the door.

How to put your best foot forward

Throughout this entire process, you may feel that the board individually and collectively is trying to pierce your defenses, seek out your hidden weaknesses and embarrass and confuse you. Actually, this is not true. They are obliged to make an appraisal of your qualifications for the job you are seeking, and they want to see you in your best light. Remember, they must interview all candidates and a non-cooperative candidate may become a failure in spite of their best efforts to bring out his qualifications. Here are 15 suggestions that will help you:

1) Be natural – Keep your attitude confident, not cocky

If you are not confident that you can do the job, do not expect the board to be. Do not apologize for your weaknesses, try to bring out your strong points. The board is interested in a positive, not negative, presentation. Cockiness will antagonize any board member and make him wonder if you are covering up a weakness by a false show of strength.

2) Get comfortable, but don't lounge or sprawl

Sit erectly but not stiffly. A careless posture may lead the board to conclude that you are careless in other things, or at least that you are not impressed by the importance of the occasion. Either conclusion is natural, even if incorrect. Do not fuss with your clothing, a pencil or an ashtray. Your hands may occasionally be useful to emphasize a point; do not let them become a point of distraction.

3) Do not wisecrack or make small talk

This is a serious situation, and your attitude should show that you consider it as such. Further, the time of the board is limited – they do not want to waste it, and neither should you.

4) Do not exaggerate your experience or abilities

In the first place, from information in the application or other interviews and sources, the board may know more about you than you think. Secondly, you probably will not get away with it. An experienced board is rather adept at spotting such a situation, so do not take the chance.

5) If you know a board member, do not make a point of it, yet do not hide it

Certainly you are not fooling him, and probably not the other members of the board. Do not try to take advantage of your acquaintanceship – it will probably do you little good.

6) Do not dominate the interview

Let the board do that. They will give you the clues – do not assume that you have to do all the talking. Realize that the board has a number of questions to ask you, and do not try to take up all the interview time by showing off your extensive knowledge of the answer to the first one.

7) Be attentive

You only have 20 minutes or so, and you should keep your attention at its sharpest throughout. When a member is addressing a problem or question to you, give him your undivided attention. Address your reply principally to him, but do not exclude the other board members.

8) Do not interrupt

A board member may be stating a problem for you to analyze. He will ask you a question when the time comes. Let him state the problem, and wait for the question.

9) Make sure you understand the question

Do not try to answer until you are sure what the question is. If it is not clear, restate it in your own words or ask the board member to clarify it for you. However, do not haggle about minor elements.

10) Reply promptly but not hastily

A common entry on oral board rating sheets is "candidate responded readily," or "candidate hesitated in replies." Respond as promptly and quickly as you can, but do not jump to a hasty, ill-considered answer.

11) Do not be peremptory in your answers

A brief answer is proper – but do not fire your answer back. That is a losing game from your point of view. The board member can probably ask questions much faster than you can answer them.

12) Do not try to create the answer you think the board member wants

He is interested in what kind of mind you have and how it works – not in playing games. Furthermore, he can usually spot this practice and will actually grade you down on it.

13) Do not switch sides in your reply merely to agree with a board member

Frequently, a member will take a contrary position merely to draw you out and to see if you are willing and able to defend your point of view. Do not start a debate, yet do not surrender a good position. If a position is worth taking, it is worth defending.

14) Do not be afraid to admit an error in judgment if you are shown to be wrong

   The board knows that you are forced to reply without any opportunity for careful consideration. Your answer may be demonstrably wrong. If so, admit it and get on with the interview.

15) Do not dwell at length on your present job

   The opening question may relate to your present assignment. Answer the question but do not go into an extended discussion. You are being examined for a *new* job, not your present one. As a matter of fact, try to phrase ALL your answers in terms of the job for which you are being examined.

Basis of Rating

   Probably you will forget most of these "do's" and "don'ts" when you walk into the oral interview room. Even remembering them all will not ensure you a passing grade. Perhaps you did not have the qualifications in the first place. But remembering them will help you to put your best foot forward, without treading on the toes of the board members.

   Rumor and popular opinion to the contrary notwithstanding, an oral board wants you to make the best appearance possible. They know you are under pressure – but they also want to see how you respond to it as a guide to what your reaction would be under the pressures of the job you seek. They will be influenced by the degree of poise you display, the personal traits you show and the manner in which you respond.

ABOUT THIS BOOK

   This book contains tests divided into Examination Sections. Go through each test, answering every question in the margin. At the end of each test look at the answer key and check your answers. On the ones you got wrong, look at the right answer choice and learn. Do not fill in the answers first. Do not memorize the questions and answers, but understand the answer and principles involved. On your test, the questions will likely be different from the samples. Questions are changed and new ones added. If you understand these past questions you should have success with any changes that arise. Tests may consist of several types of questions. We have additional books on each subject should more study be advisable or necessary for you. Finally, the more you study, the better prepared you will be. This book is intended to be the last thing you study before you walk into the examination room. Prior study of relevant texts is also recommended. NLC publishes some of these in our Fundamental Series. Knowledge and good sense are important factors in passing your exam. Good luck also helps. So now study this Passbook, absorb the material contained within and take that knowledge into the examination. Then do your best to pass that exam.

———

EXAMINATION SECTION

EXAMINATION SECTION
TEST 1

DIRECTIONS: Each question or incomplete statement is followed by several suggested answers or completions. Select the one that BEST answers the question or completes the statement. *PRINT THE LETTER OF THE CORRECT ANSWER IN THE SPACE AT THE RIGHT.*

1. Soft iron is MOST suitable for use in a   1._____

    A. permanent magnet   B. natural magnet
    C. temporary magnet   D. magneto

2. Static electricity is MOST often produced by   2._____

    A. pressure   B. magnetism   C. heat   D. friction

3. A fundamental law of electricity is that the current in a circuit is   3._____

    A. inversely proportional to the voltage
    B. equal to the voltage
    C. directly proportional to the resistance
    D. directly proportional to the voltage

4. A substance is classed as a magnet if it has   4._____

    A. the ability to conduct lines of force
    B. the property of high permeability
    C. the property of magnetism
    D. a high percentage of iron in its composition

5. If a compass is placed at the center of a bar magnet, the compass needle   5._____

    A. *points* to the geographic south pole
    B. *points* to the geographic north pole
    C. *alines* itself parallel to the bar
    D. *alines* itself perpendicular to the bar

6. When electricity is produced by heat in an iron-and-copper thermocouple, electrons   6._____
move from

    A. north to south
    B. the hot junction, through the copper, across the cold junction to the iron, and then
        to the hot junction
    C. the hot junction, through the iron, across the cold junction to the copper, and then
        return through the copper to the hot junction
    D. east to west

7. The four factors affecting the resistance of a wire are its   7._____

    A. length, material, diameter, and temperature
    B. size, length, material, and insulation
    C. length, size, relative resistance, and material
    D. size, insulation, relative resistance, and material

8. Electricity in a battery is produced by   8.____

   A. chemical action
   B. chemical reaction
   C. a chemical acting upon metallic plates
   D. all of the above

9. Resistance is ALWAYS measured in   9.____

   A. coulombs   B. henrys   C. ohms   D. megohms

10. The magnetic pole that points northward on a compass   10.____

   A. is called the north pole
   B. is actually a south magnetic pole
   C. points to the north magnetic pole of the earth
   D. indicates the direction of the north geographic pole

11. Of the six methods of producing a voltage, which is the LEAST used?   11.____

   A. Chemical action   B. Heat
   C. Friction   D. Pressure

12. As the temperature of carbon is increased, its resistance will   12.____

   A. increase   B. decrease
   C. remain constant   D. double

13. Around a magnet, the external lines of force   13.____

   A. leave the magnet from the north pole and enter the south pole
   B. often cross one another
   C. leave the magnet from the south pole and enter the north pole
   D. may be broken by a piece of iron shielding

14. When a voltage is applied to a conductor, free electrons   14.____

   A. are forced into the nucleus of their atom
   B. are impelled along the conductor
   C. unite with protons
   D. cease their movement

15. When the molecules of a substance are altered, the action is referred to as   15.____

   A. thermal   B. photoelectric
   C. electrical   D. chemical

16. When matter is separated into individual atoms, it   16.____

   A. has undergone a physical change only
   B. has been reduced to its basic chemicals
   C. retains its original characteristics
   D. has been reduced to its basic elements

17. MOST permanent magnets and all electro-magnets are   17.____

    A. classed as natural magnets
    B. manufactured in various shapes from lodestone
    C. classed as artificial magnets
    D. manufactured in various shapes from magnetite

18. When a conductor moves across a magnetic field,   18.____

    A. a voltage is induced in the conductor
    B. a current is induced in the conductor
    C. both current and voltage are induced in the conductor
    D. neither a voltage nor a current is induced

19. The nucleus of an atom contains   19.____

    A. electrons and neutrons
    B. protons and neutrons
    C. protons and electrons
    D. protons, electrons, and neutrons

20. An alnico artificial magnet is composed of   20.____

    A. magnetite, steel, and nickel
    B. cobalt, nickel, and varnish
    C. aluminum, copper, and cobalt
    D. aluminum, nickel, and cobalt

21. A material that acts as an insulator for magnetic flux is   21.____

    A. glass   B. aluminum
    C. soft iron   D. unknown today

22. The force acting through the distance between two dissimilarly-charged bodies   22.____

    A. is a chemical force
    B. is referred to as a magnetic field
    C. constitutes a flow of ions
    D. is referred to as an electrostatic field

23. An atom that has lost or gained electrons   23.____

    A. is negatively charged   B. has a positive charge
    C. is said to be ionized   D. becomes electrically neutral

24. Which of the following is considered to be the BEST conductor?   24.____

    A. Zinc   B. Copper   C. Aluminum   D. Silver

25. As the temperature increases, the resistance of most conductors also increases.   25.____
    A conductor that is an EXCEPTION to this is

    A. aluminum   B. carbon   C. copper   D. brass

KEY (CORRECT ANSWERS)

1.	C	11.	C
2.	D	12.	B
3.	D	13.	A
4.	C	14.	B
5.	C	15.	D
6.	B	16.	D
7.	A	17.	C
8.	D	18.	A
9.	C	19.	B
10.	A	20.	D

21.	D
22.	D
23.	C
24.	D
25.	B

TEST 2

DIRECTIONS: Each question or incomplete statement is followed by several suggested answers or completions. Select the one that BEST answers the question or completes the statement. *PRINT THE LETTER OF THE CORRECT ANSWER IN THE SPACE AT THE RIGHT.*

1. The dry cell battery is a _____ cell.   1._____

    A. secondary   B. polarized   C. primary   D. voltaic

2. The electrolyte of a lead-acid wet cell is   2._____

    A. sal ammoniac   B. manganese dioxide
    C. sulfuric acid   D. distilled water

3. A battery which can be restored after discharge is a _____ cell.   3._____

    A. primary   B. galvanic   C. dry   D. secondary

4. Lead-acid battery plates are held together by a   4._____

    A. glass wool mat   B. wood separator
    C. grid work   D. hard rubber tube

5. When mixing electrolyte, ALWAYS pour   5._____

    A. water into acid
    B. acid into water
    C. both acid and water into vat simultaneously
    D. first acid, then water into vat

6. When charging a battery, the electrolyte should NEVER exceed a temperature of   6._____

    A. 125° F.   B. 113° F.   C. 80° F.   D. 40° F.

7. The plates of a lead-acid battery are made of   7._____

    A. lead and lead dioxide   B. lead and lead oxide
    C. silver and peroxide   D. lead and lead peroxide

8. A battery is receiving a normal charge. It begins to gas freely.   8._____
    The charging current should

    A. be increased
    B. be decreased
    C. be cut off and the battery allowed to cool
    D. remain the same

9. A hydrometer reading is 1.265 at 92° F.   9._____
    The CORRECTED reading is

    A. 1.229   B. 1.261   C. 1.269   D. 1.301

10. In the nickel-cadmium battery, KOH is   10._____

    A. the positive plate   B. the negative plate
    C. the electrolyte   D. none of the above

11. When sulfuric acid, H_2SO_4, and water, H_2O, are mixed together, they form a   11.____

    A. gas   B. compound
    C. mixture   D. hydrogen solution

12. How many No. 6 dry cells are required to supply power to a load requiring 6 volts if the   12.____
cells are connected in series?

    A. Two   B. Four   C. Five   D. Six

13. The ordinary 6-volt lead-acid storage battery consists of how many cells?   13.____

    A. Two   B. Three   C. Four   D. Six

14. A fully-charged aircraft battery has a specific gravity reading of   14.____

    A. 1.210 to 1.220   B. 1.250 to 1.265
    C. 1.285 to 1.300   D. 1.300 to 1.320

15. What is the ampere-hour rating of a storage battery that can deliver 20 amperes continu-   15.____
ously for 10 hours?
_____ ampere-hour.

    A. 20   B. 40   C. 200   D. 400

16. The normal cell voltage of a fully-charged nickel-cadmium battery is _____ volts.   16.____

    A. 2.0   B. 1.5   C. 1.4   D. 1.0

17. The electrolyte in a mercury cell is   17.____

    A. sulfuric acid
    B. KOH
    C. potassium hydroxide, zincate, and mercury
    D. potassium hydroxide, water, and zincate

18. Concentrated sulfuric acid has a specific gravity of   18.____

    A. 1.285   B. 1.300   C. 1.830   D. 2.400

19. The number of negative plates in a lead-acid cell is ALWAYS _____ of positive plates.   19.____

    A. one greater than the number
    B. equal to the number
    C. one less than the number
    D. double the number

20. A lead-acid battery is considered fully charged when the specific gravity readings of all   20.____
cells taken at half-hour intervals show no change for _____ hour(s).

    A. four   B. three   C. two   D. one

KEY (CORRECT ANSWERS)

1.	C	11.	C
2.	C	12.	B
3.	D	13.	B
4.	C	14.	C
5.	B	15.	C
6.	A	16.	C
7.	D	17.	D
8.	B	18.	C
9.	C	19.	A
10.	C	20.	A

———

TEST 3

DIRECTIONS: Each question or incomplete statement is followed by several suggested answers or completions. Select the one that BEST answers the question or completes the statement. *PRINT THE LETTER OF THE CORRECT ANSWER IN THE SPACE AT THE RIGHT.*

1. In which direction does current flow in an electrical circuit?   1.____

   A. - to + externally, + to - internally
   B. + to - externally, + to - internally
   C. - to + externally, - to + internally
   D. + to - externally, - to + internally

2. Given the formula $P = E^2/R$, solve for E.   2.____

   A. $E = \sqrt{ER}$ B. $E = \sqrt{PR}$ C. $E = IR$ D. $E = \sqrt{P/R}$

3. Resistance in the power formula equals   3.____

   A. $R = \sqrt{I/P}$ B. $R = E/I$ C. $R = \sqrt{P \times 1}$ D. $R = E^2/P$

4. One joule is equal to   4.____

   A. 1 watt second   B. 10 watt seconds
   C. 1 watt minute   D. 10 watt minutes

5. A lamp has a source voltage of 110 v. and a current of 0.9 amps.   5.____
   What is the resistance of the lamp?

   A. 12.22 Ω   B. 122.2 Ω   C. 0.008 Ω   D. 0.08 Ω

6. In accordance with Ohm's law, the relationship between current and voltage in a simple   6.____
   circuit is that the

   A. current varies inversely with the resistance if the voltage is held constant
   B. voltage varies as the square of the applied e.m.f.
   C. current varies directly with the applied voltage if the resistance is held constant
   D. voltage varies inversely as the current if the resistance is held constant

7. The current needed to operate a soldering iron which has a rating of 600 watts at 110   7.____
   volts is

   A. 0.182 a.   B. 5.455 a.   C. 18.200 a.   D. 66.000 a.

8. In electrical circuits, the time rate of doing work is expressed in   8.____

   A. volts   B. amperes   C. watts   D. ohms

9. If the resistance is held constant, what is the relationship between power and voltage in a   9.____
   simple circuit?

   A. Resistance must be varied to show a true relationship.
   B. Power will vary as the square of the applied voltage.
   C. Voltage will vary inversely proportional to power.
   D. Power will vary directly with voltage.

10. How many watts are there in 1 horsepower?

    A. 500   B. 640   C. 746   D. 1,000

10.____

11. What formula is used to find watt-hours?

    A. $E \times T$ B. $E \times I \times T$ C. $E \times I \times \sqrt{\theta}$ D. $E \times I^2$

11.____

12. What is the resistance of the circuit shown at the right?

    A. $4.8\,\Omega$

    B. $12.0\,\Omega$

    C. $48\,\Omega$

    D. $120\,\Omega$

12.____

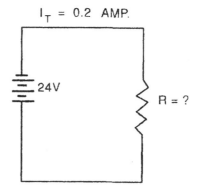

13. In the figure at the right, solve for I_T.

    A. 0.5 a.

    B. 1 a.

    C. 13 a.

    D. 169 a.

13.____

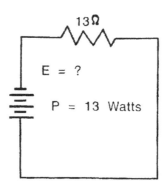

14. A simple circuit consists of one power source,

    A. and one power consuming device

    B. one power consuming device, and connecting wiring

    C. protective device, and control device

    D. one power consuming device, and protective device

14.____

15. The device used in circuits to prevent damage from overloads is called a

    A. fuse   B. switch   C. resistor   D. connector

15.____

16. What happens in a series circuit when the voltage remains constant and the resistance increases?

Current

    A. increases   B. decreases

    C. remains the same   D. increases by the square

16.____

17. Other factors remaining constant, what would be the effect on the current flow in a given circuit if the applied potential were doubled?
It would

    A. double
    C. be divided by two

    B. remain the same
    D. be divided by four

17.____

18. Which of the following procedures can be used to calculate the resistance of a load?

    A. *Multiply* the voltage across the load by the square of the current through the load
    B. *Divide* the current through the load by the voltage across the load
    C. *Multiply* the voltage across the load by the current through the load
    D. *Divide* the voltage across the load by the current through the load

18.____

19. A cockpit light operates from a 24-volt d-c supply and uses 72 watts of power. The current flowing through the bulb is _____ amps.

    A. 0.33   B. 3   C. 600   D. 1,728

19.____

20. If the resistance is held constant, what happens to power if the current is doubled?
Power is

    A. doubled
    C. halved

    B. multiplied by 4
    D. divided by 4

20.____

KEY (CORRECT ANSWERS)

1.	A	11.	B
2.	B	12.	D
3.	D	13.	B
4.	A	14.	B
5.	B	15.	A
6.	C	16.	B
7.	B	17.	A
8.	C	18.	D
9.	B	19.	B
10.	C	20.	B

TEST 4

DIRECTIONS: Each question or incomplete statement is followed by several suggested answers or completions. Select the one that BEST answers the question or completes the statement. *PRINT THE LETTER OF THE CORRECT ANSWER IN THE SPACE AT THE RIGHT.*

1. If a circuit is constructed so as to allow the electrons to follow only one possible path, the circuit is called a(n) _____ circuit.   1._____

    A. series-parallel   B. incomplete
    C. series   D. parallel

2. According to Kirchhoff's Law of Voltages, the algebraic sum of all the voltages in a series circuit is equal to   2._____

    A. zero
    B. source voltage
    C. total voltage drop
    D. the sum of the IR drop of the circuit

3. In a series circuit, the total current is   3._____

    A. always equal to the source voltage
    B. determined by the load only
    C. the same through all parts of the circuit
    D. equal to zero at the positive side of the source

4.   4._____

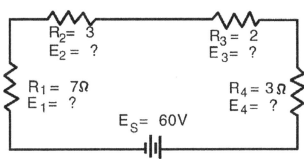

The CORRECT voltage equation for the circuit above is

    A. $E_S + E_1 + E_2 + E_3 + E_4 = 0$
    B. $E_S - E_1 - E_2 - E_3 - E_4 = 0$
    C. $E_S = -E_1 - E_2 - E_3 - E_4$
    D. $-E_S = E_1 + E_2 + E_3 + E_4$

5. Referring to the circuit shown in Question 4 above, after expressing the voltage drops around the circuit in terms of current and resistance and the given values of source voltage, the equation becomes   5._____

    A. $-60 - 71 - 31 - 21 - 31 = 0$
    B. $-60 + 71 + 31 + 21 + 31 = 0$
    C. $60 - 71 - 31 - 21 - 31 = 0$
    D. $60 + 71 + 31 + 21 + 31 = 0$

6. By the use of the correct equation, it is found that the current (I) in the circuit shown in Question 4 is of positive value. This indicates that the   6.____

    A. assumed direction of current flow is correct
    B. assumed direction of current flow is incorrect
    C. problem is not solvable
    D. battery polarity should be reversed

7.   7.____

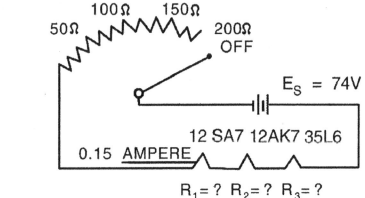

In what position would the variable rheostat in the circuit above be placed in order that the filaments of the tubes operate properly with a current flow of 0.15 ampere?
_____ position.

    A. 50Ω B. 100Ω C. 150Ω D. 200Ω

8. The power absorbed by the variable rheostat in the circuit used in Question 7 above, when placed in its proper operating position, would be _____ watts.   8.____

    A. 112.50   B. 2.25   C. 337.50   D. 450.00

9.   9.____

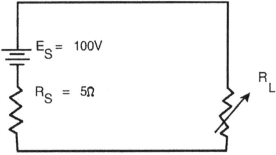

In the circuit above, maximum power would be transferred from the source to the load (R_L) if R_L were set at _____ ohms.

    A. 2   B. 5   C. 12   D. 24

10.

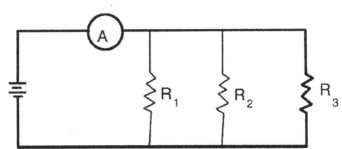

In the circuit above, if an additional resistor were placed in parallel to R_3, the ammeter reading would

10.____

A. increase
C. remain the same

B. decrease
D. drop to zero

11. In a parallel circuit containing a 4-ohm, 5-ohm, and 6-ohm resistor, the current flow is

11.____

A. *highest* through the 4-ohm resistor
B. *lowest* through the 4-ohm resistor
C. *highest* through the 6-ohm resistor
D. *equal* through all three resistors

12. Three resistors of 2, 4, and 6 ohms, respectively, are connected in parallel. Which resistor would absorb the GREATEST power?

12.____

A. The 2-ohm resistor
B. The 4-ohm resistor
C. The 6-ohm resistor
D. It will be the same for all resistors

13. If three lamps are connected in parallel with a power source, connecting a fourth lamp in parallel will

13.____

A. *decrease* E_T
C. *increase* E_T

B. *decrease* I_T
D. *increase* I_T

14.

14.____

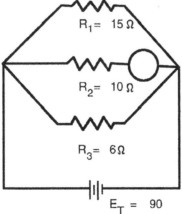

What is the current flow through the ammeter in the circuit shown above?
_____ amps.

A. 4   B. 9   C. 15   D. 28

15.

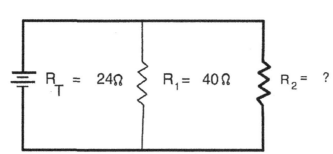

In the circuit shown above, the TOTAL resistance is 24 ohms. What is the value of R_2?
_____ ohms.

A. 16 B. 40 C. 60 D. 64

15.____

16.

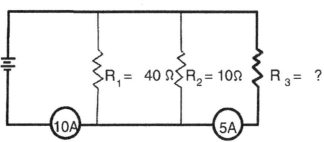

What is the source voltage of the circuit shown above?
_____ volts.

A. 40 B. 50 C. 100 D. 500

16.____

17. What is the value of R_3 in the circuit shown in Question 16 above?
_____ ohms.

A. 8 B. 10 C. 20 D. 100

17.____

18.

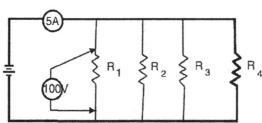

If all 4 resistors in the circuit above are of equal ohmic resistances, what is the value of R_3?
_____ ohms.

A. 5 B. 20 C. 60 D. 80

18.____

14

19.

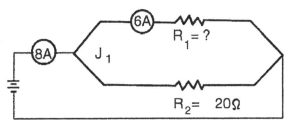

What is the value of the source voltage in the circuit above?
_____ volts

A.   20   B.   40   C.   120   D.   160

19.____

20.

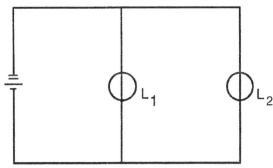

If Lamp L_2 in the circuit above should suddenly burn out, which of the statements below is CORRECT?

A.   More current would flow through lamp L_1.
B.   Source voltage would decrease.
C.   The filament resistance of lamp L_1 would decrease.
D.   Lamp L_1 would still burn normal.

20.____

21.   When referring to a circuit's conductance, you visualize the degree to which the circuit

A.   *permits* or conducts voltage
B.   *opposes* the rate of voltage changes
C.   *permits* or conducts current flow
D.   *opposes* the rate of current flow

21.____

22.

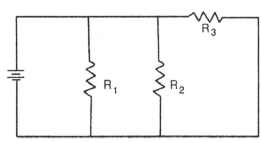

The TOTAL conductance of the circuit above would be solved by which of the equations?

A. $G_T - G_1 - G_2 - G_3 = 0$ B. $G_T + G_1 + G_2 + G_3 = 0$
C. $G_T = G_1 - G_2 - G_3$ D. $G_T = G_1 + G_2 + G_3$

22.____

23.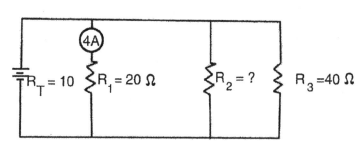

23.____

If the resistors in the circuit above are all rated at 250 watts, which resistor or resistors would overheat?

A. R_1 B. R_2 C. R_3 D. All

24.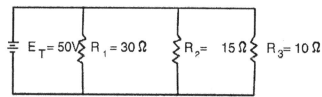

24.____

The TOTAL conductance of the circuit above is

A. 0.15G   B. 0.20G   C. 0.50G   D. 0.75G

KEY (CORRECT ANSWERS)

1. C		11. A	
2. A		12. A	
3. C		13. D	
4. B		14. B	
5. C		15. C	
6. A		16. A	
7. B		17. A	
8. B		18. D	
9. B		19. B	
10. A		20. D	

21. C
22. D
23. A
24. B

TEST 5

DIRECTIONS: Each question or incomplete statement is followed by several suggested answers or completions. Select the one that BEST answers the question or completes the statement. *PRINT THE LETTER OF THE CORRECT ANSWER IN THE SPACE AT THE RIGHT.*

1. The MINIMUM number of resistors in a compound circuit is (are)   1.____

    A. four   B. three   C. two   D. one

2.   2.____

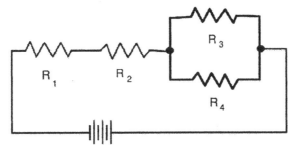

Total resistance of the circuit shown is determined by the formula

    A. $R_1R_2 + \dfrac{R_3R_4}{R_4+R_3}$ B. $R_1+R_2 + \dfrac{R_3+R_4}{R_3R_4}$

    C. $R_1+R_2 + \dfrac{R_3R_4}{R_3+R_4}$ D. $R_1+R_2 + (\dfrac{R_3R_4}{R_3+R_4})$

3.   3.____

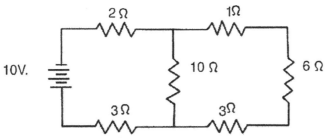

In the circuit above, what is the value of I_t?

$I_t =$ _____ amp.

    A. 1.14   B. 0.4   C. 0.667   D. 1

4. In the circuit in Question 3 above, how much power is consumed by the 6-ohm resistor?   4.____
    _____ watts.

    A. 15   B. 1.5   C. 60   D. 6

5. A voltage divider is used to   5.____

    A. provide different voltage values for multiple loads from a single source
    B. provide several voltage drops in parallel
    C. increase the voltage to the load at several taps
    D. provide tap points to alter power supplied

6. The total power supplied to the entire circuit by a voltage divider and 4 loads is the   6._____

    A. sum of the 4 loads
    B. voltage divider minus 4 loads
    C. voltage divider plus the 4 loads
    D. voltage divider only

7. The total voltage of a voltage divider is the   7._____

    A. input voltage minus the load's voltages
    B. the load's voltages only
    C. sum of the input and load voltage
    D. sum of the voltages across the divider

8. An attenuator is   8._____

    A. a network of resistors used to reduce power, voltage, or current
    B. a network of resistors to change the input voltage
    C. also called a pad
    D. used in every power circuit

9. In an attenuator, the resistors are   9._____

    A. adjusted separately
    B. connected in parallel with the load
    C. connected in series with the load
    D. ganged

10. What two conditions may be observed in a bridge circuit?   10._____

    A. T and L network characteristics
    B. No-load and full-load bridge current
    C. Unequal potential and unequal current
    D. Balance and unbalance

11.   11._____

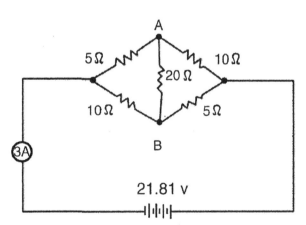

In the circuit above, how much current flows in the resistor and what is its direction?

    A. 26 a.; B to A   B. la.; A to B
    C. 0.273 a.; A to B   D. la.; B to A

12. In a three-wire distribution system, an unbalanced situation is indicated by the

    A. potential of the positive wire being equal to the negative wire
    B. positive wire carrying more amperage than the negative wire
    C. current in the neutral wire
    D. neutral wire carrying the total current

12.____

13.

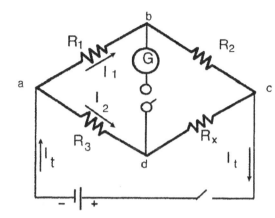

SCHEMATIC
WHEATSTONE-BRIDGE
CIRCUIT

13.____

In the figure above, the galvanometer will show zero deflection when

    A. $\dfrac{R_1}{R_2} + \dfrac{R_3}{R_x}$

    B. $R_x = \dfrac{R_1 R_3}{R_2}$

    C. $\dfrac{I_1 R_1}{I_2 R_x} = \dfrac{I_2 R_3}{I_1 R_2}$

    D. $R_x = \dfrac{R_1 R_2}{R_3}$

14. In the Wheatstone Bridge type circuit shown at the right, the bridge current is toward Point A.
The resistance of R_X is

    A. 30Ω
    B. greater than 45Ω
    C. 20Ω
    D. less than 15Ω

14.____

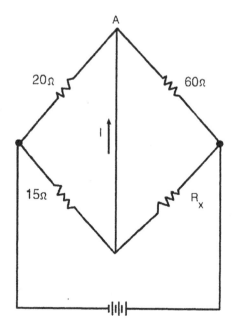

15.

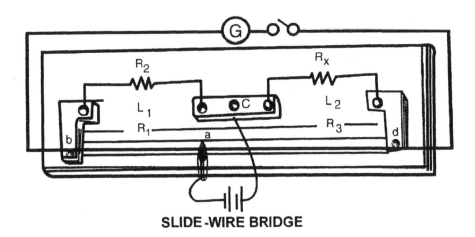

SLIDE-WIRE BRIDGE

In the slide-wire bridge shown above, L_1 is equal to

A. $L_1 = \dfrac{R_2 L_2}{R_1}$

B. $L_1 = \dfrac{R_1 + L_2}{R_2}$

C. $\dfrac{R_2}{R_1 L_2} = L_1$

D. $\dfrac{R_2 L_2}{R_x} = L_1$

15.____

16.

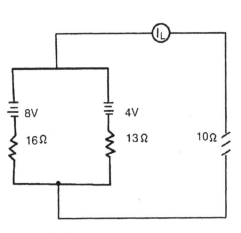

In the circuit above, I line is

A. 4.44 a.   B. 0.444 a.   C. 0.337 a.   D. 5.22 a.

16.____

17. When checking a 3-wire distribution circuit going against the direction of current flow, the IR drop is ALWAYS

A. negative
B. positive
C. not used
D. always in direction of current flow

17.____

18.

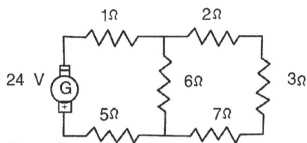

In the circuit above, the voltage drop across the 3-ohm resistor is _____ volts.

A. 2.4   B. 24   C. 9.6   D. 0.96

19. The resistance of the wire is taken into consideration in the 2- and 3-wire distribution sys-   19._____
tems because the

A. source and load are very close
B. resistance of the wire is the same throughout
C. load and source are at a considerable distance from each other
D. load must be decreased in order to determine accurate circuit values

20. What is Kirchhoff's second law as applied to 3-wire distribution circuits?   20._____

A. Sum of all the voltages is zero.
B. Algebraic sum of all the voltages about closed path is zero.
C. Algebraic sum of all voltage is zero.
D. All IR drops in the circuit are negative.

———

KEY (CORRECT ANSWERS)

1. B   11. C
2. C   12. C
3. D   13. A
4. B   14. B
5. A   15. D

6. C   16. C
7. D   17. B
8. A   18. A
9. D   19. C
10. D   20. B

———

TEST 6

DIRECTIONS: Each question or incomplete statement is followed by several suggested answers or completions. Select the one that BEST answers the question or completes the statement. *PRINT THE LETTER OF THE CORRECT ANSWER IN THE SPACE AT THE RIGHT.*

1. A mil is what part of an inch?   1.____

   A. 1/10   B. 1/100
   C. 1/1000   D. 1/1,000,000

2. The discharge (electrical leakage) that MIGHT occur from a wire carrying a high potential   2.____
   is called

   A. arcing   B. sparking
   C. static discharge   D. corona

3. Bare wire ends are spliced by the   3.____

   A. western union method   B. rat-tail joint method
   C. fixture joint method   D. all of the above

4. What is a unit conductor called that has a length of one foot and a cross-sectional area of   4.____
   one circular mil?

   A. Square mil   B. Circular mil
   C. Circular mil foot   D. Square mil foot

5. The induction-type soldering iron is commonly known as the   5.____

   A. soldering copper   B. pencil iron
   C. soldering gun   D. resistance gun

6. All good quality soldering irons operate at what temperature?   6.____

   A. 400 - 500° F.   B. 500 - 600° F.
   C. 600 - 700° F.   D. 300 - 600° F.

7. A No. 12 wire has a diameter of 80.81 mils.   7.____
   What is the area in circular mils?
   _____ cm.

   A. 6,530   B. 5,630   C. 4,530   D. 3,560

8. Dielectric strength is the   8.____

   A. opposite of potential difference
   B. ability of a conductor to carry large amounts of current
   C. ability of an insulator to withstand a potential difference
   D. strength of a magnetic field

9. To readily transfer the heat from the soldering iron tip, it FIRST should be   9.____

   A. tinned with solder
   B. allowed to form an oxide film
   C. cleaned with carbon tetrachloride
   D. allowed to heat for 25 minutes

10. A No. 12 wire has a diameter of 80.81 mils.
    What is the area in square mils?
    _____ square mils.   10._____

    A. 2,516.8   B. 5,128.6   C. 6,530   D. 8,512.6

11. Varnished cambric insulation is used to cover conductors carrying voltages above   11._____
    _____ volts.

    A. 1,000   B. 1,500   C. 15,000   D. 5,000

12. The solder splicer is used to   12._____

    A. prevent the waste of rosin core solder
    B. connect together small lengths of solder
    C. connect two conductors together
    D. none of the above

13. The conductance of a conductor is the ease with which current will flow through it.   13._____
    It is measured in

    A. ohms   B. mhos   C. henrys   D. amperes

14. Asbestos insulation loses its insulating properties when it becomes   14._____

    A. overaged
    B. overheated
    C. used over a long period of time
    D. wet

15. How are solderless connectors installed on conductors?   15._____

    A. Bolted on   B. Chemical compound
    C. Crimped on   D. All of the above

16. The factor(s) governing the selection of wire size is (are)   16._____

    A. (I^2R loss) in the line
    B. (IR drop) in the line
    C. current-carrying ability of the line
    D. all of the above

17. Enamel insulated conductors are USUALLY called   17._____

    A. magnet wire   B. high voltage wire
    C. low voltage wire   D. transmission lines

18. The advantage of solderless connectors over soldered-type connectors is that they are 18._____

    A. mechanically stronger   B. easier to install
    C. free of corrosion   D. all of the above

19. The basic requirement of any splice is that it be 19._____

    A. soldered
    B. mechanically and electrically as strong as the conductor that is spliced
    C. made with a splicer
    D. taped

20. The type of tape that is used for electrical circuits having a temperature of 175° F. or above is 20._____

    A. glass cloth
    B. plastic
    C. synthetic rubber compound
    D. impregnated cloth

KEY (CORRECT ANSWERS)

1.	C	11.	C
2.	D	12.	C
3.	D	13.	B
4.	C	14.	D
5.	A	15.	C
6.	B	16.	D
7.	A	17.	A
8.	C	18.	B
9.	A	19.	B
10.	B	20.	A

EXAMINATION SECTION
TEST 1

DIRECTIONS: Each question or incomplete statement is followed by several suggested answers or completions. Select the one that BEST answers the question or completes the statement. *PRINT THE LETTER OF THE CORRECT ANSWER IN THE SPACE AT THE RIGHT.*

1. Reversing the current flow through a coil

    A. reduces the amount of flux produced
    B. reverses its two-pole field
    C. reduces power consumed
    D. reduces eddy currents

1.____

2. The unit of magnetic flux is

    A. ampere-turn   B. gilbert
    C. intensity   D. maxwell

2.____

3. Flux in a magnetic circuit compares in an electrical circuit with

    A. voltage   B. current
    C. resistance   D. opposition

3.____

4. If a compass is placed in the vicinity of a conductor carrying d.c., the needle aligns itself

    A. in the direction of current flow in the conductor
    B. at right angles to the conductor
    C. in the general direction of the north pole
    D. in the general direction of the south pole

4.____

5. The left-hand rule for coils states: Grasping the

    A. coil with the left hand, with fingers pointing in the direction of the magnetic field, the middle finger will point to the north pole
    B. coil with the left hand, thumb pointing in the direction of the conductor movement, the fingers will point in the direction of the magnetic field
    C. conductor with the left hand, fingers pointing in the direction of the north pole, the thumb will indicate current flow
    D. coil in the left hand, fingers wrapped around in the direction of electron flow, the thumb will point towards north pole

5.____

6. The word *permeability* indicates the

    A. amount of reluctance of one centimeter-cube of air
    B. number of turns of an air core
    C. ability of a substance to conduct magnetic lines of force
    D. m.m.f. required to produce one gilbert

6.____

7. If an iron core is inserted part way into a coil and current is applied to the coil, the core will be drawn into the coil in an effort to

    A. increase reluctance of the magnetic circuit
    B. decrease the length of the magnetic circuit

7.____

C. reduce the permeability of the circuit
D. increase the residual effect

8. Current flow in a straight conductor produces   8.____

   A. hysteresis   B. magnetic lines of force
   C. a north pole   D. permeability

9. The induction of a coil depends upon the   9.____

   A. number of turns, current flow, type of core material, and ratio of coil's length to its width
   B. current, flux, and core material
   C. direction of rotation, flux, and speed
   D. permeability, reluctance, gausses, and maxwells

10. The ability of a magnetic substance to hold its magnetism after the magnetizing force has   10.____
    been removed is

    A. residual   B. retentivity
    C. hysteresis   D. permeability

11. The solenoid and plunger type of magnet is employed in various forms to control   11.____

    A. electrical equipment   B. hysteresis losses
    C. permeability   D. all of the above

12. When using the left-hand rule for a conductor,   12.____

    A. grasp the conductor with fingers pointing in the direction of current flow and thumb will indicate direction of field
    B. the compass will point in the direction of current flow and fingers will indicate direction of magnetic field
    C. grasp the conductor with the thumb extended in the direction of electron flow, the fingers will point in the direction of the magnetic lines of force
    D. reverse the current flow and thumb will point in the direction of the magnetic field

13. The magnetic circuit is determined by   13.____

    A. lines of force leaving the south pole and entering the north pole externally
    B. permeability to current and the north pole
    C. maxwells to length in centimeters and the south pole
    D. the complete path taken by magnetic lines leaving the north pole, and returning to the north pole

14. In what material is retentivity MOST apparent?   14.____

    A. Hard steel   B. Soft iron
    C. Copper   D. Wood

15. The armature type of electromagnet   15.____

    A. has a movable iron bar in its magnetic circuit
    B. uses a permanent magnet core
    C. has a hard steel core and a pivoted bar of copper
    D. has a movable iron core

16. When two parallel conductors carrying current in the same direction are placed side by side, the fields produced by both

    A. cancel each other's field
    B. push each other apart
    C. form a north pole
    D. encircle each other, drawing the conductors together

16.____

17. The equivalent Ohm's law formula for magnetic circuits is

    A. $I = \dfrac{e}{r}$ B. $R = \dfrac{I}{E}$ C. $\Phi = \dfrac{E}{R}$ D. $P = \dfrac{I}{E}$

17.____

18. Which of the following materials incurs low hysteresis loss when used for transformer cores and similar applications?

    A. Hard steel   B. Annealed steel
    C. Soft iron   D. Cast steel

18.____

19. The magnetic field around a current-carrying wire

    A. is parallel to the current flow in the conductor
    B. exists at all points along its length
    C. exists only at the beginning of electron movement
    D. moves in the direction of current flow

19.____

20. Direct current flows through a coil of wire which has an iron core. When the iron core is removed and all other factors remain unchanged, the total number of lines of force through the coil will change because

    A. changing the core material affects m.m.f.
    B. permeance has been increased
    C. reluctance has been increased
    D. the permeability of the magnetic circuit has been increased

20.____

KEY (CORRECT ANSWERS)

1. B		11. A	
2. D		12. C	
3. B		13. D	
4. B		14. A	
5. D		15. A	
6. C		16. D	
7. B		17. C	
8. B		18. C	
9. A		19. B	
10. B		20. C	

TEST 2

DIRECTIONS: Each question or incomplete statement is followed by several suggested answers or completions. Select the one that BEST answers the question or completes the statement. *PRINT THE LETTER OF THE CORRECT ANSWER IN THE SPACE AT THE RIGHT.*

1. In formula form, angular velocity as applied to voltage or current is   1._____

   A. 2ω B. $2\pi\omega$ C. $2\pi F$ D. $2F$

2. How much larger is the maximum voltage value than the effective voltage value?   2._____

   A. 1.414   B. 1.111   C. 0.707   D. 0.637

3. How many radians are in a complete circle?   3._____

   A. 0.707   B. 1.11   C. 3.14   D. 6.28

4. Magnitude of a vector is denoted by the   4._____

   A. time axis
   B. length of the line
   C. length of the line, drawn to scale
   D. length of the time axis, drawn to scale

5. Which of the following BEST defines a cycle?   5._____

   A. One alternation   B. Two alternations
   C. Three alternations   D. Four alternations

6. The MOST important value associated with sine waves of voltage or current are   6._____

   A. instantaneous   B. maximum
   C. average   D. all of the above

7. The MAXIMUM value of a single sine wave of a-c voltage is 141.4 volts. What is the   7._____
   effective value? _____ volts.

   A. 63.7   B. 70.7   C. 99.97   D. 141.4

8. Direction of a simple vector   8._____

   A. cannot be determined
   B. will indicate the reference point
   C. is indicated by an arrow at one end of the line
   D. is indicated by the magnitude

9. Frequency as applied to alternating current or voltage is the number of _____ per sec-   9._____
   ond of time.

   A. r.p.m.   B. cycles
   C. poles   D. volts generated

10. The effective value of an a-c voltage or current of sine waveform is defined in terms of the   10.____
    equivalent d.c. "_____ effect".

    A. voltage   B. current
    C. heating   D. cooling

11. The average value of a single sine wave of a-c current is 63.7 amps. What is the r.m.s.   11.____
    value? _____ amps.

    A. 63.7   B. 70.7   C. 141.4   D. 156.95

12. The instantaneous value of induced voltage of a single-phase generator   12.____

    A. will never be zero
    B. depends on the sine of the angle
    C. will always be the same
    D. depends on the cosine of the angle

13. The period of a-c voltage of sine waveform is the time required for one complete   13.____

    A. r.p.m.   B. alternation
    C. cycle   D. degree

14. The "root-mean-square" value is also known as the _____ value.   14.____

    A. average   B. peak
    C. instantaneous   D. effective

15. Two voltages of the same frequency "120 cycles per second" have their positive maxi-   15.____
    mum values displaced by 90°.
    What is the time difference between the phases? _____ sec.

    A. 0.00208   B. 0.00416   C. 0.02080   D. 0.04160

16. Positive rotation of a vector is   16.____

    A. clockwise
    B. counterclockwise
    C. either clockwise or counterclockwise
    D. neither clockwise nor counterclockwise

17. The effective generated voltage of a single-phase a-c generator may be obtained by the   17.____
    formula

    A. $E = 1.111 \ \Phi \ fD10^{-8}$ B. $E = 2.22 \ \Phi \ fN^{-6}$
    C. $E = 1.111 \ \Phi \ FD^{-6}$ D. $E = 2.22 \ \Phi \ fN^{-8}$

18. Most a-c voltmeters and ammeters are calibrated in _____ values.   18.____

    A. r.m.s.   B. average
    C. peaks   D. instantaneous

19. A radian is ALWAYS equal to   19.____

    A. the circumference of the circle   B. the radius of the circle
    C. π D. 60 degrees

20. Angular velocity is symbolized by the Greek letter   20._____

    A. gamma γ B. mu μ C. omega ω D. beta β

21. If an active conductor's length is doubled, the   21._____

    A. pole length is cut in half
    B. flux per pole is cut in half
    C. generated voltage is doubled
    D. generated voltage is tripled

22. The "form factor" in most cases refers to the ratio of   22._____

    A. average value to maximum value
    B. instantaneous value to maximum value
    C. r.m.s. value to effective value
    D. r.m.s. value to average value

23. Conductor size in an a-c circuit is based on _____ current.   23._____

    A. instantaneous   B. maximum
    C. average   D. effective

24. The term "angular velocity," as applied to electricity, refers to the number of   24._____

    A. radians per second a voltage vector rotates
    B. radians per minute a voltage vector rotates
    C. degrees averaged together
    D. degrees subtracted from the radians

25. Vectors indicate   25._____

    A. direction
    B. magnitude
    C. time, direction, and magnitude
    D. magnitude and direction

KEY (CORRECT ANSWERS)

1.	C		11.	B
2.	A		12.	B
3.	D		13.	C
4.	C		14.	D
5.	B		15.	B
6.	D		16.	B
7.	C		17.	D
8.	C		18.	A
9.	B		19.	B
10.	C		20.	C

21.	C
22.	D
23.	D
24.	A
25.	D

TEST 3

DIRECTIONS: Each question or incomplete statement is followed by several suggested answers or completions. Select the one that BEST answers the question or completes the statement. *PRINT THE LETTER OF THE CORRECT ANSWER IN THE SPACE AT THE RIGHT.*

1. Inductance is the property of an electric circuit that   1._____

   A. opposes any change in the applied voltage through that circuit
   B. opposes any change in the current through that circuit
   C. aids any change in the applied voltage through that circuit
   D. aids any change in the current through that circuit

2. A coil has a resistance of 22 ohms, and, in 0.1 second after the switch is closed, the current has reached 63.2% of its final value.   2._____
   The value of inductance (L) is _____ henries.

   A. 0.22   B. 0.44   C. 2.20   D. 4.40

3. When a capacitor's counter e.m.f. has risen to equal the battery voltage, the current is   3._____

   A. maximum in the circuit
   B. at 63.2% of its maximum Ohm's law value in the circuit
   C. zero in the circuit
   D. at 36.8% of its maximum Ohm's law value in the circuit

4. The total capacitance of two 100-microfarad capacitors connected in series is _____   4._____
   microfarads.

   A. 25   B. 50   C. 100   D. 200

5. When the magnetic field is collapsing, the induced e.m.f.   5._____

   A. aids and tends to prolong the impressed current
   B. opposes the impressed current
   C. has no effect upon the impressed current
   D. causes the impressed current to go immediately to zero

6. To increase the time required for the current to reach its maximum Ohm's law value in a   6._____
   series resistance and inductance circuit, it is necessary to

   A. increase the resistance
   B. decrease the resistance
   C. decrease the inductance
   D. increase the applied voltage

7. In a simple capacitor, the plate area is 2 square inches, the dielectric material is mica,   7._____
   and the distance between the plates is 0.01 inch. To increase the capacitance,

   A. increase the distance between the plates
   B. change dielectric material from mica to paraffin paper
   C. decrease the plate area
   D. change dielectric material from mica to flint glass

8. What is the total capacitance of two 200-microfarad capacitors connected in series with each other and both in parallel with a 50-microfarad capacitor? _____ microfarads.   8.____

   A. 50   B. 250   C. 100   D. 150

9. The unit of inductance is the   9.____

   A. ohm   B. farad   C. henry   D. coulomb

10. The coefficient of coupling of two coils is   10.____

    A. increased by turning one coil axis at right angles to the other coil axis
    B. greatly increased with the addition of a soft iron core
    C. generally higher in an air core circuit than in an iron core circuit
    D. almost unity on a diamagnetic core

11. Factors that determine the capacitance of parallel-electrode capacitors are   11.____

    A. area of the plates and the type of dielectric
    B. thickness of the plates, type and thickness of the dielectric
    C. type and thickness of the dielectric and the plate area
    D. thickness of the dielectric, area of the plate, and the direction of the current flow

12. The time constant of a resistance-capacitance circuit is   12.____

    A. the time required to discharge a capacitor to 36.8% of its final voltage
    B. the time required to charge a capacitor to 36.8% of its maximum voltage
    C. equal to the circuit capacitance divided by the circuit resistance
    D. equal to the circuit resistance divided by the circuit capacitance

13. The voltage due to self-induction   13.____

    A. can only occur when the conductor is wound in the form of a coil
    B. is produced when the strength of the magnetic field changes
    C. is produced by moving a conductor through a magnetic field
    D. cannot occur in a direct-current circuit

14. If two coils are positioned with respect to each other so as to have unity coefficient of coupling and the inductance of coil A equals coil B, what is the mutual inductance between the two coils?   14.____

    A. Equal to the inductance of coil A
    B. One-half of the inductance of coil A
    C. Double the inductance of coil A
    D. Equal to the square root of the inductance of coil A

15. The capacitance of a capacitor is inversely proportional to the   15.____

    A. frequency of the applied voltage
    B. dielectric constant
    C. active plate area
    D. distance between the plates

16. A 40-microfarad capacitor in series with 2,000 ohms is connected to a 200-volt source. The time constant is _____ second.   16.____

   A. 0.05   B. 0.08   C. 0.50   D. 0.80

17. To increase the inductance of a coil,   17.____

   A. increase the permeability of the core material
   B. increase the length of the coil
   C. increase the magnitude of the current flow through the coil
   D. decrease the cross-sectional area of the coil

18. What is the total inductance (L_t) of two coils connected in parallel when the coefficient of coupling is zero?   18.____

   A. $L_t = L_1 + L_2$ B. $L_t = L_1$

   C. $L_t = \dfrac{1}{L_1} + \dfrac{1}{L_2}$ D. $L_t = \dfrac{L_1 L_2}{L_1 + L_2}$

19. The charge that is stored in a capacitor depends upon   19.____

   A. voltage divided by the capacitance
   B. voltage multiplied by the capacitance
   C. capacitance divided by the voltage
   D. capacitance multiplied by the resistance

20. When selecting a capacitor for use in a circuit, its working voltage should be AT LEAST   20.____

   A. 10% greater than the highest voltage to be applied to it
   B. equal to the highest voltage to be applied to it
   C. 30% greater than the highest voltage to be applied to it
   D. 50% greater than the highest voltage to be applied to it

21. A battery, a switch, a resistor, and a coil are connected in series. What happens at the instant the switch is closed? The   21.____

   A. voltage across the resistor is maximum
   B. voltage across the coil is maximum
   C. current in the circuit is maximum
   D. voltage across the resistor and the coil are minimum

22. Capacitance is the property of an electric circuit that   22.____

   A. opposes any change of current in the circuit
   B. opposes any change of voltage in the circuit
   C. is not affected by a change of voltage
   D. aids any change of current in the circuit

23. When capacitors are connected in parallel, the resulting capacitance is the

    A. sum of the individual capacitances
    B. reciprocal of the sum of reciprocals of the individual capacitors
    C. sum of the individual reciprocals of the capacitors
    D. reciprocal of the sum of capacitances

23.____

24. The time constant of an inductive-resistive circuit is

    A. that time required for a direct current to rise one-half of its maximum value
    B. a method of determining how much current would flow at the end of one second
    C. the product of the resistance and the inductance of a circuit
    D. the time in seconds required for the current to rise to 63.2% of its final Ohm's law value

24.____

25. When capacitors are connected in series, the resulting capacitance is found by

    A. a rule similar to that for combining parallel resistors
    B. a rule similar to that for combining resistors in series
    C. dividing the applied voltage by the total resistance of series circuit
    D. multiplying the applied voltage by the total resistance of series circuit

25.____

KEY (CORRECT ANSWERS)

1.	B		11.	C
2.	C		12.	A
3.	C		13.	B
4.	B		14.	A
5.	A		15.	D
6.	B		16.	B
7.	D		17.	A
8.	D		18.	D
9.	C		19.	B
10.	B		20.	D

21. B
22. B
23. A
24. D
25. A

TEST 4

DIRECTIONS: Each question or incomplete statement is followed by several suggested answers or completions. Select the one that BEST answers the question or completes the statement. *PRINT THE LETTER OF THE CORRECT ANSWER IN THE SPACE AT THE RIGHT.*

1. When frequency is increased in an inductive circuit, the current flow will   1._____

    A. increase because of greater inductive voltage
    B. increase because of less inductive voltage
    C. decrease because of greater inductive voltage
    D. decrease because of less inductive voltage

2. The unit of measurement for reactive power is the   2._____

    A. Volt Amp (VA)
    B. Volt Amp Wattage (VAW)
    C. Volt Amp Reactive (VAR)
    D. Volt Amp Kilo Watt (VAKW)

3. The prime factors that determine inductive reactance are   3._____

    A. frequency and current
    B. frequency and inducted voltage
    C. inductance and frequency
    D. inductance and voltage

4. What are the prime factors affecting capacitive reactance?   4._____

    A. Frequency and capacitance
    B. Frequency and inductance
    C. Frequency and resistance
    D. Frequency squared

5. The reaction of an inductor to any change in current is known as inductive   5._____

    A. reactance
    B. voltage
    C. current
    D. resistance

6. What two quantities comprise the total power of an a-c circuit?   6._____

    A. Apparent power and VARS
    B. True power and VARS
    C. True power and VAWS
    D. True power and power factor

7. Power factor is the   7._____

    A. percentage of apparent power expended in heat
    B. amount of apparent power in an a-c circuit
    C. amount of apparent power plus true power
    D. efficiency of a circuit expressed as an angle

8. The unit of measurement for inductive reactance is the   8._____

    A. ohm   B. volt   C. ampere   D. henry

9. What is the power factor of a pure capacitive circuit?   9.____

    A. 70.7%   B. 86.6%   C. 100%   D. 0%

10. The self-induced voltage in a coil depends on the   10.____

    A. voltage applied
    B. inductive reactance
    C. c.e.m.f.
    D. current change in the coil

11. What is the path for current flow through a capacitor?   11.____

    A. Does not actually flow through
    B. From negative plate to positive plate
    C. From positive plate to negative plate
    D. From dielectric to plates

12. Power is described as the rate at which   12.____

    A. work is being done
    B. energy is being used
    C. energy is being expended
    D. all of the above are produced

13. What is the power characteristic of a positive inductive circuit?   13.____

    A. Positive power is the largest.
    B. Positive and negative power are equal.
    C. Negative power is the largest.
    D. Negative power is the smallest.

14. The vector sum of X_C and R in a series R-C circuit is the total   14.____

    A. opposition to voltage in the circuit
    B. capacitive reactance in the circuit
    C. resistance in the circuit
    D. opposition to current flow in the circuit

15. Self-induced voltage in an inductor will ALWAYS oppose   15.____

    A. the applied voltage by 180 degrees
    B. circuit current
    C. the applied voltage by 90 degrees
    D. the circuit current by 180 degrees

16. What is the value of apparent current flow in a capacitive circuit when it is FIRST ener-   16.____
gized?

    A. No current flow in a capacitive circuit
    B. Minimum
    C. Maximum
    D. Zero

17. What is the phase relationship between current and voltage in a resistive circuit?   17._____

    A. 90° phase difference
    B. 0° phase difference
    C. Out of phase
    D. Cannot be determined without numerical value of R

18. Voltage and current are considered to be out of phase with each other in a pure inductive   18._____
circuit by what amount? Current

    A. leads voltage by 90°   B. lags voltage by 90°
    C. leads voltage by 180°   D. lags voltage by 180°

19. What is the phase relationship between current and voltage in a pure capacitive circuit?   19._____

    A. No phase angle
    B. Current lags voltage by 90°
    C. Voltage leads current by 90°
    D. Voltage lags current by 90°

20. The phase angle between current and voltage in a circuit containing both resistive and   20._____
inductive elements is

    A. greater than 0° but less than 90°
    B. a constant 45°
    C. 90° at all times
    D. 0° because X_L and R are equal

21. In the formula for capacitive reactance, the symbol "C" represents capacitance in   21._____

    A. farads   B. micromicrofarads
    C. microfarads   D. ohms

22. What is the effect on capacitor voltage when frequency is increased? Voltage   22._____

    A. increases   B. decreases
    C. not affected   D. is minimum

23. What is impedance?   23._____

    A. Opposition to current flow in an a-c circuit created by resistance and reactances
    B. Resistance of an a-c circuit
    C. Vector sum of voltage drops in an a-c circuit
    D. Current divided by voltage in an a-c circuit

24. When voltages are out of phase, the total voltage can be found by adding   24._____

    A. arithmetically   B. vectorially
    C. peak value   D. average values

25. The number of radians per second traversed by an alternating-voltage vector is
    CLOSELY related to its   25.____

    A. current sine wave   B. voltage sine wave
    C. frequency   D. none of the above

KEY (CORRECT ANSWERS)

1.	C		11.	A
2.	C		12.	D
3.	C		13.	B
4.	A		14.	D
5.	A		15.	A
6.	B		16.	C
7.	A		17.	B
8.	A		18.	B
9.	D		19.	D
10.	D		20.	A

21.	A
22.	B
23.	A
24.	B
25.	C

TEST 5

DIRECTIONS: Each question or incomplete statement is followed by several suggested answers or completions. Select the one that BEST answers the question or completes the statement. *PRINT THE LETTER OF THE CORRECT ANSWER IN THE SPACE AT THE RIGHT.*

1. When resistive, inductive, and capacitive elements are connected in series,   1._____

   A.   they lose their individual characteristics
   B.   their individual characteristics remain unchanged
   C.   the inductance component is always the largest
   D.   the capacitive component is always the largest

2. In a circuit containing both X_C and X_L, if the difference between X_C and X_L increases, the total   2._____

   A.   impedance decreases
   B.   impedance increases
   C.   impedance remains the same
   D.   resistance increases

3. In a 60-cycle a-c circuit, with an inductor of 0.053 microhenry and a resistance of 50 ohms connected in series, the impedance would be _____ ohms.   3._____

   A.   539   B.   5.39   C.   53.9   D.   19.97

4. The effective resistance of a circuit may be defined as the ratio of the   4._____

   A.   true power absorbed by the circuit to the square of the effective current flowing
   B.   apparent power absorbed by the circuit to the square of the effective current flowing
   C.   true power absorbed by the circuit to the square of the total resistance in the circuit
   D.   apparent power absorbed by the circuit to the square of the total resistance in the circuit

5. In a series circuit, when X_C and X_L are equal,   5._____

   A.   line voltage leads line current by an unknown $\angle \theta$
   B.   line current leads line voltage by an unknown $\angle \theta$
   C.   total impedance is minimum
   D.   total impedance is maximum

6. To find true power, use the formula   6._____

   A.   T.P. = E x 1   B.   T.P. = E x 1 x cos $\angle \theta$

   C.   T.P. = E^2 ÷ cos $\angle \theta$ D.   T.P. = E x 1 x sin $\angle \theta$

7. A low-loss inductor has a low   7._____

   A. X_L at high frequencies   B.   current at low frequencies
   C.   inductance   D.   resistance

8. The MOST inefficient method of voltage reduction, from the standpoint of power loss, is a(n)   8._____

    A.   capacitor in series with the load
    B.   inductor in series with the load
    C.   capacitor and an inductor in series with the load
    D.   resistor in series with the load

9. The formula for finding the loss factor of a capacitor is the dielectric constant   9._____

    A.   times the power factor
    B.   divided by the power factor
    C.   times the apparent power
    D.   times the true power

10. A phase difference between E and I causes   10._____

    A.   true power to increase
    B.   apparent power to increase
    C.   true power to decrease
    D.   apparent power to decrease

11. The energy component of a current flowing in an R-L circuit is the current flowing through the   11._____

    A.   inductor and resistor   B.   inductor
    C.   resistor   D.   power source

12. Corona loss is the result of   12._____

    A.   emission of electrons from the surface of a conductor
    B.   electron collision inside a conductor
    C.   overheating a high-frequency conductor
    D.   none of the above

13. To find total true power in a parallel circuit, first find the true power in each branch and then   13._____

    A.   add the power in all branches arithmetically
    B.   add the power in all branches using the parallelogram method
    C.   multiply the voltage times the current
    D.   multiply the square of the current times the resistance

14. The hypotenuse of the power triangle represents   14._____

    A.   true power   B.   VARS
    C.   apparent power   D.   none of the above

15. To find a circuit's power factor in percent, use the formula   15._____

    A. $P.F. = \dfrac{AP}{TP} \times 100$ B. $P.F. = \cos \angle \theta$

    C. $P.F. = $ angle in degrees x 100   D. $P.F. = \dfrac{E \times I \times \cos \angle \theta}{E \times I} \times 100$

16. Corona loss can be held to a satisfactory low value by 16.____

    A. avoiding sharp points, bends, and turns
    B. using low voltages
    C. using large diameter conductors
    D. all of the above

17. In a parallel circuit with a lagging power factor, to improve the power factor, 17.____

    A. increase the inductance
    B. put an inductor in parallel with the rest of the circuit
    C. put a capacitor in parallel with the rest of the circuit
    D. decrease the resistance

18. The non-energy component of an a-e circuit is 18.____

    A. true power   B. reactive power
    C. apparent power   D. none of the above

19. The formula for computing R - L - C in series is 19.____

    A. $Z = R_T + X_L + X_C$
    B. $Z = R + X_L - X_C$
    C. $Z^2 = R^2 + (X_L^2 - X_C^2)$
    D. $Z = R^2 + (X_L^2 - X_C^2)$

20. One radian is equal to 20.____

    A. $\dfrac{180}{2\pi}$ B. 2π C. 1.414   D. $\dfrac{360}{2\pi}$

21. Skin effect describes the tendency of 21.____

    A. d-c conductors to carry the circuit current on their surfaces
    B. a-c conductors to carry the circuit current on their surfaces
    C. both a-c and d-c conductors to carry the circuit current on their surfaces
    D. none of the above

22. The current in an a-c parallel circuit varies 22.____

    A. inversely with the cos $\angle\theta$

    B. directly with the cos $\angle\theta$

    C. inversely with the sine $\angle\theta$

    D. directly with the sine $\angle\theta$

23. In a circuit containing X_C and X_L, if X_C is larger,

23.____

    A. the voltage would lead the current
    B. the current would lead the voltage
    C. there would be no phase difference
    D. true power is maximum

24. The effective resistance of a capacitor dissipated in heat in the

24.____

    A. positive capacitor plate
    B. negative capacitor plate
    C. dielectric
    D. leads connecting the capacitor in the circuit

25. When loops of wire are formed into a coil and current is passed through this coil,

25.____

    A. the result is a permanent magnet
    B. each turn will cancel the magnetic field of each adjacent turn
    C. the magnetic field of each turn of wire links with the fields of adjacent turns
    D. permeability decreases to minimum

KEY (CORRECT ANSWERS)

1.	B		11.	C
2.	B		12.	A
3.	C		13.	A
4.	A		14.	C
5.	C		15.	D
6.	B		16.	D
7.	D		17.	C
8.	D		18.	B
9.	A		19.	C
10.	C		20.	D

21. B
22. A
23. B
24. C
25. C

TEST 6

DIRECTIONS: Each question or incomplete statement is followed by several suggested answers or completions. Select the one that BEST answers the question or completes the statement. *PRINT THE LETTER OF THE CORRECT ANSWER IN THE SPACE AT THE RIGHT.*

1. In a D'Arsonval type meter, the PRIMARY purpose of the iron core is to   1._____

    A. dampen coil movement
    B. concentrate the flux between the core and the pole piece
    C. concentrate the flux between the core and the hairsprings
    D. weaken the flux between the core and the pole piece

2. The D'Arsonval movement operates on the principle of   2._____

    A. mutual induction
    B. repulsion
    C. magnetic repulsion and attraction
    D. magnetic attraction

3. In order to measure large currents with the D'Arsonval ammeter,   3._____

    A. the meter must be made more rugged
    B. an increased number of turns must be put on the moving coil
    C. shunts are used
    D. the pointer must be lengthened

4. The PRIMARY purpose of the megger is to measure   4._____

    A. milliohms   B. kilohms
    C. megohms   D. microhms

5. A moving iron-vane meter works on the principle of   5._____

    A. induction   B. repulsion
    C. conduction   D. attraction

6. When hairsprings are used in a D'Arsonval type meter, they   6._____

    A. serve as conductors
    B. are wound oppositely and provide restoring forces
    C. are attached to the ends of the bobbin
    D. produce all of the above

7. The metal ribbons attached to the moving coil in the galvanometer have no force on them   7._____
    when the

    A. north pole of the moving coil is close to the south pole of the horseshoe magnet
    B. north pole of the moving coil is as close as possible to the north pole of the horse-
        shoe magnet
    C. north pole of the moving coil is 90° from the north pole of the horseshoe magnet
    D. south pole of the moving coil is as close as possible to the south pole of the horse-
        shoe magnet

8. When shunts are used with an ammeter, they 8.____

   A. must be located within the case
   B. must be located outside the case
   C. may be located either inside or outside the case
   D. reduce the accuracy of the movement

9. The power supply for a megger comes from 9.____

   A. two flashlight batteries
   B. a hand-driven generator
   C. any 115 v. wall plug
   D. the aircraft battery

10. The iron-vane meter can be used on 10.____

   A. a.c. only   B. a.c. and d.c.
   C. d.c. only   D. rectified a.c.

11. The Weston meter uses the principle of operation of the 11.____

   A. D'Arsonval galvanometer
   B. Thompson incline coil
   C. iron vane
   D. V.T.V.M.

12. Current-measuring instruments MUST always be connected in 12.____

   A. parallel with a circuit
   B. series with a circuit
   C. series-parallel with a circuit
   D. delta with the shunt

13. If the pointer fails to come back to zero when the megger is not in use, 13.____

   A. the megger is out of calibration
   B. this is normal operation
   C. the hairsprings are burned out
   D. the pointer is stuck

14. When using ammeters, 14.____

   A. reverse polarity must be used
   B. + or - polarity can be used
   C. polarity should be observed
   D. regardless of polarity, the instrument cannot be damaged because it is grounded

15. For measuring resistances of multimillions of ohms, use a(n) 15.____

   A. TS 297 multimeter   B. ohmmeter with high scales
   C. megger   D. combustion volt ammeter

16. Dampening is accomplished in the iron-vane meter by 16.____

   A. hairsprings   B. the hermetically sealed case
   C. an aluminum bobbin   D. an aluminum vane

17. Balance springs on each end of the shaft of the Weston ammeter   17.____

    A. are used to carry current to the moving coil
    B. are not balanced due to temperature change
    C. provide a turning force for the pointer
    D. are factory adjusted and must not be re-adjusted

18. The electrodynamometer-type meter employs   18.____

    A. two permanent magnets
    B. one permanent magnet and one electromagnet
    C. two fixed coils and one movable permanent magnet
    D. none of the above

19. With the ohmmeter setting on R x 1, it takes 0.01 ma. to deflect the pointer to half scale.   19.____
    If the meter were set on R x 100, how much would it take to deflect the pointer to half
    scale? _____ ma.

    A. 0.1   B. 0.01   C. 0.001   D. 1.0

20. Electrodynamometer-type meters   20.____

    A. never utilize shunts
    B. utilize four coils, all of which are movable
    C. are seldom used in the laboratory because they are not accurate enough
    D. are not as sensitive as the D'Arsonval meter

21. Meggers provided aboard ships are usually rated at _____ volts.   21.____

    A. 250   B. 500   C. 750   D. 1,000

22. The voltage developed in the thermocouple-type meter depends on the   22.____

    A. material of which the wires are made
    B. direction of current flow
    C. frequency of the heater voltage
    D. type of meter movement

23. A multimeter contains a   23.____

    A. voltmeter and wattmeter
    B. voltmeter and frequency meter
    C. voltmeter, ohmmeter, and milliammeter
    D. voltmeter, ammeter, and ohmmeter

24. In the iron-vane power factor meter, the spiral springs   24.____

    A. are eliminated   B. return the pointer to zero
    C. oppose torque   D. carry current to coils A and B

25. Instruments that are used to measure voltage and current regardless of circuit ratings   25.____
    are

    A. instrument transformers   B. autotransformers
    C. electrodynamometers   D. D'Arsonvals

KEY (CORRECT ANSWERS)

1.	B		11.	A
2.	C		12.	B
3.	C		13.	B
4.	C		14.	C
5.	B		15.	C
6.	D		16.	D
7.	B		17.	A
8.	C		18.	D
9.	B		19.	B
10.	B		20.	D

21.	B
22.	A
23.	C
24.	A
25.	A

———

EXAMINATION SECTION
TEST 1

DIRECTIONS: Each question or incomplete statement is followed by several suggested answers or completions. Select the one that BEST answers the question or completes the statement. *PRINT THE LETTER OF THE CORRECT ANSWER IN THE SPACE AT THE RIGHT.*

1. An a-c armature is ALWAYS the   1.____

   A. rotating part of the generator
   B. stationary part of the generator
   C. conductors into which voltage is induced
   D. conductors through which d-c exciter current flows

2. The armature windings of a 2-phase a-c generator are physically placed so that the   2.____
   induced voltages are out of phase by

   A. 30°   B. 60°   C. 90°   D. 120°

3. When connecting a 3-phase a-c generator for delta operation, the delta closure voltage   3.____
   should be

   A. line voltage
   B. phase voltage
   C. approximately zero volts
   D. less than phase voltage

4. With no load on the secondary, the current in the primary is   4.____

   A. zero
   B. limited only by the resistance of the winding
   C. determined by c.e.m.f. of secondary
   D. determined by c.e.m.f. of primary

5. The a-c field is ALWAYS the   5.____

   A. rotating part of the generator
   B. stationary part of the generator
   C. conductors into which voltage is induced
   D. conductors through which d-c exciter current flows

6. The voltage induced into the armature windings is maximum when the field poles are   6.____

   A. in the neutral plane
   B. opposite the armature poles
   C. between the armature poles
   D. rotating at a high speed

7. The output frequency of an a-c generator is dependent upon the   7.____

   A. number of poles and phases
   B. rotor speed and phases

C. number of poles and the speed of the prime mover
D. number of poles and the rotor speed

8. The load rating of an a-c generator is determined by the   8.____

   A. internal heat it can withstand
   B. load it can carry continuously
   C. load it is capable of supplying
   D. overload it can carry for a specified time only

9. In a 2-phase, 3-wire a-c generator, the formula for line voltage is $E_L =$ 9.____

   A. $\dfrac{E_P}{\cos 45^\circ}$ B. $\dfrac{E_P}{\tan 45^\circ}$ C. $E_P \times 0.707$ D. $E_P \times 1.73$

10. The voltage output of an a-c generator is controlled by   10.____

   A. regulating the speed of the prime mover
   B. varying the d-c exciter voltage
   C. varying the reluctance of the air gap
   D. shorting out part of the armature windings

11. The PRIMARY reason for connecting transformers wye-wye is to   11.____

   A. double the input voltage
   B. double the primary current
   C. invert the frequency
   D. decrease line losses by high voltage with low current in the line

12. The purpose of the d-c generator is to excite the   12.____

   A. a-c armature   B. a-c field
   C. d-c armature   D. a-c and d-c field

13. A 3-phase wye-connected a-c generator is used to produce _____ current, _____ volt-   13.____
    age.

   A. high; low   B. low; low
   C. low; high   D. high; high

14. Two types of instrument transformers are   14.____

   A. step-up and step-down
   B. potential and high voltage
   C. potential and current
   D. auto and power

15. The output of a rotating field a-c generator is taken from   15.____

   A. sliprings and brushes
   B. commutator bars and brushes
   C. fixed terminals
   D. none of the above

16. Aircraft transformers are designed for 400 c.p.s. because   16._____

    A. of the 400-c.p.s. supply available in the aircraft
    B. the higher frequency permits savings of size and weight
    C. it is more stable than lower frequencies
    D. it has a higher average current flow

17. The closure voltage of a delta-connected transformer secondary is   17._____

    A. 0 volts   B. phase voltage
    C. line voltage   D. line voltage x 1.73

18. The revolving field type a-c generator is MOST widely used because of   18._____

    A. low armature current
    B. improved safety features
    C. low field current through fixed terminals
    D. high power from armature through sliprings

19. When using an a-c generator on a 3-phase, 4-wire system, the neutral wire 19._____

    A. maintains equal current in each phase
    B. maintains equal power in each phase
    C. maintains equal voltage in each phase
    D. has no current flow when the loads are unbalanced

20. The three principal parts of a transformer are its   20._____

    A. core, primary windings, and secondary windings
    B. primary, load, and magnetic flux
    C. primary windings, secondary windings, and magnetic flux
    D. mutual induction, magnetic flux, and windings

21. A-c generators are classified   21._____

    A. as to construction
    B. as to power output
    C. according to type of prime mover
    D. according to load connections

22. The principle of operation of a transformer is   22._____

    A. electromagnetic induction
    B. varying a conductor in a magnetic field
    C. mutual induction
    D. thermionic emission

KEY (CORRECT ANSWERS)

1.	C		11.	D
2.	C		12.	B
3.	C		13.	C
4.	D		14.	C
5.	D		15.	C
6.	B		16.	B
7.	D		17.	A
8.	A		18.	B
9.	A		19.	C
10.	B		20.	A

21. C
22. C

TEST 2

DIRECTIONS: Each question or incomplete statement is followed by several suggested answers or completions. Select the one that BEST answers the question or completes the statement. *PRINT THE LETTER OF THE CORRECT ANSWER IN THE SPACE AT THE RIGHT.*

1. The variable resistance placed in the rotor circuit of the form-wound rotor is for the purpose of _____ control.

   A. speed
   B. frequency
   C. voltage
   D. starting torque

   1.____

2. The MOST common method of starting a synchronous motor is

   A. with a separate d-c motor
   B. with a cage-rotor winding
   C. manually
   D. by applying d-c to the rotor

   2.____

3. Why does the capacitor motor have a higher starting torque than a split-phase motor? It has

   A. a higher power factor
   B. no displacement between start and main winding currents
   C. less displacement between start and main winding currents
   D. greater displacement between its start and main winding currents

   3.____

4. The synchronous speed of an induction motor is the

   A. speed at which the rotor turns
   B. speed of the rotating field
   C. frequency of the rotor current
   D. slip in percent of rotor r.p.m.

   4.____

5. Near synchronous speed, the

   A. voltage induced into the rotor is very small
   B. voltage induced into the rotor is large
   C. applied voltage on the stator is zero
   D. rotor frequency is maximum

   5.____

6. What circumstances cause a lagging power factor?

   A. I_s lags resultant E by 90^0 - I_s lags E_a by angle θ
   B. I_s leads resultant E by 90^0 - I_s leads E_a by angle θ
   C. Resultant E lags Is by 90^0 - I_s lags E_a by angle ϕ
   D. E_c leads I_s by 90^0 - I_s leads E_a by angle ϕ

   6.____

7. What is the direction of rotation of the shaded-pole motor in respect to the sweeping field?

   A. With the sweeping field
   B. Against the sweeping field

   7.____

    C.   Toward the unshaded tip
    D.   Depends on direction motor was started

8. Increasing the number of poles in an induction motor   8.____

    A.   increases the field speed
    B.   decreases the field speed
    C.   decreases the motor's rated torque
    D.   causes the frequency of line E to drop

9. The rotor voltage is proportional to the   9.____

    A.   strength of the magnetic field
    B.   number of conductors on the stator
    C.   angle at which lines of force are cut
    D.   difference in rotor speed and the speed of the rotating field

10. The MOST common type of starter used on board ship for a-c motors is the   10.____

    A.   autotransformer   B.   secondary capacitor
    C.   primary resistor   D.   across-the-line

11. In the repulsion induction motor, what is the position of the brushes in relation to the stator polar axis for maximum torque?   11.____

    A. 15° B. 25° C. 45° D. 90°

12. Increasing the frequency of the voltage applied to an induction motor causes the   12.____

    A.   field speed to decrease
    B.   field speed to increase
    C.   rotor torque to decrease
    D.   stator current to increase

13. The purpose of the iron rotor core is to   13.____

    A.   decrease motor weight
    B.   produce eddy currents
    C.   reduce air gap reluctance
    D.   decrease permeability

14. The frequency of rotor current varies directly with the   14.____

    A.   applied voltage
    B.   resistance of the rotor
    C.   slip
    D.   number of windings on the stator

15. The efficiency of a motor is equal to the   15.____

    A.   torque output at synchronous speed
    B.   amount of current in the rotor
    C.   horsepower of the motor
    D.   ratio of its output power to its input power

16. The type of starter used when it is necessary to limit the starting current of an a-c motor   16._____
    is the

    A. autotransformer   B. secondary resistor
    C. primary resistor   D. primary capacitor

17. The type of starter used for speed control of an a-c motor is the   17._____

    A. secondary resistor   B. open transition
    C. closed transition   D. primary resistor

18. Motor action is BEST analyzed by applying   18._____

    A. Fleming's right-hand rule
    B. the magnetic laws of polarity
    C. Lenz's law for self-induced voltage
    D. the left-hand motor rule

19. A synchronous motor is NOT self-starting due to   19._____

    A. its lack of a rotating magnetic field
    B. inertia of the rotor
    C. magnetic locking action between rotor and stator fields
    D. its low power factor

20. The single-phase a-c motor is NOT self-starting because there is   20._____

    A. inertia in the rotor
    B. no high starting torque
    C. no revolving magnetic field
    D. a magnetic lock between the rotor and stator

21. In the a-c series motor, how are hysteresis losses minimized?   21._____
    By use of

    A. high frequency voltage   B. laminations only
    C. hard iron   D. silicon steel

22. The direction of rotation of an induction motor is   22._____

    A. opposite the rotating field direction
    B. same as direction of rotating field
    C. determined by the number of poles
    D. determined by the location of its brushes

23. A synchronous motor differs from an induction motor in that it   23._____

    A. is not self-starting
    B. requires an a-c and a d-c power supply
    C. may be used for power factor correction
    D. all of the above

24. How can the direction of rotation of a split-phase induction motor be reversed?   24.____
    Reverse

    A. leads of main winding
    B. leads of start windings
    C. leads of one phase
    D. any two leads

25. Fractional horsepower a-c series motors are called _____ motors.   25.____

    A. induction   B. synchronous
    C. universal   D. shaded-pole

KEY (CORRECT ANSWERS)

1.	D	11.	B
2.	B	12.	B
3.	D	13.	C
4.	B	14.	C
5.	A	15.	D
6.	A	16.	C
7.	A	17.	A
8.	B	18.	D
9.	D	19.	B
10.	D	20.	C

21. D
22. B
23. D
24. B
25. C

TEST 3

DIRECTIONS: Each question or incomplete statement is followed by several suggested answers or completions. Select the one that BEST answers the question or completes the statement. *PRINT THE LETTER OF THE CORRECT ANSWER IN THE SPACE AT THE RIGHT.*

1.   A d-c generator is a rotating machine that converts _____ energy.   1.____

   A.   electrical energy to mechanical
   B.   mechanical energy to electrical
   C.   low mechanical energy to a higher level of mechanical
   D.   low electrical energy to a higher level of electrical

2.   Commutator segments are insulated from each other by   2.____

   A.   small strips of wood   B.   a rubber insert
   C.   laminated varnish   D.   sheet mica

3.   The brushes that carry the current from the commutator to the external circuit are made   3.____
   of

   A.   carbon and lead   B.   carbon and graphite
   C.   graphite and lead   D.   graphite and zinc

4.   The heat-radiating ability of very small armature conductors, as compared to large arma-   4.____
   ture conductors, is

   A.   the same   B.   higher
   C.   lower   D.   there is no relation

5.   The degree that the neutral plane of a generator will shift under load is _____ the load.   5.____

   A.   inversely proportional to
   B.   proportional to
   C.   always less than proportional to
   D.   independent of

6.   D-c generators are classified according to the manner in which   6.____

   A.   they are used
   B.   the field windings are connected to the load
   C.   the armature circuit is connected to the load
   D.   the field windings are connected to the armature circuit

7.   The ONLY type of compound generator commonly used is the   7.____

   A.   over compounded   B.   flat compounded
   C.   stabilized shunt   D.   cumulative compounded

8.   On one end of the tilted plate regulator, the graphite plates are separated by mica spac-   8.____
   ers, while on the other end they are separated by

   A.   platinum contacts   B.   silver contacts
   C.   zinc contacts   D.   a carbon shoe

9. In the rocking disk regulator, when the terminal voltage of the generator starts to fall, the disk movement   9._____

   A. opens the circuit to the solenoid
   B. short-circuits more of the resistors
   C. short-circuits less of the resistors
   D. completes the circuit to the solenoid

10. The 3-wire generator is similar to the 2-wire generator except that the armature winding is tapped at _____ degrees.   10._____

   A. 30 mechanical   B. 90 electrical
   C. 180 electrical   D. 30 electrical

11. The name given to the mechanical power source used to turn the armature of a d-c generator is the   11._____

   A. motor driver   B. machine driver
   C. prime mover   D. rotor

12. Flashover between the commutator segments in a high-voltage d-c generator is prevented by   12._____

   A. reducing the number of segments
   B. increasing the number of segments
   C. reducing the number of field coils
   D. increasing the number of field coils

13. The distance between the two sides of a coil in a d-c generator armature is called   13._____

   A. coil pitch   B. commutator pitch
   C. pole span   D. pole pitch

14. The effects of armature reaction in a generator are reduced by the use of   14._____

   A. commutating windings
   B. interpoles
   C. commutating windings and interpoles
   D. compensating windings and commutating poles

15. The need for shifting the brushes of a d-c generator as its load changes has been eliminated by the use of   15._____

   A. interpoles   B. commutating poles
   C. compensating windings   D. larger brushes

16. A shunt generator will build up to full terminal voltage with no external load connected to it due to   16._____

   A. the large conductors used in the armature
   B. motor action of the generator
   C. interpoles
   D. self-excitation

17. The percent regulation of a generator having a no-load e.m.f. of 220 volts and a full-load   17._____
    e.m.f. of 215 volts is APPROXIMATELY

    A. 3%   B. 45%   C. 0.02%   D. 2%

18. The purpose of the vibrator-type current limiter is to automatically limit the output current   18._____
    of the generator to its

    A. preset value   B. minimum rated value
    C. maximum rated value   D. saturation point

19. The main differences between shipboard d-c generators and aircraft d-c generators are   19._____

    A. size, rating, and appearance
    B. size, appearance, and function
    C. size and rating only
    D. appearance, rating, and function

20. The part of a d-c generator into which the working voltage is induced is the   20._____

    A. yoke   B. field poles
    C. armature   D. commutator

21. Power lost in heat in the windings due to the flow of current through the copper is known   21._____
    as

    A. eddy current loss   B. hysteresis loss
    C. copper loss   D. none is correct

22. Compensating windings are imbedded in the pole faces parallel to the armature conduc-   22._____
    tors and are electrically connected with the armature windings in

    A. parallel
    B. series-parallel
    C. series
    D. numbers equal to the number of armature conductors

23. As armature current of a generator increases, motor reaction force   23._____

    A. decreases
    B. remains the same
    C. increases
    D. has no relation to armature current

24. The small variable shunt connected across the series field coils, to permit adjustment of   24._____
    the degree of compounding, is a

    A. diverter   B. divider   C. resistor   D. rheostat

25. The MAJOR difference between various voltage regulator systems is merely the method   25._____
    by which _____ controlled.

    A. field circuit resistance and current are
    B. armature circuit resistance is
    C. load circuit resistance is
    D. armature current and load resistance are

KEY (CORRECT ANSWERS)

1.	B	11.	C
2.	D	12.	B
3.	B	13.	A
4.	B	14.	D
5.	B	15.	A
6.	D	16.	D
7.	C	17.	D
8.	B	18.	C
9.	B	19.	A
10.	C	20.	C

21.	C
22.	C
23.	C
24.	A
25.	A

TEST 4

DIRECTIONS: Each question or incomplete statement is followed by several suggested answers or completions. Select the one that BEST answers the question or completes the statement. *PRINT THE LETTER OF THE CORRECT ANSWER IN THE SPACE AT THE RIGHT.*

1. The MOST convenient method of determining the direction of induced motion of a current-carrying conductor in a magnetic field is by   1.____

    A. applying the right-hand rule for motors
    B. applying the left-hand rule for motors
    C. using a small permanent magnet
    D. observation of the location of the conductor

2. The formula for torque developed by a motor is T =   2.____

    A. $\dfrac{K_t}{\phi I_a}$ B. $K_t^2 \phi I_a$ C. $K_t \phi I_a^2$ D. $K_t \phi I_a$

3. The effective voltage (E_{eff}) drop in a motor's armature is determined by E_{eff} =   3.____

    A. E_{app} + c.e.m.f.   B. E_{app} x c.e.m.f.

    C. E_{app} - c.e.m.f.   D. $\dfrac{\text{c.e.m.f.}}{E_{app}}$

4. Which of the following is TRUE regarding the speed regulation of a shunt motor? It has a _____ speed characteristic under _____ loads.   4.____

    A. constant; varying   B. varying; varying
    C. varying; constant   D. none of the above

5. The PRIMARY advantage of the differentially compounded motor is that it(s)   5.____

    A. is stable under heavy loads
    B. speed regulation is very good if load is not excessive
    C. has good speed regulation under varying loads
    D. will start under a heavy load

6. If the no-load speed of a shunt motor is 1,800 r.p.m. and the full-load speed is 1,475 r.p.m., the speed regulation is   6.____

    A. 18%   B. 22%   C. 2.2%   D. 1.8%

7. The input power of a series motor is the product of the applied voltage and   7.____

    A. counter e.m.f.
    B. torque
    C. current through the armature and the field
    D. current through the armature and counter e.m.f.

8. The disadvantage of the time-element automatic starter is that the   8.____
   - A. cost is high
   - B. wiring is complicated
   - C. construction is too heavy to be practical
   - D. motor is not protected on overload

9. The starting resistor of the shunt current-limit starter is connected in _____ with the   9.____
   _____.
   - A. parallel; motor armature
   - B. series; accelerating conductor
   - C. series; field winding of the motor
   - D. series; armature of the motor

10. A motor which has an output of 820 watts and an input of 960 watts has an efficiency of   10.____
    APPROXIMATELY
    - A. 90%   B. 85%   C. 75%   D. 70%

11. The horsepower developed by a motor depends MAINLY upon which of the following two   11.____
    factors?
    - A. Speed and voltage   B. Speed and torque
    - C. Torque and voltage   D. Torque and watts

12. A series motor is more adaptable where a   12.____
    - A. small variation of torque and speed is needed
    - B. wide variation of torque but a small variation of speed is needed
    - C. wide variation of torque is required, and wide variations in speed are allowable
    - D. constant speed is needed

13. Cumulative compound motors are BEST suited for use where   13.____
    - A. small starting torque is required
    - B. small changes in speed can be tolerated
    - C. the load may be removed from the motor with safety
    - D. constant speed under varying load is required

14. What is the output power in watts of a shunt motor of 1 horsepower operating on 100   14.____
    volts at 910 r.p.m., armature current of 9 amps, and a line current of 10 amps?
    _____ watts.
    - A. 98.4   B. 472   C. 646   D. 815

15. The counter e.m.f. of a motor is zero when the   15.____
    - A. motor is at rated speed
    - B. armature is not turning
    - C. motor is almost up to rated speed
    - D. armature has just begun to turn

16. The operation of the c.e.m.f. starter depends upon the   16.____

    A. size of the orifice in the dashpot
    B. c.e.m.f. developed across the armature
    C. accelerating contacts
    D. interlocking relays

17. In a shunt current-limit starter, the number of starting resistors that are commonly used is   17.____

    A. one   B. two or three
    C. five or six   D. more than ten

18. The speed of a motor with no load, with an increase of resistance in series with the field winding, will   18.____

    A. not be affected   B. decrease
    C. increase   D. fluctuate rapidly

19. The generated voltage (c.e.m.f.) of a motor   19.____

    A. opposes the impressed (source) voltage
    B. opposes any change in load
    C. aids the impressed (source) voltage
    D. none of the above

20. When a load is applied to a shunt motor, which one of the following will happen?
Speed _____, c.e.m.f. goes _____.   20.____

    A. decreases; up   B. increases; down
    C. increases; up   D. decreases; down

21. On a time-element starter, what determines the speed with which the resistance is cut out?   21.____

    A. Size of the orifice in the dashpot
    B. Counter e.m.f. of the armature
    C. Interlocking relays
    D. Accelerating contacts

22. The coil of the accelerating contactor of the shunt current-limit starter is caused to become energized by which of the following when the motor speeds up?   22.____

    A. Series relay contacts closing
    B. Series relay contacts opening
    C. The no-voltage release
    D. Holding relay contacts

23. In the series current-limit starter, the flux is prevented from closing the contactor before it has time to lock open by   23.____

    A. an open coil
    B. the spring tension of the contacts
    C. the starting resistor
    D. a short-circuited coil

24. The d-c motor armature whose speed is to be controlled by the Ward-Leonard system is   24.____
fed by a

   A. 3-phase motor
   B. d-c supply in parallel with a rheostat
   C. d-c generator
   D. rectifier

25. In the rocking disk regulator, when the terminal voltage of the generator starts to fall, the   25.____
solenoid is weakened and the weight rocks the disk

   A. upward   B. to the left
   C. to the right   D. downward

KEY (CORRECT ANSWERS)

1. A		11. B		
2. D		12. C		
3. C		13. C		
4. A		14. D		
5. B		15. B		
6. B		16. B		
7. C		17. B		
8. D		18. C		
9. D		19. A		
10. B		20. D		

21. A
22. A
23. D
24. C
25. D

TEST 5

DIRECTIONS: Each question or incomplete statement is followed by several suggested answers or completions. Select the one that BEST answers the question or completes the statement. *PRINT THE LETTER OF THE CORRECT ANSWER IN THE SPACE AT THE RIGHT.*

1. A wattmeter is connected in a circuit with the current coil _____ with the load.   1.____

   A. and the potential coil in parallel
   B. in parallel and the potential coil in series
   C. in series and the potential coil in parallel
   D. and the potential coil in series

2. A metallic rectifier is a device that   2.____

   A. converts d.c. to a.c.
   B. offers high opposition to current in two directions
   C. is classed as a unidirectional conductor
   D. has two good conductors of electricity

3. The amperage rating of the secondary windings of a current transformer is rated at _____ amps.   3.____

   A. 400   B. 12   C. 5   D. 2,000

4. In the iron-vane power factor meter, the vanes are magnetized by current flowing in   4.____

   A. coil A
   B. coil B
   C. coil C
   D. all three coils simultaneously

5. In a wattmeter, if the voltage or current safe rating is exceeded, the meter   5.____

   A. reading may not indicate overload
   B. will peg to the right of the scale
   C. will not be affected
   D. will not indicate power factor

6. The path for current flow through a rectifier cell is   6.____

   A. from the conductor, across the barrier layer, through the semiconductor
   B. from the semiconductor, across to the barrier layer, through the conductor
   C. in the direction of the arrow
   D. through the fin assembly

7. In a capacitor bridge, to find the value of an unknown capacitor, what is used to bring the circuit into balance?   7.____

   A. Two variable capacitors
   B. Capacitive reactance of capacitors
   C. Two resistors
   D. Two potentiometers

8. A watt-hour meter reads the product as   8.____

    A. energy and time   B. power and current
    C. power and time   D. power and energy

9. Under normal conditions, the fin assembly in a rectifier is used to   9.____

    A. apply uniform pressure to reduce internal resistance
    B. carry current
    C. create resistance
    D. dissipate excess heat

10. When using the vibrating-reed frequency meter, if the frequency of the current is 112   10.____
cycles, the reed will be marked _____ c.p.s.

    A. 55   B. 56   C. 60   D. 112

11. In the iron-vane power factor meter, the spiral springs   11.____

    A. are eliminated
    B. return the pointer to zero
    C. oppose torque
    D. carry current to coils A and B

12. Instruments for measuring high voltage circuits become inaccurate when connected   12.____
directly to high voltage because of

    A. electrostatic forces acting on the transformer
    B. inexpensiveness of instrument indicators
    C. high hysteresis effect on indicating element
    D. electrostatic forces acting on indicating element

13. The normal efficiency of a copper-oxide rectifier is from   13.____

    A. 25% to 55%   B. 55% to 65%
    C. 85% to 100%   D. 65% to 85%

14. In the moving-disk frequency meter, the magnetic field tends to produce rotation toward   14.____

    A. coil A   B. the magnetizing coil
    C. the shorted coil   D. coil B

15. When reading a watt-hour meter, the dials are read   15.____

    A. from the next highest number that the needle has just passed
    B. left to right
    C. right to left
    D. and subtracted

16. Instruments that are used to measure voltage and current regardless of circuit ratings   16.____
are

    A. instrument transformers   B. autotransformers
    C. electrodynamometers   D. D'Arsonvals

17. A D'Arsonval d-c type instrument can be converted to read a.c. by using   17._____

    A. a bridge rectifier unit
    B. four rectifier cells connected in series
    C. a selenium rectifier
    D. a copper-oxide rectifier

18. In the moving-disk frequency meter, the current through coil B varies   18._____

    A. inversely with the frequency
    B. directly with the frequency
    C. because it is connected in parallel
    D. because inductive reactance is constant

19. A safety precaution to follow when using a potential transformer is to   19._____

    A. ground the secondary
    B. ground the primary
    C. insulate for high current
    D. connect it in series with the line

20. The primary of a current transformer is always connected in   20._____

    A. series with the primary
    B. series with the line
    C. parallel with the line
    D. parallel with the power source

21. The wattmeter is a(n)   21._____

    A. D'Arsonval meter   B. electrodynamometer
    C. potential coil meter   D. iron-vane meter

22. A power factor meter measures the   22._____

    A. phase angle between current and voltage
    B. sine of the phase angle between current and voltage
    C. ratio of apparent power to true power
    D. ratio of true power to apparent power

23. The secondary of a current transformer should NOT be open-circuited because   23._____

    A. of high current in the primary
    B. of high voltage in the secondary
    C. of low current in the primary
    D. it is not grounded

24. In the crossed-coil power factor meter, circuit continuity to the coils is provided by   24._____

    A. stationary current coil   B. the resistor
    C. the inductor   D. three spiral springs

25. In the carbon-pile type regulator, the mechanical pressure on the carbon pile is applied   25.____
    by the

    A. wafer spring
    B. potential coil
    C. iron core of the potential coil
    D. rheostat

KEY (CORRECT ANSWERS)

1.	C	11.	A
2.	C	12.	D
3.	C	13.	D
4.	C	14.	C
5.	A	15.	C
6.	A	16.	A
7.	D	17.	A
8.	C	18.	A
9.	D	19.	A
10.	B	20.	B

21.	B
22.	D
23.	B
24.	D
25.	A

EXAMINATION SECTION
TEST 1

DIRECTIONS: Each question or incomplete statement is followed by several suggested answers or completions. Select the one that BEST answers the question or completes the statement. *PRINT THE LETTER OF THE CORRECT ANSWER IN THE SPACE AT THE RIGHT.*

1. When control current is sufficient to saturate the core, inductance _____ and reactance _____.   1.____

    A.   increases; decreases   B.   decreases; increases
    C.   increases; increases   D.   decreases; decreases

2. The power handling capacity of magnetic amplifiers has been improved PRIMARILY because of the development of   2.____

    A.   dry-disk rectifiers   B.   high-quality steels
    C.   electron amplifier tubes   D.   high-wattage resistors

3. When the inductive reactance of the load winding is decreased, load and load voltage _____.   3.____

    A.   current rises; drops
    B.   current drops; rises
    C.   circuit impedance drops;rises
    D.   circuit impedance rises;rises

4. Doubling the number of turns on a coil will   4.____

    A.   double the inductance
    B.   decrease the inductance by one-half
    C.   increase the inductance as the square of the turns
    D.   have no effect on inductance

5. Which of the following is a disadvantage of a magnetic amplifier?   5.____

    A.   High efficiency
    B.   Ruggedness
    C.   It has no moving parts
    D.   It is not useful at high frequencies

6. When a magnetic amplifier is operating at the knee of the magnetization curve, a small increase in control current will   6.____

    A.   cause a large increase in flux density
    B.   desaturate the core
    C.   increase permeability of the core
    D.   decrease inductance of the load winding

7. Transformer action between the a-c load windings and d-c control winding is   7.____

    A.   necessary to increase amplification
    B.   desired in order to reduce the required control current
    C.   desired to increase response time
    D.   not desired

8. Which of the following is considered an advantage of a magnetic-amplifier circuit over a vacuum-tube circuit?   8._____

    A. Little distortion   B. Frequency response time
    C. Shock resistance   D. Impedance matching

9. Current flow in the load circuit can be increased by   9._____

    A. *increasing* the impedance of the circuit
    B. *decreasing* the permeability of the core
    C. *increasing* the permeability of the core
    D. *decreasing* the control current

10. The BASIC control action of a magnetic amplifier depends upon   10._____

    A. variations in the load impedance
    B. changes in inductance
    C. type of core material
    D. construction of the core

11. Permeability of a substance is defined as the   11._____

    A. ease with which it conducts magnetic lines of flux
    B. opposition it offers to a-c current flow
    C. opposition it offers to d-c current flow
    D. ease with which it retains magnetic properties

12. Which of the following is an advantage of a magnetic amplifier?   12._____

    A. It has a time delay associated with magnetic effects
    B. The output waveform is not an exact reproduction of the input waveform
    C. No warm-up time
    D. It cannot handle low-level signals

13. Rectifiers are placed in the control circuits to prohibit current flow in the control winding   13._____
    during the

    A. warm-up time   B. gating half cycle
    C. reset half cycle   D. complete cycle

14. Silicon steel cores were not satisfactory for saturable reactors because of _____ satura-   14._____
    tion flux density and _____ hysteresis losses.

    A. low; high   B. high; high
    C. low; low   D. high; low

15. An important advantage of controlling circuit current by an adjustable inductor is   15._____

    A. low circuit power factor
    B. high circuit power factor
    C. absence of heat loss in the control element
    D. high heat loss in the control element

16. Operating the reactor core in the region of saturation for a portion of each cycle will cause the circuit gain to

    16.____

    A. hold steady
    C. decrease

    B. fluctuate rapidly
    D. increase

KEY (CORRECT ANSWERS)

1.	D	9.	B
2.	B	10.	B
3.	C	11.	A
4.	C	12.	C
5.	D	13.	B
6.	D	14.	A
7.	D	15.	C
8.	C	16.	D

TEST 2

DIRECTIONS: Each question or incomplete statement is followed by several suggested answers or completions. Select the one that BEST answers the question or completes the statement. *PRINT THE LETTER OF THE CORRECT ANSWER IN THE SPACE AT THE RIGHT.*

1. The direction of rotation of a capacitor motor can be reversed by   1.____

    A. reversing connection to the noncapacitor phase
    B. reversing connection to the capacitor phase
    C. reversing source power connections
    D. shifting the capacitor from one phase to the other

2. A synchro transmitter is connected to a synchro motor   2.____

    A. mechanically   B. magnetically
    C. directly   D. electrically

3. If S2 and either S1 or S3 are reversed at the receiver, the rotor will   3.____

    A. reverse direction with no error
    B. be 180° in error
    C. be 120° in error
    D. not be affected

4. A BASIC synchro system is used to   4.____

    A. transmit position information
    B. control drive motors
    C. control large amounts of current
    D. transfer energy

5. To reverse the direction of rotation of the rotor of the receiver (with no error), reverse   5.____

    A. S1 and S2   B. R1 and R2
    C. S2 and S3   D. S1 and S3

6. A control transformer synchro uses a _____ rotor.   6.____

    A. squirrel cage   B. drum wound
    C. salient pole   D. lap wound

7. The purpose of the compensating windings is to create a magnetomotive force to _____ current m.m.f.   7.____

    A. counterbalance the armature load
    B. aid the armature load
    C. counterbalance the control field
    D. aid the control field

8. The a-c servomotor is a _____ motor.   8.____

    A. 3 Φ induction   B. 1Φ repulsion induction
    C. 1Φ induction   D. 1Φ series

9. A synchro is comparable to a   9.____

    A. single-phase transformer   B. generator
    C. synchronous motor   D. three-phase transformer

10. Synchro generators and motors are usually NOT interchangeable because   10.____

    A. they are not electrically identical
    B. they are not mechanically identical
    C. the generator is larger than the motor
    D. the generator operates at a higher voltage

11. The essential components of a servomechanism are _____ controller and _____.   11.____

    A. input; transmitter
    B. input; receiver
    C. output; transmitter
    D. output; input controller

12. The differential synchro transmitter uses a rotor having _____ coil(s).   12.____

    A. a single
    B. three separately connected
    C. three wye-connected
    D. three delta-connected

13. With both rotors in the same position and maximum voltage induced in winding S2, there   13.____
is _____ current flow in _____.

    A. *minimum;* the system
    B. *maximum;* the system
    C. *minimum;* stator windings
    D. *maximum;* stator windings

14. Driving the follow-up center tap rotor from the electrical zero position causes a voltage to   14.____
be induced into the rotor by the excited stator.
This voltage will be _____ with the voltage generated by the _____ controller.

    A. in phase; input   B. out of phase; output
    C. in phase; output   D. out of phase; input

15. The generator and motor rotors are connected   15.____

    A. in parallel   B. in series
    C. to separate sources   D. by mutual inductance

16. The stator voltages are   16.____

    A. in phase and subtractive
    B. out of phase and subtractive
    C. in phase and additive
    D. out of phase and additive

17. The motor rotor will follow the generator rotor because of   17.____

    A. magnetic coupling   B. induced e.m.f.
    C. c.e.m.f.   D. generator movement

18. The windings of the synchro stators are displaced from each other by   18.____

    A. 45°   B. 90°   C. 120°   D. 240°

19. An amplidyne is a(n)   19.____

    A. a-c amplifier   B. d-c amplifier
    C. ac-dc amplifier   D. d-c servomotor

20. The rotor of a synchro MUST continuously draw current to   20.____

    A. produce heat
    B. maintain a magnetized rotor
    C. set up a reference voltage
    D. produce an induced voltage in the stator

21. Synchro systems will be at a null when induced e.m.f.'s are   21.____

    A. in phase and equal   B. out of phase and equal
    C. in phase and not equal   D. out of phase and not equal

22. The amplidyne drive motor is USUALLY a _____ motor.   22.____

    A. d-c compound
    B. d-c series
    C. one-phase a-c induction
    D. three-phase a-c induction

KEY (CORRECT ANSWERS)

1.	D	11.	D
2.	D	12.	C
3.	C	13.	A
4.	A	14.	B
5.	D	15.	A
6.	B	16.	A
7.	A	17.	A
8.	D	18.	C
9.	A	19.	B
10.	B	20.	B
21.	A		
22.	D		

TEST 3

DIRECTIONS: Each question or incomplete statement is followed by several suggested answers or completions. Select the one that BEST answers the question or completes the statement. *PRINT THE LETTER OF THE CORRECT ANSWER IN THE SPACE AT THE RIGHT.*

1. A molded capacitor on which the top row of dots (left to right) is silver, brown, and gray and the bottom row (left to right) is yellow, gold, and orange will have a value of _____ mfd.

    A. 0.018   B. 18   C. 0.183   D. 183

1.____

2. Electrical drawings which show the electric wiring for a building or other structure are called

    A. electrical layouts
    B. elementary wiring diagrams
    C. schematic wiring diagrams
    D. isometric wiring diagrams

2.____

3. The electrical symbol used to indicate a potentiometer is

    A.   B.

    C.   D.

3.____

4. The lower left dot in a five-dot capacitor indicates the

    A. multiplier   B. tolerance
    C. working voltage   D. characteristic

4.____

5. Small power transformer primary leads a.re color coded

    A. red   B. black   C. green   D. yellow

5.____

6. The temperature coefficient of a ceramic capacitor is indicated by the

    A. first dot   B. last dot   C. first band   D. last band

6.____

7. A carbon resistor color coded red, blue, green, and gold would indicate a tolerance of

    A. 2%   B. 5%   C. 10%   D. 20%

7.____

8. A carbon resistor color coded brown, black, and silver has a resistance value of

    A. 0.01Ω B. 0.1Ω C. 1Ω D. 10Ω

8.____

9. The secondary high voltage windings of a small power transformer are color coded

    A. black   B. green   C. white   D. red

9.____

10. Before making any adjustments on a faulty circuit, the maintenance man should

    A. check all resistors and capacitors in the circuit
    B. make sure he understands what the circuit is supposed to do in normal operation
    C. check the circuit power supply
    D. observe the circuit's faulty operation

10.____

11. The value of a radial carbon resistor with a red end, blue body, and an orange dot would   11.____
be

   A. 26,000Ω ± 20%   B. 6,300Ω ± 20%
   C. 3,600Ω ± 20%   D. 62,000Ω ± 20%

12. The drawings MOST often used in maintenance work are   12.____

   A. master electrical drawings and schematics
   B. schematics and wiring diagrams
   C. wiring diagrams and isometric drawings
   D. isometric drawings and schematics

13. In a standard circuit drawing 1 milli-ampere, the power rating of a 4-megohm resistor   13.____
should be _____ watts.

   A. 3   B. 4   C. 5   D. 6

14. A molded capacitor on which the top row of dots (left to right) is red, violet, and yellow   14.____
and the bottom row of dots (left to right) is green, silver, and orange will have a voltage
rating of _____ volts.

   A. 200   B. 300   C. 400   D. 500

15. The type of diagram that is consulted to find location and interconnection of parts is   15.____
called a _____ diagram.

   A. schematic   B. master   C. wiring   D. pictorial

16. In what direction does current flow in a circuit?   16.____
From

   A. left to right
   B. right to left
   C. the negative terminal to the positive
   D. the positive terminal to the negative

———————

KEY (CORRECT ANSWERS)

1.	A		9.	D
2.	A		10.	B
3.	C		11.	D
4.	A		12.	B
5.	B		13.	D
6.	C		14.	D
7.	B		15.	C
8.	B		16.	C

EXAMINATION SECTION
TEST 1

DIRECTIONS: Each question or incomplete statement is followed by several suggested answers or completions. Select the one that BEST answers the question or completes the statement. *PRINT THE LETTER OF THE CORRECT ANSWER IN THE SPACE AT THE RIGHT.*

1.   The one of the following which is a unit of inductance is the   1.____

    A.   millihenry   B.   microfarad   C.   kilohm   D.   weber

2.   Of the following, the BEST conductor of electricity is   2.____

    A.   aluminum   B.   copper   C.   silver   D.   iron

3.   A voltage of 1000 microvolts is the SAME as   3.____

    A.   1,000 volts   B.   0.100 volts
    C.   0.010 volts   D.   0.001 volts

4.   The function of a rectifier is SIMILAR to that of a(n)   4.____

    A.   inverter   B.   relay   C.   commutator   D.   transformer

5.   A 9-ohm resistor rated at 225 watts is used in a 120-volt circuit. In order not to exceed the rating of the resistor, the MAXIMUM current, in amperes, which can flow through the circuit is   5.____

    A.   2   B.   3   C.   4   D.   5

6.   The number of circular mils in a conductor 0.036 inch in diameter is   6.____

    A.   6   B.   36   C.   72   D.   1296

7.   The color of the label on most commercially available 250-volt cartridge fuses of 15-amperes or less capacity is   7.____

    A.   green   B.   blue   C.   red   D.   yellow

8.   Assume that a two-microfarad capacitor is connected in parallel with a three-microfarad capacitor. The resulting capacity, in microfarads, is   8.____

    A.   2/3   B.   6/5   C.   3/2   D.   5

9.   The speed of the rotating magnetic field in a 12-pole 60-cycle stator is   9.____

    A.   1800 rpm   B.   1200 rpm   C.   720 rpm   D.   D 600 rpm

10.   The transformer connection *generally* used to convert from three-phase to two-phase by means of two transformers is the   10.____

    A.   Scott or T   B.   V or Open delta
    C.   Wye-Delta   D.   Delta-Wye

11. The conductance, in mhos, of a circuit whose resistance is one ohm is   11.____

    A. 1/10   B. 1   C. 10   D. 100

12. Assume that a 220-volt, 25 cycle, A.C., e.m.f. is impressed across a circuit consisting of a   12.____
25-ohm resistor in series with a 30-microfarad capacitor. The current in this circuit, in
amperes, is, *most nearly,*

    A. 0.5   B. 0.8   C. 1.0   D. 1.5

13. An ammeter has a full scale deflection with a current of 0.010 amperes and an internal   13.____
resistance of 20 ohms.
In order for the ammeter to have a full scale deflection with a current of 10 amperes
and not damage its movement, a shunt should be used having a value of

    A. 10 ohms   B. 0.2 ohms   C. 0.02 ohms   D. 0.01 ohms

14. American Wire Gage (A.W.G.) wire size numbers are set so that the resistance of wire   14.____
per 1,000 ft. doubles with every increase of

    A. one gage number   B. two gage numbers
    C. three gage numbers   D. four gage numbers

15. In an ideal transformer for transforming or "stepping down" the voltage from 1200 volts to   15.____
120 volts, the turns ratio is

    A. 10:1   B. 12:1   C. 1:12   D. 1:10

16. When a lead-acid battery is fully charged, the negative plate consists of lead   16.____

    A. peroxide   B. sponge   C. sulfate   D. dioxide

17. Improving the commutation of a D.C. generator is MOST often done by using   17.____

    A. a rheostat in series with the equalizer
    B. an equalizer alone
    C. a compensator
    D. interpoles

18. In a wave-wound armature, the MINIMUM number of commutator brushes necessary is   18.____

    A. two times the number of poles
    B. two, regardless of the number of poles
    C. one-half times the number of poles
    D. four, regardless of the number of poles

19. A three-phase induction motor runs hot with all stator coils at the same temperature. The   19.____
trouble which would cause this condition is that

    A. the motor is running single phase
    B. the motor is overloaded
    C. a part of the motor windings is inoperative
    D. the rotor bars are loose

20. Where constant speed is required, the one of the following motors that should be used is   20._____
    a

    A. wound-rotor motor   B. series motor
    C. compound motor   D. shunt motor

21. To reverse the direction of rotation of a 3-phase induction motor,   21._____

    A. the field connections should be reversed
    B. the armature connections should be reversed
    C. any two line leads should be interchanged
    D. the brushes should be shifted in the direction opposite to that of the armature rotation

22. The speed of a wound-rotor motor may be increased by   22._____

    A. *decreasing* the resistance in the secondary circuit
    B. *increasing* the resistance in the secondary circuit
    C. *decreasing* the shunt field current
    D. *increasing* the series field resistance

23. The one of the following methods which can be used to increase the slip of the rotor in a   23._____
    single-phase shaded-pole motor, is the

    A. reversal of the leads of the field winding
    B. addition of capacitors in series with the starting winding
    C. reduction of the impressed voltage
    D. addition of more capacitors in parallel with the starting winding

24. The direction of rotation of a single-phase A.C. repulsion motor may be reversed by   24._____

    A. interchanging the two line leads to the motor
    B. interchanging the leads to the main winding
    C. interchanging the leads to the starting winding
    D. moving the brushes to the other side of the neutral position

25. The torque developed by a D.C. series motor is   25._____

    A. *inversely proportional* to the square of the armature current
    B. *proportional* to the square of the armature current
    C. *proportional* to the armature current
    D. *inversely proportional* to the armature current

KEY (CORRECT ANSWERS)

1.	A		11.	B
2.	C		12.	C
3.	D		13.	C
4.	C		14.	C
5.	D		15.	A
6.	D		16.	B
7.	B		17.	D
8.	D		18.	B
9.	D		19.	B
10.	A		20.	D

21.	C
22.	A
23.	C
24.	D
25.	B

TEST 2

DIRECTIONS: Each question or incomplete statement is followed by several suggested answers or completions. Select the one that BEST answers the question or completes the statement. *PRINT THE LETTER OF THE CORRECT ANSWER IN THE SPACE AT THE RIGHT.*

1. The one of the following which is MOST commonly used to clean a commutator is   1.____

   A. emery cloth   B. graphite
   C. a smooth file   D. fine-grit sandpaper

2. The type of motor which requires BOTH A.C. and D.C. for operation is the   2.____

   A. compound motor   B. universal motor
   C. synchronous motor   D. squirrel-cage motor

3. Compensators are used for starting large   3.____

   A. shunt motors   B. series motors
   C. induction motors   D. compound motors

4. The device MOST frequently used to correct low lagging power factor is a(n)   4.____

   A. solenoid   B. induction regulator
   C. induction motor   D. synchronous motor

5. Of the following motors, the one with the HIGHEST starting torque is the   5.____

   A. compound motor   B. series motor
   C. shunt motor   D. split phase motor

6. The approximate efficiency of a 60-cycle, 6-pole induction motor running at 1050 rpm and having a synchronous speed of 1200 rpm, is   6.____

   A. 67.0%   B. 78.5%   C. 87.5%   D. 90.0%

7. The MAIN contributing factor to motor starter failures *usually* is   7.____

   A. overloading   B. dirt
   C. bearing trouble   D. friction

8. The neutral or grounded conductors in branch circuit wiring must be identified by being colored   8.____

   A. black or brown   B. black with white traces
   C. white with black traces   D. white or natural gray

9. The SMALLEST radius for the inner edge of any field bend in a 1-inch rigid or flexible conduit when type R wire is being used, is   9.____

   A. 3 inches   B. 5 inches   C. 6 inches   D. 10 inches

10. Thermal cutouts used to protect a motor against overloads may have a current rating of not more than   10.____

    A. the starting current of the motor
    B. 125% of the full-load current rating of the motor

C.   the full-load current of the motor

D.   the current-carrying capacity of the branch circuit conductors

11.   The MAXIMUM size of EMT permitted is   11.____

   A.   4 inches   B.   3 1/2 inches   C.   3 inches   D.   2 inches

12.   The type of equipment which is defined as a set of conductors originating at the load side   12.____
   of the service equipment and supplying the main and/or one or more secondary distribution centers, is a

   A.   sub-feeder   B.   feeder   C.   main   D.   service cable

13.   The SMALLEST size rigid conduit that may be used in wiring is   13.____

   A.   3/8 inch   B.   1/2 inch   C.   3/4 inch   D.   1 inch

14.   An enclosed 600-volt cartridge fuse must be of the knife-blade contact type if its ampere   14.____
   rating is

   A.   20   B.   40   C.   60   D.   80

15.   An insulated ground for fixed equipment should be color coded   15.____

   A.   yellow
   B.   green or green with a yellow stripe
   C.   blue or blue with a yellow stripe
   D.   black

16.   Of the following, the meter that CANNOT be used to measure A.C. voltage is the   16.____

   A.   electrodynamic voltmeter   B.   electrostatic voltmeter
   C.   D'Arsonval voltmeter   D.   thermocouple voltmeter

17.   Of the following, an instrument frequently used to measure high insulation resistance is   17.____
   a(n)

   A.   tong-test ammeter   B.   megger
   C.   ohmmeter   D.   electrostatic voltmeter

18.   When using a voltmeter in testing an electric circuit, the voltmeter should be placed in   18.____

   A.   *series* with the circuit
   B.   *parallel* with the circuit
   C.   *parallel* or in *series* with a current transformer, depending on the current
   D.   *series* with the active element

19.   The MINIMUM number of wattmeters necessary to measure the power in the load of a   19.____
   balanced 3-phase, 4-wire system, is

   A.   1   B.   2   C.   3   D.   4

20.   An instrument that measures electrical energy is the   20.____

   A.   current transformer   B.   watthour meter
   C.   dynamometer   D.   wattmeter

21. The one of the following items which can be used to *properly* test an armature for a   21.____
shorted coil is a

   A. neon light   B. megger
   C. growler   D. pair of series test lamps

22. The instrument that measures loads at the load terminals, averaged over specified time   22.____
periods, is the

   A. coulomb meter   B. wattmeter
   C. demand meter   D. var-hour meter

23. A multiplier is usually used to increase the range of   23.____

   A. voltmeter   B. watthour meter
   C. wheatstont bridge   D. Nernst bridge

24. The instrument used to indicate the phase relation between the voltage and the current   24.____
of an A.C. circuit is called a

   A. power factor meter   B. synchroscope
   C. phase indicator   D. var-hour meter

25. Except where busways are entering or leaving service or distribution equipment, the bot-   25.____
tom of the busway enclosure for all horizontal busway runs should be kept at a MINIMUM
height above the floor of

   A. 4 feet   B. 6 feet   C. 8 feet   D. 10 feet

―――――――

KEY (CORRECT ANSWERS)

1.	D	11.	D
2.	C	12.	B
3.	C	13.	B
4.	D	14.	D
5.	B	15.	B
6.	C	16.	C
7.	B	17.	B
8.	D	18.	B
9.	C	19.	A
10.	B	20.	B

21.	C
22.	C
23.	A
24.	A
25.	C

―――――――

TEST 3

DIRECTIONS: Each question or incomplete statement is followed by several suggested answers or completions. Select the one that BEST answers the question or completes the statement. *PRINT THE LETTER OF THE CORRECT ANSWER IN THE SPACE AT THE RIGHT.*

1. The lubricant *commonly* used to make it easier to pull braid-covered cable into a duct is   1._____

    A. soapstone   B. soft soap
    C. heavy grease   D. light oil

2. Of the following, the conductor insulation which may be used in wet locations is type   2._____

    A. RH   B. RHH   C. RHW   D. RUH

3. Assume that at a certain distribution point you notice that among several of the conductors entering the same raceway, some have a half-inch band of yellow tape, while the others do not. The conductors with the yellow tape are all   3._____

    A. grounded   B. ungrounded   C. A.C.   D. D.C.

4. Conductors of the same length, same circular mil area and type of insulation, may be run in multiple   4._____

    A. under no circumstances
    B. if each conductor is #4 or larger
    C. if each conductor is #2 or larger
    D. if each conductor is #1/0 or larger

5. In order to keep conduits parallel where several parallel runs of conduit of varying size are installed through 45 or 90 degree bends, it is BEST to   5._____

    A. bend conduit on the job
    B. use standard factory-made elbows
    C. use flexible connectors to adjust runs
    D. bend conduit at the factory

6. The BEST way to join two lengths of conduit which cannot be turned is to   6._____

    A. use a split adapter
    B. use a conduit union ("Erickson")
    C. cut running threads on one end of one length of the conduit
    D. cut running threads on the ends of both lengths of conduit

7. When an electrical splice is wrapped with both rubber tape and friction tape, the MAIN purpose of the friction tape is to   7._____

    A. protect the rubber tape
    B. provide additional insulation
    C. build up the insulation to the required thickness
    D. increase the strength of the splice

8. Assume that explosion-proof wiring is required in a certain area. Conduits entering an enclosure in this area which contains apparatus that may produce arcs, sparks or high temperature, should be provided with

    A. a cable terminator
    B. an approved sealing compound
    C. couplings with three full threads engaged
    D. insulated bushings

8.____

9. If installed in dry locations, wireways may be used for circuits of **not more than**

    A. 208 volts   B. 440 volts   C. 600 volts   D. 1100 volts

9.____

10. An interior wiring circuit has two conductors, one white and one black. Assume that it becomes necessary to add a third conductor as a switch leg. The color of the THIRD conductor should be

    A. blue   B. red   C. green   D. natural gray

10.____

11. Keyless lampholders rated at 1500 watts have bases which are classed as

    A. Intermediate   B. Medium   C. Mogul   D. Admedium

11.____

12. In precast cellular concrete floor raceways, the LARGEST conductor which may be installed, except by special permission, is

    A. No. 2   B. No. 0   C. No. 00   D. No. 000

12.____

13. The conductor insulation which may be used for fixture wire is type

    A. TF   B. TW   C. TA   D. RW

13.____

14. Multiple fuses are permissible

    A. under no circumstances
    B. for conductors longer than 1/0
    C. for conductors larger than 2/0
    D. for conductors larger than 4/0

14.____

15. In loosening a nut, a socket wrench with a ratchet handle should be used in preference to other types of wrenches if

    A. the nut is out of reach
    B. the turning space for the handle is limited
    C. the nut is worn
    D. greater leverage is required

15.____

16. Solders used for electrical connections are alloys of

    A. tin and lead   B. tin and zinc
    C. lead and zinc   D. tin and copper

16.____

17. Another name for a pipe wrench is a

    A. crescent wrench   B. torque wrench
    C. Stillson wrench   D. monkey wrench

17.____

18. The tool used to cut raceways is a hacksaw with fine teeth, *commonly* called a   18._____

    A.   crosscut saw   B.   keyhole saw
    C.   rip saw   D.   tube saw

19. Lead expansion anchors are MOST commonly used to fasten conduit to a   19._____

    A.   wooden partition wall   B.   plaster wall
    C.   solid concrete wall   D.   gypsum wall

20. The use of "running" threads when coupling two sections of conduit is   20._____

    A.   always good practice
    B.   good practice only when installing enameled conduit
    C.   good practice only if it is impossible to turn one of the conduits
    D.   always poor practice

21. A quick-break knifeswitch is often used rather than a standard knifeswitch of the same   21._____
rating because the quick-break knife switch

    A.   resists burning due to arcing at the contact points
    B.   is easier to install and align
    C.   is simpler in construction
    D.   can carry a higher current without over-heating

22. The tip of a soldering iron is made of copper because   22._____

    A.   copper is a very good conductor of heat
    B.   solder will not stick to other metals
    C.   it is the cheapest metal available
    D.   the melting point of copper is very high

23. Good practice requires that cartridge fuses be removed from their clips by using a fuse   23._____
puller rather than the bare hand. The reason for using the fuse puller is that the

    A.   bare hand may be burned or otherwise injured
    B.   fuse is less likely to break
    C.   fuse clips may be damaged when pulled
    D.   use of the bare hands slows down removal of fuse and causes arcing

24. The frame of a portable electric tool should be grounded in order to   24._____

    A.   reduce leakage from the winding
    B.   prevent short circuits
    C.   reduce the danger of overheating
    D.   prevent the frame from becoming alive to ground

25. The LEAST desirable device for measuring the dimensions of an electrical equipment   25._____
cabinet containing live equipment, is a

    A.   wooden yardstick
    B.   six-foot folding wooden ruler
    C.   twelve-inch plastic ruler
    D.   six-foot steel tape

KEY (CORRECT ANSWERS)

1.	A		11.	C
2.	C		12.	B
3.	D		13.	A
4.	D		14.	A
5.	A		15.	B
6.	B		16.	A
7.	A		17.	C
8.	B		18.	D
9.	C		19.	C
10.	B		20.	D

21.	A
22.	A
23.	A
24.	D
25.	D

———

TEST 4

DIRECTIONS: Each question or incomplete statement is followed by several suggested answers or completions. Select the one that BEST answers the question or completes the statement. *PRINT THE LETTER OF THE CORRECT ANSWER IN THE SPACE AT THE RIGHT.*

1. If three equal resistance coils are connected in parallel, the resistance of this combination is **equal to**   1._____

    A.   one-third the resistance of one coil
    B.   the resistance of one coil
    C.   three times the resistance of one coil
    D.   nine times the resistance of one coil

2. The voltage to neutral of a 3-phase, 4-wire system, is 120 volts. The line-to-line voltage is   2._____

    A.   208 volts   B.   220 volts   C.   230 volts   D.   240 volts

3. Three 6-ohm resistances are connected in Y across a 3-phase circuit. If a current of 10 amperes flows through each resistance, the TOTAL power in watts drawn by this load is, *most nearly,*   3._____

    A.   600   B.   1200   C.   1800   D.   2400

4. A conduit in an outlet box should be provided with a locknut   4._____

    A.   on the outside and bushing on the inside
    B.   and bushing on the inside
    C.   on the inside and bushing on the outside
    D.   and bushing on the inside

5. If the current in a single-phase, 120-volt circuit is 10 amperes and a wattmeter in this circuit reads 1080 watts, the power factor is, *most nearly,*   5._____

    A.   1.11   B.   .9   C.   .8   D.   .7

6. It is poor practice to use a file without a handle because the   6._____

    A.   file may be dropped and damaged
    B.   unprotected end may mar the surface being filed
    C.   user may be injured
    D.   file marks will be too deep

7. If a 60-cycle, 4-pole squirrel-cage, induction motor has a slip of 5%, its speed is, *most nearly,*   7._____

    A.   1800 rpm   B.   1795 rpm   C.   1750 rpm   D.   1710 rpm

8. The PROPER way to reverse the direction of rotation of a 3-phase wound rotor induction motor is to   8._____

    A.   reverse two leads between the rotor and the control resistances
    B.   shift the brushes
    C.   reverse two supply leads
    D.   open one rotor lead

9. Sulphuric acid should **always** be poured into the water when new electrolyte for a lead-acid battery is prepared. The reason for this precaution is to   9.____

    A. *avoid* splattering of the acid
    B. *avoid* explosive fumes
    C. *prevent* corrosion of the mixing vessel
    D. *prevent* clotting of the acid

10. The direction of rotation of a d.c. shunt motor can be reversed PROPERLY by   10.____

    A. reversing the two supply leads
    B. shifting the position of the brushes
    C. reversing the connections to both the armature and the field
    D. reversing the connections to the field

Questions 11-13.

DIRECTIONS: Questions 11 to 13, inclusive, refer to this excerpt from the electrical code on the subject of grounding electrodes.

Each buried plate electrode shall present not less than two square feet of surface to the exterior soil. Electrodes of plate copper shall be at least .06 inch in thickness. Electrodes of iron or steel plate shall be at least one-quarter inch in thickness. Electrodes of iron or steel pipe shall be galvanized and not less than three-quarter inch in internal diameter. Electrodes of rods of steel or iron shall be at least three-quarter inch minimum cross-section dimension... Driven electrodes of pipes or rods... shall be driven to a depth of at least eight feet regardless of the size or number of electrodes used... Each electrode used shall be separated at least six feet from any other electrode including those used for signal circuits, radio, lightning rods or any other purposes.

11. According to the above paragraph, all grounding electrodes MUST be   11.____

    A. of plate copper
    B. of iron pipe
    C. at least three-quarter inch minimum cross-section dimension
    D. separated at least six feet from any other electrode

12. According to the above paragraph, the one of the following electrodes which meets the code requirements is a(n)   12.____

    A. copper plate 12" X 18" X .06"
    B. steel plate 14" X 24" X .06"
    C. copper plate 12" X 24" X .06"
    D. iron plate 12" X 18" X .25'"

13. According to the above paragraph, the one of the following electrodes which meets the code requirements is   13.____

    A. plain iron pipe, 1" in internal diameter, driven to a depth of 10 feet
    B. galvanized iron pipe, 3/4" in internal diameter, driven to a depth of 6 feet
    C. plain steel pipe, 1" in internal diameter, driven to a depth of 7 feet
    D. galvanized steel pipe, 3/4" in internal diameter, driven to a depth of 9 feet

14. With reference to armature windings, lap windings are often called   14.____

    A. ring windings   B. multiple windings
    C. series windings   D. toroidal windings

15. The question refers to the diagram below.   15.____

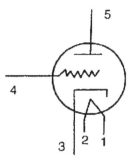

    The element numbered 4 is usually called the

    A. plate   B. grid   C. filament   D. cathode

16. To properly mount an outlet box on a concrete ceiling, it is BEST to use   16.____

    A. expansion screw anchors   B. wooden plugs
    C. wood screws   D. masonry nails

17. A d.c. motor takes 30 amps, at 110 volts and has an efficiency of 90%. The horsepower   17.____
    available at the pulley is, *approximately*,

    A. 5   B. 4   C. 3   D. 2

18. If the armature current drawn by a series motor doubles, the torque   18.____

    A. remains the same   B. doubles
    C. becomes 4 times as great   D. becomes 8 times as great

19. The full load current, in amperes, of a 110-volt, 10 H.P., d.c. motor having an efficiency of   19.____
    80% is, *approximately*,

    A. 62   B. 85   C. 99   D. 133

Questions 20-21.

DIRECTIONS: Questions 21 and 22 are to be answered in accordance with the diagram
             below.

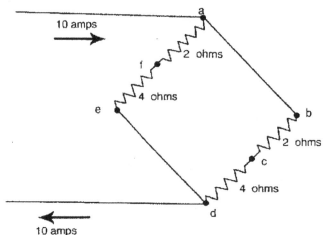

20. With reference to the above diagram, the voltage difference between points c and f is, *most nearly,*

    A. 40 volts   B. 20 volts   C. 10 volts   D. 0 volts

20.____

21. With reference to the above diagram, the current flowing through the resistance c d is, *most nearly,*

    A. 10 amperes   B. 5 amperes   C. 4 amperes   D. 2 amperes

21.____

Questions 22-25.

DIRECTIONS: Questions 22 through 25, inclusive, refer to the diagram below

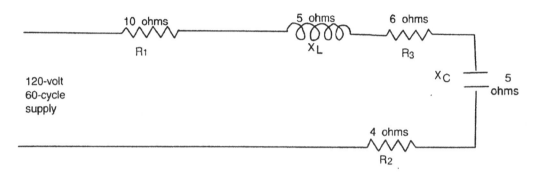

22. The value of the impedance in ohms of the above circuit is, *most nearly,*

    A. 60   B. 30   C. 25   D. 20

22.____

23. The current, in amperes, flowing in the above circuit is, *most nearly,*

    A. 2   B. 3   C. 6   D. 8

23.____

24. The potential drop, in volts, across R_3 is, *most nearly,*

    A. 12   B. 18   C. 36   D. 48

24.____

25. The power, in watts, consumed in the above circuit is, *most nearly,*

    A. 1080   B. 720   C. 180   D. 80

25.____

KEY (CORRECT ANSWERS)

1.	A		11.	D
2.	A		12.	C
3.	C		13.	D
4.	A		14.	B
5.	B		15.	B
6.	C		16.	A
7.	D		17.	B
8.	C		18.	C
9.	A		19.	B
10.	D		20.	D

21.	B
22.	D
23.	C
24.	C
25.	B

———

TEST 5

DIRECTIONS: Each question or incomplete statement is followed by several suggested answers or completions. Select the one that BEST answers the question or completes the statement. *PRINT THE LETTER OF THE CORRECT ANSWER IN THE SPACE AT THE RIGHT.*

1. The heat dissipation, W, in a resistor having a resistance of R ohms connected across a supply of E volts, is proportional to E^2/R.
   If R is reduced to one-half of its former value and E is doubled, the heat dissipation in this resistor is *now*

   A. 8W   B. 2W   .C. 4W   D. 1/2W

   1.____

2. Solder commonly used for electrical work is composed, *most likely,* of

   A. lead and tin   B. antimony and zinc
   C. lead and zinc   D. silver and antimony

   2.____

3. A condenser having a capacitance of 3 microfarads is connected in parallel with a condenser having a capacitance of 2 microfarads. The combination is equal to a single condenser having a capacitance, in microfarads, of, *most nearly,*

   A. 5/6   B. 6/5   C. 5   D. 6

   3.____

4. Of the following units, the one which is a unit of inductance is the

   A. maxwell   B. henry   C. weber   D. oersted

   4.____

5. The tool *commonly* used for bending conduit of small sizes is called a

   A. mandrel   B. bending wrench   C. hickey   D. kinker

   5.____

6. If a cartridge fuse clip makes contact with its fuse with much less than normal spring tension, the result would MOST likely be that the

   A. fuse will immediately burn out
   B. voltage at the supply will be high
   C. voltage at the load will be high
   D. clips will become warm

   6.____

7. Of the following units, the one which is a unit of work or energy is the

   A. joule   B. faraday   C. coulomb   D. farad

   7.____

8. The one of the following substances which is the BEST conductor of electricity is

   A. iron   B. aluminum   C. tin   D. copper

   8.____

9. The formula for the resistance of one branch of a wye which is equivalent to a given delta

   is $R_a = \dfrac{A}{A+B+C}$.

   If A = B = C = 3, the value of R_a is, *most nearly,*

   A. 1   B. 3   C. 6   D. 9

   9.____

10. When a splice is soldered, flux is used to 10.____

    A. act as a binder   B. lubricate the surfaces
    C. keep the surfaces clean   D. prevent rapid loss of heat

11. A 2000 ft. cable which has an insulation resistance of 180 megohms is cut in half. The 11.____
insulation resistance of one of the 1000-ft. lengths will be, *most nearly,*

    A. 720 megohms   B. 360 megohms
    C. 90 megohms   D. 45 megohms

12. The area in circular mils of a piece of bare copper wire whose diameter is 0.1" is, *most* 12.____
nearly,

    A. 780   B. 1,000   C. 7,800   D. 10,000

13. The resistance of a piece of copper wire is 13.____

    A. *directly* proportional to its diameter
    B. *inversely* proportional to its length
    C. *directly* proportional to the square of its diameter
    D. *inversely* proportional to its cross-sectional area

14. If an incandescent lamp is operated at a voltage which is higher than its rated voltage, 14.____
the

    A. lumens output will be less than rated value
    B. current drawn will be less than rated value
    C. power consumed will be less than rated value
    D. life of the lamp will be less than rated value

15. The one of the following that is BEST suited to fight electrical fires is a 15.____

    A. CO_2 fire extinguisher   B. soda-acid fire extinguisher
    C. foam fire extinguisher   D. very fine spray of water

16. In order to get MAXIMUM power output from a battery, the external resistance should 16.____
equal

    A. zero
    B. one-half of the internal resistance of the battery
    C. the internal resistance of the battery
    D. twice the internal resistance of the battery

17. A voltmeter with a scale range of 0-5 has a resistance of 500 ohms. The resistance, in 17.____
ohms, of a multiplier for this instrument which will give it a range of 0 to 150 volts is, *most*
nearly,

    A. 750   B. 2,500   C. 14,500   D. 75,000

18. The one of the following items which is *commonly* used to increase the range of a d.c. 18.____
ammeter is a

    A. ceramicon   B. shunt
    C. current transformer   D. bridging transformer

19. Continuity of the conductors in an electrical circuit can be determined *conveniently* in the field by means of a(n)   19.____

    A. bell and battery set   B. Maxwell bridge
    C. Preece test   D. ammeter

Questions 20-25.

DIRECTIONS: Questions 20 to 25, inclusive, refer to the symbols of the A.S.A. which are listed below.

1. (D)   6. [F]○   11. (W)   16. (symbol)

2. (symbol)   7. [•]   12. [WH]   17. (c)

3. (F)   8. S_2 13. (B)   18. (symbol)

4. (•)   9. [F]   14. —///—   19. [SC]

5. (symbol)$_3$ 10. (symbol)   15. [P]   20. S_{mc}

20. A push button is designated by the symbol numbered   20.____

    A. 4   B. 7   C. 13   D. 15

21. A fire alarm station is designated by the symbol numbered   21.____

    A. 3   B. 6   C. 9   D. 10

22. A duplex convenience outlet is designated by the symbol numbered   22.____

    A. 1   B. 2   C. 5   D. 17

23. A battery is designated by the symbol numbered   23.____

    A. 10   B. 13   C. 16   D. 18

24. A double pole switch is designated by the symbol numbered   24.____

    A. 1   B. 2   C. 8   D. 15

25. The designation for a 3-wire circuit is numbered   25.____

    A. 3   B. 5   C. 11   D. 14

KEY (CORRECT ANSWERS)

1.	A		11.	B
2.	A		12.	D
3.	C		13.	D
4.	B		14.	D
5.	C		15.	A
6.	D		16.	C
7.	A		17.	C
8.	D		18.	B
9.	A		19.	A
10.	C		20.	B

21.	C
22.	B
23.	C
24.	C
25.	D

TEST 6

DIRECTIONS: Each question or incomplete statement is followed by several suggested answers or completions. Select the one that BEST answers the question or completes the statement. *PRINT THE LETTER OF THE CORRECT ANSWER IN THE SPACE AT THE RIGHT.*

1. A good magnetic material is

   A. aluminum   B. iron   C. brass   D. carbon

   1.____

2. A thermo-couple is a device for

   A. changing frequency   B. changing d.c. to a.c.
   C. measuring temperature   D. heat insulation

   2.____

3. It is desired to operate a 6-volt lamp from a 120-volt a.c source. This can be done with the LEAST waste of power by using a

   A. series resistor   B. rectifier
   C. step-down transformer   D. rheostat

   3.____

4. Rosin is a material *generally* used

   A. in batteries   B. as a dielectric
   C. as a soldering flux   D. for high voltage insulation

   4.____

5. A milliampere is

   A. 1000 amperes   B. 100 amperes
   C. .01 ampere   D. .001 ampere

   5.____

6. A compound motor usually has

   A. only a shunt field   B. only a series field
   C. no brushes   D. both a shunt and a series field

   6.____

7. To connect a d.c. voltmeter to measure a voltage higher than the scale maximum, use a

   A. series resistance   B. shunt
   C. current transformer   D. voltage transformer

   7.____

8. The voltage applied to the terminals of a storage battery to charge it CANNOT be

   A. rectified a.c.   B. straight d.c.
   C. pulsating d.c.   D. ordinary a.c.

   8.____

9. When two unequal condensers are connected in parallel, the

   A. total capacity is decreased
   B. total capacity is increased
   C. result will be a short-circuit
   D. smaller one will break down

   9.____

10. A megohm is

   A. 10 ohms   B. 100 ohms
   C. 1000 ohms   D. 1,000,000 ohms

   10.____

11. Of the following, the poorest conductor of electricity is   11.____

    A. brass   B. lead   C. an acid solution D. slate

12. A flashlight battery, a condenser, and a flashlight bulb are connected in series with each   12.____
    other. If the bulb burns brightly and steadily, then the condenser is

    A. open-circuited   B. short-circuited
    C. good   D. fully charged

13. A kilowatt of power will be taken from a 500-volt d.c. supply by a load of   13.____

    A. 200 amperes   B. 20 amperes   C. 2 amperes   D. 0.2 ampere

14. A commutator is used on a shunt generator in order to   14.____

    A. step-up voltage   B. step-up current
    C. change a.c. to d.c.   D. control generator speed

15. The number of cells connected in series in a 6-volt storage battery of the lead-acid type   15.____
    is

    A. 2   B. 3   C. 4   D. 5

16. A 15-ampere circuit breaker as compared to a 15-ampere plug fuse   16.____

    A. can be reclosed   B. is cheaper
    C. is safer   D. is smaller

17. Lengths of rigid conduit are connected together to make up a long run by means of   17.____

    A. couplings   B. bushings   C. hickeys   D. lock nuts

18. BX is *commonly* used to indicate   18.____

    A. rigid conduit without wires
    B. flexible conduit without wires
    C. insulated wires covered with flexible steel armor
    D. insulated wires covered with a non-metallic covering

19. Good practice is to cut BX with a   19.____

    A. hacksaw   B. 3-wheel pipe cutter
    C. bolt cutter   D. heavy pliers

20. Silver is used for relay contacts in order to   20.____

    A. improve conductivity   B. avoid burning
    C. reduce costs   D. avoid arcing

21. Rigid conduit is fastened on the inside of the junction box by means of   21.____

    A. a bushing   B. a locknut
    C. a coupling   D. set-screw clamps

22. Of the following, the material which can BEST withstand high temperature is   22.____

    A. plastic   B. enamel   C. fiber   D. mica

23. A lead-acid type of storage battery exposed to freezing weather is *most likely* to freeze when the   23.____

    A. battery is fully charged   B. battery is complete discharged
    C. water level is low   D. cap vent holes are plugged

24. An important reason making it poor practice to put telephone wires in the same conduit with a.c. power lines is that   24.____

    A. power will be lost from the a.c. line
    B. the conduit will overheat
    C. the wires may be confused
    D. the telephone circuits will be noisy

25. In a loaded power circuit, it is MOST dangerous to   25.____

    A. *close* the circuit with a circuit breaker
    B. *close* the circuit with a knife switch
    C. *open* the circuit with a knife switch
    D. *open* the circuit with a circuit breaker

KEY (CORRECT ANSWERS)

1. B	11. D
2. C	12. B
3. C	13. C
4. C	14. C
5. D	15. B
6. D	16. A
7. A	17. A
8. D	18. C
9. B	19. A
10. D	20. A

21. A
22. D
23. B
24. D
25. C

TEST 7

DIRECTIONS: Each question or incomplete statement is followed by several suggested answers or completions. Select the one that BEST answers the question or completes the statement. *PRINT THE LETTER OF THE CORRECT ANSWER IN THE SPACE AT THE RIGHT.*

1. When fastening electrical equipment to a hollow tile wall, it is good practice to use   1.____
   A. toggle bolts   B. wood screws
   C. nails   D. ordinary bolts and nuts

2. Of the following, the MOST important reason for keeping the oil in a transformer tank   2.____
   moisture-free is to prevent
   A. rusting   B. voltage breakdown
   C. freezing of the oil   D. overheating

3. A voltmeter is generally connected to a high potential a.c. bus through a(n)   3.____
   A. auto-transformer   B. potential transformer
   C. resistor   D. relay

4. The HIGHEST total voltage which can be measured by using two identical 0-300 volt   4.____
   range d.c. meters connected in series would be
   A. 150 volts   B. 300 volts   C. 450 volts   D. 600 volts

5. Transistors are MAINLY employed in electrical circuits to take the place of   5.____
   A. resistors   B. condensers   C. inductances   D. vacuum tubes

6. The MINIMUM number of 10-ohm,1-ampere resistors which would   6.____
   be required to give an equivalent resistance of 10 ohms capable of carrying a 2-
   ampere load is
   A. 2   B. 3   C. 4   D. 5

7. To increase the current measuring range of an ammeter, the equipment *commonly*   7.____
   employed is a
   A. series resistor   B. shunt
   C. short-circuiting switch   D. choke

8. If a 10-watt lamp and a 100-watt lamp, each rated at 120 volts, are connected in series to   8.____
   a 240-volt source, then the voltage *across* the 10-watt lamp will be
   A. zero   B. about 24 volts
   C. exactly 120 volts   D. much more than 120 volts

9. If the load on the secondary of a small 10 to 1 step-up transformer is 100 watts, then the   9.____
   power being taken by the *primary* from the power line
   A. is less than 100 watts
   B. is exactly 100 watts
   C. is more than 100 watts
   D. may be more or less than 100 watts depending on the nature of the load

10. A 1/2-ohm, a 2-ohm, a 5-ohm, and a 25-ohm resistor are connected in series to a power source. The resistor which will consume the MOST power is the   10.____

   A. 1/2-ohm   B. 2-ohm   C. 5-ohm   D. 25-ohm

11. With respect to 60-cycle current, it is CORRECT to say that one cycle takes   11.____

   A. 1/60th of a second   B. 1/30th of a second
   C. 1/60th of a minute   D. 1/30th of a minute

12. A rheostat is used in the field circuit of a shunt generator to control the   12.____

   A. generator speed   B. load
   C. generator voltage   D. power factor

13. If a condenser has a safe working voltage of 250 volts d.c. then it would be *most likely* to break down if used across a   13.____

   A. 250-volt,60-cycle a.c. line   B. 250-volt d.c. line
   C. 240-volt battery   D. 120-volt, 25-cycle a.c. line

14. Transformer cores are generally made up of thin steel lamin-ations. The MAIN purpose of this is to   14.____

   A. reduce the transformer losses
   B. reduce the initial cost of the transformer
   C. increase the weight of the transformer
   D. prevent voltage breakdown in the transformer

15. The MAIN reason for using copper tips in soldering irons is that copper   15.____

   A. is a good heat conductor   B. is a good electrical conductor
   C. has a low melting point   D. is very soft

16. Five identical electric fans, each rated at 120-volts d.c., are connected in series with each other on a 600-volt circuit. If one fan develops an open circuit, then   16.____

   A. the remaining fans will run, but at slow speed
   B. the remaining fans will run, but at above normal speed
   C. only one fan will run
   D. none of the fans will run

17. The pressure of a carbon brush on a commutator is measured with a   17.____

   A. spring balance B. feeler gage   C. taper gage   D. wire gage

18. A non-inductive carbon resistor consumes 50 watts when connect ted across a 120-volt d.c.source. If it is connected across a 120-volt a.c. source, the power consumed by the resistor will be nearest to   18.____

   A. 30 watts   B. 40 watts   C. 50 watts   D. 60 watts

19. Of the following, the combination of lamps which will draw the MOST current from a stan-dard 120-volt branch circuit is one with   19.____

   A. three 150-watt lamps   B. one 300-watt lamp
   C. four 100-watt lamps   D. six 50-watt lamps

20. A condenser is sometimes connected across contact points which make and break a d.c.   20.____
    circuit in order to reduce arcing of the points. The condenser produces this effect
    because it

    A. discharges when the contacts open
    B. charges when the contacts open
    C. charges while the contacts are closed
    D. discharges when the contacts are closed

————

KEY (CORRECT ANSWERS)

1.	A	11.	A
2.	B	12.	C
3.	B	13.	A
4.	D	14.	A
5.	D	15.	A
6.	C	16.	D
7.	B	17.	A
8.	D	18.	C
9.	C	19.	A
10.	D	20.	B

————

EXAMINATION SECTION
TEST 1

DIRECTIONS: Each question or incomplete statement is followed by several suggested answers or completions. Select the one that BEST answers the question or completes the statement. *PRINT THE LETTER OF THE CORRECT ANSWER IN THE SPACE AT THE RIGHT.*

1. The one of the following items which is used to test the electrolyte of a battery is a(n)   1.____

   A. manometer   B. hydrometer   C. electrometer   D. hygrometer

2. The one of the following instruments which CANNOT be used to measure the current in   2.____
   both a.c. circuits and d.c. circuits *without* additional equipment is a(n)

   A. D'Arsonval galvanometer
   B. hot wire ammeter
   C. iron vane ammeter
   D. electro-dynamometer type ammeter

3. A growler is *commonly* used to test   3.____

   A. relays   B. armatures   C. cable joints   D. rectifiers

4. In cutting a large stranded copper cable with a hacksaw, the PRIMARY reason for using   4.____
   a blade with fine teeth rather than one with coarse teeth is

   A. that using a coarse blade overheats the copper
   B. to avoid making too wide a cut
   C. that the coarse blade bends too easily
   D. to avoid snagging or pulling the strands

5. Toggle bolts are MOST commonly used to fasten an outlet box to a   5.____

   A. solid brick wall   B. solid concrete wall
   C. plaster or tile wall   D. wooden partition wall

6. Laminated sheet steel is *usually* used to make up transformer cores in order to minimize   6.____

   A. copper loss   B. weight
   C. hysterisis loss   D. eddy current loss

Questions 7-9.

DIRECTIONS: Questions 7 to 9, inclusive, refer to the diagram below.

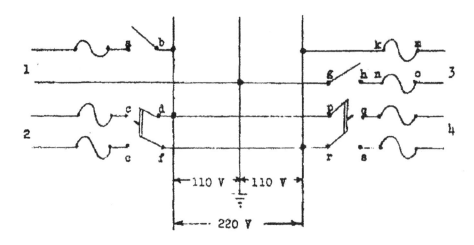

7. Circuit No. 3 in the above diagram   7._____

    A. supplies 220 volts to the load
    B. would be correctly wired if there were a direct connection instead of a fuse between points k and m
    C. would be correctly wired if there were a direct connection instead of a fuse between points n and o
    D. would be correctly wired if the switch and fuse were eliminated and replaced by a direct connection between g and o

8. Circuit No. 4 in the above diagram   8._____

    A. is not properly fused as it should have only one fuse in the hot leg
    B. supplies 220 volts to the load
    C. is grounded if, with the switch open, test lamps light when placed between points p and r
    D. is shorted if, with the switch open, test lamps light when placed between points p and r

9. Circuit No. 1 in the above diagram   9._____

    A. supplies 220 volts to the load
    B. is grounded if a pair of test lamps light when placed between point b and ground
    C. is not properly fused as it should have a fuse in each leg
    D. is shorted if, with the switch open, a pair of test lamps light when placed between points a and b

10. An ideal transformer which has 1 ampere in the primary and 10 amperes in the second-   10._____
ary MUST have

    A. 10 volt amperes in the primary
    B. a ratio of primary turns to secondary turns of 1 to 10
    C. 10 volt amperes in the secondary
    D. a ratio of primary turns to secondary turns of 10 to 1

11. In soldering electric wires, rosin is used in preference to acid as a flux PRIMARILY because rosin is   11._____

    A. a dry powder   B. non-conducting
    C. non-corrosive   D. a strong electrolyte

12. The one of the following items which should be used to test whether a circuit is a.c. or d.c. is a   12._____

    A. pair of test lamps   B. hot wire ammeter
    C. psychrometer   D. neon light

13. An ideal transformer has 200 volts impressed across its primary. If the primary current is 10 amperes,   13._____

    A. the ratio of primary turns to secondary turns is 20 to 1
    B. the ratio of primary turns to secondary turns is 1 to 20
    C. there are approximately 2 KVA in the secondary
    D. the secondary voltage is 20 volts

14. To control a lamp independently from five locations, the one of the following groups of switches which is required is: 14._____

    A. Four 3-way switches and one 4-way switch
    B. Three 3-way and two 4-way switches
    C. Two 3-way and three 4-way switches
    D. Two single-pole, single throw switches and three 4-way switches

Questions 15-20.

DIRECTIONS: Questions 15 to 20, inclusive, refer to the terms listed below which are defined in the electrical code.

1. Appliance	9. Periodic duty	17. Service
2. Branch Circuit	10. Short time duty	18. Service cable
3. Connected load	11. Varying duty	19. Service conductor
4. Concealed	12. Enclosed	20. Service drop
5. Computed load	13. Equipment	21. Service Entrance conductors
6. Device	14. Feeder	22. Sub-feeder
7. Demand factor	15. Isolated	23. Scalable
8. Intermittent duty	16. Mains	24. Rating

15. The one term in the above which is defined as a unit of an electrical system, other than a conductor, which is intended to carry but not consume electrical energy, is numbered   15._____

    A. 1   B. 6   C. 13   D. 19

16. The one term in the above which is defined as that portion of the wiring system extending beyond the final overcurrent device protecting the circuit, is numbered   16._____

    A. 2   B. 14   C. 16   D. 22

17. The one term in the above which is defined as that portion of the overhead service conductors between the last pole and the first point of attachment to the building, is numbered
17.____

    A. 17   B. 18   C. 20   D. 21

18. The one term in the above which is defined as rendered inaccessible by the structure or finish of the building, is numbered
18.____

    A. 4   B. 12   C. 15   D. 23

19. The one term in the above which is defined as a requirement of service that demands operation at loads, and for intervals of time, both of which may be subject to wide variation, is numbered
19.____

    A. 8   B. 9   C. 10   D. 11

20. The one term in the above which is defined as the sum of the continuous ratings of the load consuming apparatus connected to the system or part of the system under consideration, is numbered
20.____

    A. 3   B. 5   C. 7   D. 24

21. In electrical tests, a megger is calibrated to read
21.____

    A. amperes   B. ohms   C. volts   D. watts

22. Metal cabinets for lighting circuits are grounded in order to
22.____

    A. save insulating material
    B. provide a return for the netural current
    C. eliminate short circuits
    D. minimize the possibility of shock

23. In an a.c. circuit containing only resistance, the power factor will be
23.____

    A. zero   B. 50% lagging   C. 50% leading   D. 100%

24. The size of fuse for a two-wire lighting circuit using No. 14 wire should NOT exceed
24.____

    A. 15 amperes   B. 20 amperes
    C. 25 amperes   D. 30 amperes

25. When working near acid storage batteries, extreme care should be taken to guard against sparks MAINLY because a spark may
25.____

    A. cause an explosion
    B. set fire to the electrolyte
    C. short-circuit a ceil
    D. ignite the battery case

KEY (CORRECT ANSWERS)

1.	B		11.	C
2.	A		12.	D
3.	B		13.	C
4.	D		14.	C
5.	C		15.	B
6.	D		16.	A
7.	D		17.	C
8.	B		18.	A
9.	D		19.	D
10.	D		20.	A

21.	B
22.	D
23.	D
24.	A
25.	A

TEST 2

DIRECTIONS: Each question or incomplete statement is followed by several suggested answers or completions. Select the one that BEST answers the question or completes the statement. *PRINT THE LETTER OF THE CORRECT ANSWER IN THE SPACE AT THE RIGHT.*

1. If a blown fuse in an existing lighting circuit is replaced by another of the same rating which also blows, the PROPER maintenance procedure is to   1._____

    A. use a higher rating fuse
    B. cut out some of the outlets in the circuit
    C. check the circuit for grounds or shorts
    D. install a renewable fuse

2. The number of fuses required in a three-phase, four-wire branch circuit with grounded neutral is   2._____

    A. one   B. two   C. three   D. four

3. The electrodes of the common dry cell are carbon *and*   3._____

    A. zinc   B. lead   C. steel   D. tin

4. An electrician's hickey is used to   4._____

    A. strip insulation off wire   B. pull cable through conduits
    C. thread metallic conduit   D. bend metallic conduit

5. A group of wire sizes that is CORRECTLY arranged in the order of increasing current-carrying capacity is: 5._____

    A. 6; 12; 3/0   B. 12; 6; 3/0   C. 3/0; 12; 6   D. 3/0; 6; 12

6. The metal which is the BEST conductor of electricity is   6._____

    A. silver   B. copper   C. aluminum   D. nickel

7. If the two supply wires to a d.c. series motor are reversed, the motor will   7._____

    A. run in the opposite direction   B. not run
    C. run in the same direction   D. become a generator

8. Before doing work on a motor, to prevent accidental starting, you should   8._____

    A. short-circuit the motor leads   B. remove the fuses
    C. block the rotor   D. ground the frame

9. The material *commonly* used for brushes on d.c. motors is   9._____

    A. copper   B. carbon   C. brass   D. aluminum

10. The conductors of a two-wire No. 12 armored cable used in an ordinary lighting circuit are _____ insulated.   10._____

    A. stranded and rubber   B. solid and rubber
    C. stranded and cotton   D. solid and cotton

11. The rating, 125V.-10A.; 250V.-5A., *commonly* applies to a   11.____

    A. snap switch   B. lamp   C. conductor   D. fuse

12. Commutators are found on   12.____

    A. alternators   B. d.c. motors
    C. transformers   D. circuit breakers

13. A proper *use* for an electrician's knife is to   13.____

    A. cut wires
    B. pry out a small cartridge fuse
    C. mark the place where a conduit is to be cut
    D. skin wires

14. A d.c. device taking one milliampere at one kilovolt takes a *total* power of one   14.____

    A. milliwatt   B. watt   C. kilowatt   D. megawatt

15. In connection with electrical work, it is GOOD practice to   15.____

    A. scrape the silvery coating from a wire before soldering
    B. nick a wire in several places before bending it around a terminal
    C. assume that a circuit is alive
    D. open a switch to check the load

16. Mica is *commonly* used as an insulation   16.____

    A. for cartridge fuse cases
    B. between commutator bars
    C. between lead acid battery plates
    D. between transformer steel laminations

17. The function of a step-down transformer is to *decrease* the   17.____

    A. voltage   B. current   C. power   D. frequency

18. A conduit run is MOST often terminated in a(n)   18.____

    A. coupling   B. elbow   C. bushing   D. outlet box

19. In long conduit runs, pull boxes are *sometimes* installed at intermediate points to   19.____

    A. avoid using couplings
    B. support the conduit
    C. make use of short lengths of conduit
    D. facilitate pulling wire

20. A rheostat would LEAST likely be used in connection with the operation of   20.____

    A. transformers   B. motors
    C. generators   D. battery charging M.G. sets

21. The fiber bushing inserted at the end of a piece of flexible metallic conduit prevents   21.____

    A. moisture from entering the cable
    B. the rough edges from cutting the insulation
    C. the wires from touching each other
    D. the wires from slipping back into the armor

22. Portable lamp cord is MOST likely to have   22.____

    A. paper insulation   B. solid wire
    C. armored wire   D. stranded wire

23. Thermal relays are used in motor circuits to protect a-gainst   23.____

    A. reverse current   B. overspeed
    C. overvoltage   D. overload

24. It is GOOD practice to connect the ground wire for a building electrical system to a   24.____

    A. vent pipe   B. steam pipe
    C. cold water pipe   D. gas pipe

25. The MOST practical way to determine in the field the *approximate* length of insulated   25.____
wire in a large coil is to

    A. unreel the wire and measure it with a 6-foot rule
    B. find another coil with the length marked on it and compare
    C. count the turns and multiply by the average circumference
    D. weigh the coil and compare it with a 1000-ft. coil

KEY (CORRECT ANSWERS)

1.	C		11.	A
2.	C		12.	B
3.	A		13.	D
4.	D		14.	B
5.	B		15.	C
6.	A		16.	B
7.	C		17.	A
8.	B		18.	D
9.	B		19.	D
10.	B		20.	A

21.	B
22.	D
23.	D
24.	C
25.	C

TEST 3

DIRECTIONS: Each question or incomplete statement is followed by several suggested answers or completions. Select the one that BEST answers the question or completes the statement. *PRINT THE LETTER OF THE CORRECT ANSWER IN THE SPACE AT THE RIGHT.*

1. The property of an electric circuit tending to prevent the flow of current and, at the same time, causing electric energy to be converted into heat energy, is called   1.____

   A. conductance   B. inductance
   C. resistance   D. reluctance

2. If a certain length of copper wire is elongated by stretching and its volume does not change, it then can be said that, for a fixed volume, the resistance of this conductor varies *directly* as   2.____

   A. the square of its length
   B. its length
   C. the cube of its length
   D. the square root of its length

3. The property of a circuit or of a material which tends to permit the flow of an electric current is called   3.____

   A. conductance   B. inductance
   C. resistance   D. reluctance

4. The equivalent resistance in ohms of a circuit having four resistances, respectively, 1, 2, 3, and 4 ohms in parallel, is   4.____

   A. 14.8   B. 10   C. 4.8   D. .48

5. The area in square inches of one circular mil is   5.____

   A. $(\pi / 4) (0.001)^2$ B. $4\pi \,(.01)$
   C. $(0.001)^2$ D. $(0.01)^2$

6. The current through a field rheostat is 5 amperes and its resistance is 10 ohms. The power lost as heat in the rheostat is, *approximately,*   6.____

   A. 500 watts   B. 250 watts   C. 125 watts   D. 50 watts

7. A d.c. motor takes 30 amps at 220 volts and has an efficiency of 80%. The horsepower available at the pulley is, *approximately,*   7.____

   A. 10   B. 7   C. 5   D. 2

8. A tap is a tool *commonly* used to   8.____

   A. remove broken screws   B. cut internal threads
   C. cut external threads   D. smooth the ends of conduit

9. Lead covering is used on conductors for   9.____

   A. heat prevention   B. explosion protection
   C. grounding   D. moisture proofing

10. The one of the following tools which is run through a conduit to clear it before wire is pulled through is a(n)   10.____

    A. auger   B. borer   C. stop   D. mandrel

11. A pothead as used in the trade is a   11.____

    A. pot to heat solder
    B. cable terminal
    C. protective device used for cable splicing
    D. type of fuse

12. Resistance measurements show that an electro-magnet coil consisting of 90 turns of wire having an average diameter of 8 inches is shorted. The length of wire, in feet, required to rewind this coil is, *approximately,*   12.____

    A. 110   B. 190   C. 550   D. 2280

13. An inexpensive and portable instrument *commonly* used for detecting the presence of static electricity is the   13.____

    A. neon-tube electrical circuit tester   B. gauss meter
    C. photo-electric cell   D. startometer

14. A coil of wire is connected to an a.c. source of supply. If an iron bar is placed in the center of this coil, it will affect the magnetic circuit in such a way that the   14.____

    A. inductance of the coil will increase
    B. power taken by the coil will increase
    C. coil will draw more current
    D. impedance of the coil will decrease

15. The electrolyte used with the Edison nickel-iron-alkaline cell is   15.____

    A. sulphuric acid   B. nitric acid
    C. potassium hydroxide   D. lead peroxide

16. The D'Arsonval galvanometer principle used in sensitive current-measuring instruments is *nothing more than*   16.____

    A. the elongation of a wire- due to the flow of current
    B. two coils carrying current reacting from one another
    C. the dynamic reaction of an aluminum disc due to eddy currents
    D. a coil turning in a magnetic field

17. With reference to armature windings, lap windings are *often* called   17.____

    A. series windings   B. cascade windings
    C. multiple or parallel windings   D. ring windings

18. With reference to armature windings, wave windings are *often* called   18.____

    A. series windings   B. cascade windings
    C. multiple or parallel windings   D. ring windings

19. Polarization in a dry cell causes the reduction in the current capacity of the cell after it has delivered current for some time. A remedy for polarization is to bring oxidizing agents into intimate contact with the cell cathode. A chemical agent *commonly* used for this purpose is   19.____

     A.   potash   B.   manganese dioxide
     C.   lead carbonate   D.   acetylene

20. The e.m.f. inducted in a coil is GREATEST where the magnetic field within the coil is   20.____

     A.   constant   B.   increasing
     C.   decreasing   D.   changing most rapidly

21. The BRIGHTNESS of incandescent lamps is *commonly* rated in   21.____

     A.   foot candles   B.   kilowatts   C.   lumens   D.   watts

22. The effect of eddy currents in a.c. magnetic circuits may be *reduced* by   22.____

     A.   laminating the iron used
     B.   making the magnet core of solid steel
     C.   making the magnet core of solid cast iron
     D.   inserting brass rings around the magnet core

23. The direction of rotation of a single-phase repulsion induction motor can be *reversed* by   23.____

     A.   reversing two supply leads
     B.   shifting the position of the brushes
     C.   changing the connections to the field
     D.   changing the connections to the armature

24. Underexciting the d.c. field of a synchronous motor will cause it to   24.____

     A.   slow down
     B.   speed up
     C.   draw lagging current
     D.   be unable to carry full normal load

25. A certain 6-pole 60-cycle induction motor has a slip of 5% when operating at a certain load. The *actual* speed of this motor under these conditions is, *most nearly,*   25.____

     A.   1200 rpm   B.   1140 rpm   C.   570 rpm   D.   120 rpm

———————

KEY (CORRECT ANSWERS)

1. C		11. B	
2. A		12. B	
3. A		13. A	
4. D		14. A	
5. A		15. C	
6. B		16. D	
7. B		17. C	
8. B		18. A	
9. D		19. B	
10. D		20. D	

21. C
22. A
23. B
24. C
25. B

TEST 4

DIRECTIONS: Each question or incomplete statement is followed by several suggested answers or completions. Select the one that BEST answers the question or completes the statement. *PRINT THE LETTER OF THE CORRECT ANSWER IN THE SPACE AT THE RIGHT.*

Questions 1-4.

DIRECTIONS: Questions 1 to 4, inclusive, refer to the diagram below.

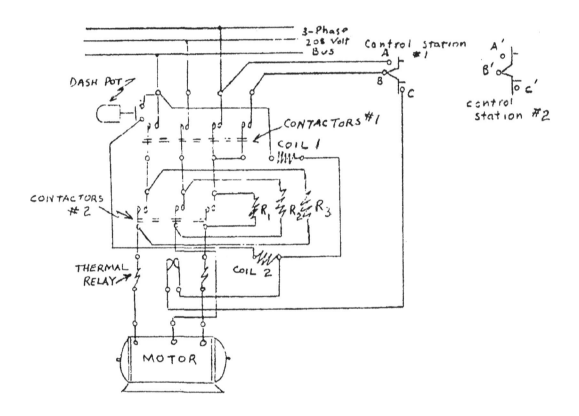

The above is a wiring diagram of a resistance starting controller for a.c. motors. This type of starter limits the starting current by means of equal resistances in each line wire leading to the motor. These resistances are automatically shunted out after the motor has gained full speed connecting the motor directly across the lines.

Station #2 may be added to Station #1 by connecting the start buttons in parallel and the stop buttons in series.

1.   When the starting button is pressed,   1._____

   A.   contactor coil #1 is immediately energized, causing contactors #1 to close
   B.   contactor coil #2 is immediately energized, causing contactors #2 to close

    C.   contactor coil #1 is energized, but contactors #1 close only after contactors #2 close

    D.   both contactors #1 and contactors #2 close at the same time

2.   The motor shown in the above diagram is a 3-phase   2._____

    A.   wound rotor induction motor
    B.   squirrel-cage induction motor
    C.   capacitator-type induction motor
    D.   synchronous motor

3.   When the motor current becomes excessive, the thermal relay will actuate and cause   3._____

    A.   contactors #1 to open first
    B.   contactors #2 to open first
    C.   contactors #1 and contactors #2 to open simultaneously
    D.   the dash pot to energize coil #2

4.   To add control station #2 to the circuit,   4._____

    A.   A is connected to A^1, lead to C is disconnected and connected to C^1, and C is connected to B^1
    B.   A is connected to A^1, C to C, and B to B^1
    C.   lead to B is disconnected and connected to B^1, A^1 to B, and C to C^1
    D.   A is connected to B^1, A^1 to B, and C to C^1

Questions 5-12.

DIRECTIONS: Questions 5 to 12, inclusive, refer to the electric wiring plan below.

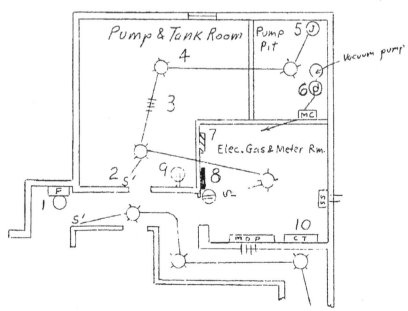

PART OF BUILDING CELLAR PLAN

5. Symbol numbered 1 represents a   5.____

    A. local fire alarm gong   B. bell
    C. buzzer   D. local fire alarm station

6. Symbol numbered 2 represents a   6.____

    A. 3-way switch   B. 2-way switch
    C. single pole switch   D. push button switch and pilot

7. Symbol numbered 3 represents a   7.____

    A. flexible conduit
    B. the number of phases
    C. the number of conductors in the conduit
    D. the size of wire in the conduit

8. Symbol numbered 4 represents a   8.____

    A. drop cord   B. lamp holder
    C. floor outlet   D. ceiling outlet

9. Symbol numbered 5 represents a   9.____

    A. telephone jack   B. junction box
    C. Jandus fixture   D. convenience outlet

10. Symbol numbered 6 represents a   10.____

    A. doorbell   B. drop cord   C. transformer   D. motor

11. Symbol numbered 7 represents a(n)   11.____

    A. power panel   B. telephone box
    C. interconnection cabinet   D. voltmeter

12. Symbol numbered 8 represents a(n)   12.____

    A. meter panel   B. interconnection cabinet
    C. lighting panel   D. underfloor duct

Questions 13-16.

DIRECTIONS: Questions 13 to 16, inclusive, refer to the diagram below.

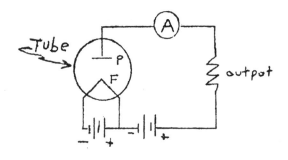

Figure I

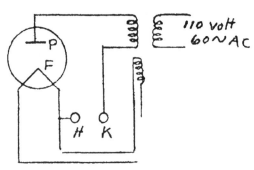

Figure II

13. With reference to Figure I, the flow of electrons is   13.____

    A. blocked by the negative filament
    B. blocked by the negative plate
    C. from F to P
    D. from P to F

14. Figure II represents the diagram of a(n)   14.____

    A. rectifier   B. amplifier
    C. oscillator   D. voltage doubler

15. With reference to Figure II, under normal operating conditions, terminal   15.____

    A. H is negative
    B. H is alternately plus or minus
    C. K is positive
    D. H is positive

16. The tube in the above diagram (Figure I) is a *commonly* used symbol for a   16.____

    A. tetrode   B. heptode   C. pentode   D. diode

17. A 10" pulley revolving at 950 rpm is belted to a 20" pulley. The rpm of the 20" pulley is,   17.____
most nearly,

    A. 1900   B. 1425   C. 950   D. 475

18. A battery composed of 5 cells, each having an e.m.f. of 1.5 volts and an internal resis-   18.____
tance of .1 ohm, is connected to a .5 ohm resistance. If the cells are all in parallel, the
current in amperes drawn from the battery is, *most nearly,*

    A. 2.88   B. 3.00   C. 12.50   D. 14.50

19. The MAXIMUM power delivered by a battery is obtained when the external resistance of   19.____
the battery is made

    A. two times as large as its internal resistance
    B. one-half as large as its internal resistance
    C. one-quarter as large as its internal resistance
    D. equal to its internal resistance

20. A voltmeter is connected across the terminals of a certain battery. The difference   20.____
between the open-circuit voltage and the voltage when current is taken from the battery
is the

    A. internal voltage drop in the battery
    B. external voltage drop of the battery
    C. emf of the battery
    D. drop in voltage across the load resistance

Questions 21-22.

DIRECTIONS: According to the electrical code, the number of wires, running through or terminating in an outlet or junction box, shall be limited according to the free space within the box and the size of the wires. For combinations NOT found in a table provided for the selection of junction boxes, the code gives the following table:

Size of Conductor		Free Space Within Box for Each Conductor
No	. 14	2 cubic inches
No	. 12	2.25 cubic inches
No	. 10	2.5 cubic inches
No	. 8	3 cubic inches

21. In accordance with the above information, the MINIMUM size of box, in inches, for nine No. 12 wires is   21._____

   A. 1 1/2 X 4 square   B. 1 1/2 X 3 square
   C. 2 X 3 square   D. 2 X 4 square

22. With reference to the above information, the MINIMUM size of box, in inches, for four No. 8 wires and four No. 10 wires is   22._____

   A. 1 1/2 X 4 square   B. 1 1/2 X 3 square
   C. 2 X 3 square   D. 2 X 4 square

23. The current, in amperes, drawn from a battery cell having an e.m.f. of 3 volts and an internal resistance of 0.02 ohm when connected to an external resistance of 0.28 ohm is, *most nearly*,   23._____

   A. 5   B. 10   C. 15   D. 20

24. The term OPEN CIRCUIT means that   24._____

   A. the wiring is exposed
   B. the fuse is located outdoors
   C. the circuit has one end exposed
   D. all parts of the circuit (or path) are not in contact

25. The direction of rotation of a 3-phase wound rotor induction motor can be *reversed* by   25._____

   A. interchanging the connections to any two rotor terminals
   B. interchanging the connections to any two stator terminals
   C. interchanging the connections to the field
   D. shifting the position of the brushes

KEY (CORRECT ANSWERS)

#	Ans		#	Ans
1.	A		11.	A
2.	B		12.	C
3.	C		13.	C
4.	A		14.	A
5.	A		15.	D
6.	C		16.	D
7.	C		17.	D
8.	D		18.	A
9.	B		19.	D
10.	D		20.	A

21. A
22. A
23. B
24. D
25. B

TEST 5

DIRECTIONS: Each question or incomplete statement is followed by several suggested answers or completions. Select the one that BEST answers the question or completes the statement. *PRINT THE LETTER OF THE CORRECT ANSWER IN THE SPACE AT THE RIGHT.*

Questions 1-4.

DIRECTIONS: Questions 1 through 4, inclusive, refer to the diagram below.

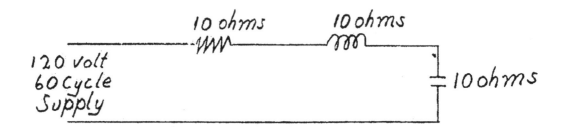

1.   The value of the impedance, in ohms, of the above circuit is, *most nearly,*   1.____

    A.   30   B.   10   C.   3.33   D.   1.73

2.   The current, in amperes, flowing in the above circuit is, *most nearly,*   2.____

    A.   4   B.   6   C.   12   D.   18

3.   The power, in watts, consumed in the above circuit is, *most nearly,*   3.____

    A.   480   B.   635   C.   720   D.   1440

4.   The voltage drop across the 10-ohm resistance is, *most nearly,*   4.____

    A.   10V   B.   40V   C.   60V   D.   120V

Questions 5-6.

DIRECTIONS: Questions 5 and 6 are to be answered in accordance with the information in the paragraph below.

In the year 1914, a circuit was produced in which an electric current showed no diminution in strength 5 hours after the e.m.f. was removed. The current was induced magnetically in a short-circuited coil of lead wire at -270°C, produced by liquid helium, and the inducing source was removed. This experiment indicates that the resistance of lead was practically zero at this extremely low temperature.

5.   In accordance with the above paragraph, the current in the short-circuited lead wire MUST have been   5.____

    A.   electro-static current   B.   induced current
    C.   leading current   D.   lagging current

6. According to the above paragraph, the resistance of lead   6.____

     A. is practically zero at -270°C
     B. is practically infinity at -270°C

7. A form of metal *suitable* for carrying electrical current, such as a wire or cable, is called a(n)   7.____

     A. raceway   B. trough   C. conductor   D. appliance

8. In accordance with the electrical code, the MINIMUM size of the wire used on a 15-ampere circuit is   8.____

     A. No. 16   B. No. 14   C. No. 12   D. No. 10

9. In cutting conduit, the pressure applied on a hacksaw should be on   9.____

     A. the forward stroke only
     B. the return stroke only
     C. the forward and return strokes equally
     D. either the forward or return stroke, depending on the material

10. To measure the diameter of wire *most* accurately, it is BEST to use a   10.____

     A. wire gauge   B. depth gauge
     C. micrometer   D. microtome

11. To measure the speed of an armature directly in rpm, it is BEST to use a   11.____

     A. tachometer   B. chronometer
     C. bolometer   D. manometer

12. The PRIMARY purpose for the use of oil in certain transformers is   12.____

     A. for lubrication
     B. to reduce the permeability
     C. to provide insulation and aid in cooling
     D. as a rust inhibitor

13. A single-throw switch should be mounted in such a way that, to open the switch, the blade MUST move   13.____

     A. to the right   B. upward
     C. to the left   D. downward

14. Of the following, the metal MOST commonly used as a filament in electric lamps is   14.____

     A. platinum   B. tungsten   C. manganin   D. constantin

15. Of the following tools, the one MOST commonly used to cut holes in masonry is the   15.____

     A. star drill   B. auger   C. router   D. reamer

16. Resistance coils having a small resistance temperature coefficient, are made with a wire of a metal alloy called   16.____

     A. mallacca   B. massicot   C. manganin   D. malachite

17. For lead-acid type storage batteries, the *normal* battery potential is calculated on the basis of   17.____

    A. 12 volts per cell   B. 6 volts per cell
    C. 3 volts per cell   D. 2 volts per cell

18. Fluorescent lamps, while designed for alternating-current operation, can be used on a direct-current circuit if a specially designed d.c. auxiliary *and*   18.____

    A. parallel condenser of currect value are employed
    B. series condenser of correct value are employed
    C. parallel resistance of correct value are employed
    D. series resistance of correct value are employed

19. A transformer bank composed of three single-phase transformers is to be connected delta-delta. The primary side is first connected, but, before making the last secondary connection, the transformer should be tested for   19.____

    A. an open-circuit   B. a grounded-circuit
    C. a cross-circuit   D. the proper phase relation

20. As a safety measure, water should not be used to extinguish fires involving electrical equipment. The MAIN reason is that water   20.____

    A. is ineffective on electrical fires
    B. may transmit current and shock to the user
    C. may destroy the insulation property of wire
    D. may short-circuit the equipment

21. The SMALLEST number of wires necessary to carry 3-phase current is   21.____

    A. 2 wires   B. 3 wires   C. 4 wires   D. 5 wires

22. A 5-ampere d.c. ammeter may be *safely* used on a 50-ampere circuit provided the   22.____

    A. correct size current transformer is used
    B. proper size shunt is used
    C. proper circuit series resistance is used
    D. proper size multiplier is used

23. As used in the electrical code, the term "device" refers to   23.____

    A. an electrical appliance which does not have moving parts
    B. a unit of an electrical system other than a conductor which is intended to carry but not consume electrical energy
    C. current consuming equipment
    D. an accessory which is intended primarily to perform a mechanical rather than an electrical function

24. The difference of electrical potential between two wires of a circuit is its   24.____

    A. voltage   B. resistance   C. amperage   D. wattage

25. On long straight horizontal conduit runs, it is GOOD practice to use   25.____

    A. expansion joints   B. universal joints
    C. isolation joints   D. insulation joints

126

KEY (CORRECT ANSWERS)

1.	B		11.	A
2.	C		12.	C
3.	D		13.	D
4.	D		14.	B
5.	B		15.	A
6.	A		16.	C
7.	C		17.	D
8.	C		18.	D
9.	A		19.	D
10.	C		20.	B

21.	B
22.	B
23.	B
24.	A
25.	A

TEST 6

DIRECTIONS: Each question or incomplete statement is followed by several suggested answers or completions. Select the one that BEST answers the question or completes the statement. *PRINT THE LETTER OF THE CORRECT ANSWER IN THE SPACE AT THE RIGHT.*

1. A circular mil is a measure of   1.____

    A. area   B. length   C. volume   D. weight

2. In electrical tests, a megger is calibrated to read   2.____

    A. amperes   B. ohms   C. volts   D. watts

3. Metal cabinets for lighting circuits are grounded in order to   3.____

    A. save insulating material
    B. provide a return for the neutral current
    C. eliminate short circuits
    D. minimize the possibility of shock

4. In an a.c. circuit containing only resistance, the power factor will be   4.____

    A. zero   B. 50% lagging   C. 50% leading   D. 100%

5. The size of fuse for a two-wire lighting circuit using No. 14 wire should NOT exceed   5.____

    A. 15 amperes   B. 20 amperes
    C. 25 amperes   D. 30 amperes

6. When working near acid storage batteries, extreme care should be taken to guard against   6.____
   sparks MAINLY because a spark may

    A. cause an explosion
    B. set fire to the electrolyte
    C. short-circuit a cell
    D. ignite the battery case

7. If a blown fuse in an existing lighting circuit is replaced by another of the same rating   7.____
   which also blows, the PROPER maintenance procedure is to

    A. use a higher rating fuse
    B. cut out some of the outlets in the circuit
    C. check the circuit for grounds or shorts
    D. install a renewable fuse

8. The number of fuses required in a three-phase, four-wire, branch circuit, with grounded   8.____
   neutral, is

    A. one   B. two   C. three   D. four

9. The electrodes of the common dry cell are carbon *and*   9.____

    A. zinc   B. lead   C. steel   D. tin

10. An electrician's hickey is used to

    A. strip insulation off wire
    B. pull cable through conduits
    C. thread metallic conduit
    D. bend metallic conduit

10.____

11. A group of wire sizes that is *correctly* arranged in the order of INCREASING current-carrying capacity is:

    A. 6;12;3/0   B. 12;6;3/0   C. 3/0;12;6   D. 3/0;6;12

11.____

Questions 12-19.

DIRECTIONS: Questions 12 to 19 inclusive refer to the figures below. Each question gives the proper figure to use with that question.

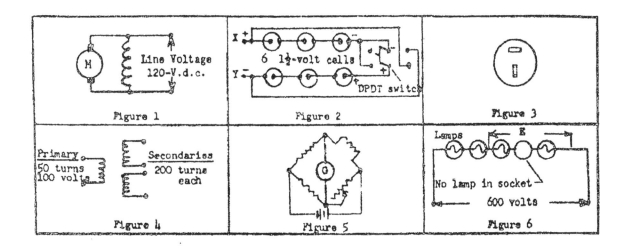

12. Figure 1 shows the standard diagram for a(n)

    A. synchronous motor   B. shunt motor
    C. series motor   D. induction motor

12.____

13. In Figure 1, if the line current is 5 amperes, the energy consumed by the motor if in continuous operation for 3 hours, is _____ watthours.

    A. 200   B. 600   C. 1800   D. 9000

13.____

14. In Figure 2, with the DPDT switch closed to the right, the voltage between X and Y is

    A. 0   B. 1 1/2   C. 4 1/2   D. 9

14.____

15. In Figure 2, with the DPDT closed to the left, the voltage between X and Y is

    A. 9   B. 4 1/2   C. 1 1/2   D. 0

15.____

16. The convenience outlet shown in Figure 3 is used, particularly, for a device which

    A. is polarized   B. is often disconnected
    C. takes a heavy current   D. vibrates

16.____

17. In Figure 4,the MAXIMUM secondary voltage possible by the interconnecting the secondaries is _____ volts.

    A. 50   B. 200   C. 400   D. 800

18. Figure 5 shows a Wheatstone bridge which is used to measure

    A. voltage   B. resistance   C. current   D. power

19. In Figure 6,with one of the five good lamps removed from its socket as indicated, the voltage E is *nearest* to

    A. 240   B. 0   C. 600   D. 360

20. The metal which is the BEST conductor of electricity is

    A. silver   B. copper   C. aluminum   D. nickel

21. If the two supply wires to a d.c.series motor are reversed, the motor will

    A. run in the opposite direction   B. not run
    C. run in the same direction   D. become a generator

22. Before doing work on a motor,to prevent accidental starting you *should*

    A. short circuit the motor leads   B. remove the fuses
    C. block the rotor   D. ground the frame

23. The material *commonly* used for brushes on d.c. motors is

    A. copper   B. carbon   C. brass   D. aluminum

24. The conductors of a two-wire,No.12,armored cable used in an ordinary lighting circuit are

    A. stranded and rubber insulated
    B. solid and rubber insulated
    C. stranded and cotton insulated
    D. solid and cotton insulated

25. The rating,125C.-10A,; 250V.-5A., *commonly* applies to a

    A. snap switch   B. lamp   C. conductor   D. fuse

KEY (CORRECT ANSWERS)

1.	A		11.	B
2.	B		12.	B
3.	D		13.	C
4.	D		14.	C
5.	A		15.	A
6.	A		16.	A
7.	C		17.	D
8.	C		18.	B
9.	A		19.	C
10.	D		20.	A

21.	C
22.	B
23.	B
24.	B
25.	A

———

EXAMINATION SECTION
TEST 1

DIRECTIONS: Each question or incomplete statement is followed by several suggested answers or completions. Select the one that BEST answers the question or completes the statement. *PRINT THE LETTER OF THE CORRECT ANSWER IN THE SPACE AT THE RIGHT.*

1. A set of conductors originating at the load side of the service equipment and supplying the main and/or one or more secondary distribution centers is commonly called a
   A. circuit
   B. line
   C. cable
   D. feeder

   1.____

2. A 5-microfarad condenser is charged by putting 100 volts d.c. across its terminals. If this condenser is now placed across another condenser which has the same capacity rating and is identical in every other respect, the NEW voltage across these two condensers is *most nearly*
   A. 100
   B. 75
   C. 50
   D. 25

   2.____

3. A synchronous condenser, so far as construction and appearance is concerned, *closely* resembles a(n)
   A. electrolytic condenser B.   synchronous motor
   C. synchroscope   D. wound rotor induction motor

   3.____

4. In an electric spot welding machine, the primary winding contains 200 turns of #10 wire and the secondary contains one turn made up of laminated copper sheeting.
   When the primary current is 5 amperes, the current, in amperes, passing through the metal to be welded is *approximately*
   A. 100
   B. 200
   C. 500
   D. 1000

   4.____

5. With reference to an electric spot welding machine, the metal BEST suited to be united by spot welding is
   A. copper
   B. zinc
   C. lead
   D. iron

   5.____

6. Two steel bars "G" and "H" have equal dimensions but one of them is a magnet and the other an ordinary piece of soft steel. In order to find out which one of the two bars is the magnet, you would touch the point midway between the ends of bar "G" with one end of bar "H". Then, if bar "H" tends to
   A. *pull* bar "G," bar "H" is not the magnet
   B. *pull* bar "G," bar "H" is the magnet
   C. *repel* bar "G," bar "H" is the magnet
   D. *repel* bar "G," bar "H" is not the magnet

   6.____

7. The MAIN purpose of a cutting fluid used in threading electrical conduits is to   7.____
    A. prevent the formation of electrolytic pockets
    B. improve the finish of the thread
    C. wash away the chips
    D. prevent the eventual formation of rust

8. If a certain electrical job requires 212 feet of ½" rigid conduit, the number   8.____
    of lengths that you should requisition is
    A. 16   B. 18   C. 20   D. 22

9. The number of threads per inch *commonly* used for ½" electrical conduit is   9.____
    A. 15   B. 14   C. 13   D. 12

10. For mounting a heavy pull box on a hollow tile wall, it is BEST to use   10.____
    A. lag screws   B. masonry nails
    C. toggle bolts   D. expansion shields

11. For mounting an outlet box on a concrete ceiling, it is BEST to use   11.____
    A. ordinary wood screws   B. masonry nails
    C. expansion screw anchors   D. toggle bolts

12. The electrical code states that incandescent lamps shall not be equipped   12.____
    with medium bases if above 1500 watts; special approved bases or other
    devices shall be used.
    In accordance with the above statement, the lamp base that you should use for
    a 750 watt incandescent lamp is the _____ base.
    A. medium   B. candelabra   C. intermediate   D. mogul

13. In order to remove rough edges after cutting, all ends of conduit should be   13.____
    A. filed   B. sanded   C. reamed   D. honed

14. Where a conduit enters a box, in order to protect the wire from abrasion,   14.____
    you should use an approved
    A. coupling   B. close nipple C. locknut   D. bushing

15. The MAXIMUM number of No. 10 type R conductors permitted in a ¾"   15.____
    conduit is
    A. 8   B. 6   C. 4   D. 2

16. A large switch which opens automatically when the current *exceeds* a   16.____
    predetermined limit is called a
    A. disconnect   B. contactor
    C. circuit breaker   D. limit switch

17. The flux *commonly* used for soldering electrical wires is   17.____
    A. rosin   B. borax   C. zinc chloride D. tallow

18. The cost of the electrical energy consumed by a 50-watt lamp burning for   18.____
    100 hours as compared to that consumed by a 100-watt lamp burning for 50
    hours is
    A. four times as much   B. three times as much
    C. twice as much   D. the same

19. Pneumatic tools are run by   19.____
    A. electricity   B. steam
    C. compressed air   D. oil

20. It is required to make a right angle turn in a conduit run in which there are 20.____
    already 3 quarter bends following the last pull box. The fitting BEST suited to
    properly do this is a(n)
    A. cross   B. tee   C. union   D. ell

21. A 10,000 ohms resistance in an electronic timing switch burned out and   21.____
    must be replaced. The service manual states that this resistance should have
    an accuracy of 5%. This means that the value of the new resistance should
    differ from 10,000 ohms by NOT more than ____ ohms.
    A. 50   B. 150   C. 300   D. 500

22. Of the following, the A.W.G. size of single conductor bare copper wire which   22.____
    has the LOWEST resistance per foot is
    A. #40   B. #10   C. #00   D. #0

23. The voltage output of 6 ordinary flashlight dry cells of the zinc-carbon type, 23.____
    when connected in parallel with each other, will be *approximately* _____ volts.
    A. 1.5   B. 3   C. 9   D. 12

24. Full load current for a 5-ohm, 20-watt resistor is   24.____
    A. 4   B. 3   C. 2   D. 1

25. An auto-transformer could NOT be used to   25.____
    A. step-up voltage   B. step-down voltage
    C. act as a choke cell   D. change a.c. frequency

KEY (CORRECT ANSWERS)

1.	D	11.	C
2.	C	12.	D
3.	B	13.	C
4.	D	14.	D
5.	D	15.	C
6.	B	16.	C
7.	B	17.	A
8.	D	18.	D
9.	B	19.	C
10.	C	20.	D

21.	D
22.	C
23.	A
24.	C
25.	D

TEST 2

DIRECTIONS: Each question or incomplete statement is followed by several suggested
answers or completions. Select the one that BEST answers the question or
completes the statement. *PRINT THE LETTER OF THE CORRECT ANSWER
IN THE SPACE AT THE RIGHT.*

1.   A resistor is connected across a supply of "E" volts. The heat produced   1.____
in this resistor is proportion to I^2R. If R is reduced in value, the heat produced
in this resistor now
   A. increases   B. decreases
   C. remains the same   D. is indeterminate

2.   A d.c. shunt generator has developed some trouble. You find that there is   2.____
an open armature coil. As a *temporary* measure, you should
   A. use new brushes having a thickness of at least 3 commutator segments
   B. bridge the two commutator bars across which the open coil is connected
   C. use new brushes having a thickness of at least 4 commutator segments
   D. disconnect the open coil from the commutator

3.   A cable composed of two insulated stranded conductors laid parallel, having   3.____
a common cover is called a _____ cable.
   A. twin   B. duplex   C. concentric   D. sector

4.   If two equal resistance coils are connected in parallel, the resistance of this   4.____
combination is *equal* to
   A. the resistance of one coil   B. ½ the resistance of one coil
   C. twice the resistance of one coil   D. ¼ the resistance of one coil

5.   A condenser whose capacity is one microfarad is connected in parallel with   5.____
a condenser whose capacity is 2 microfarads. This combination is equal to a
single condenser having a capacity, in microfarads, of *approximately*
   A. 2/3   B. 1   C. 3   D. 3/2

Questions 6-7.

DIRECTIONS: Questions 6 and 7 are to be answered on the basis of the diagram sketched
below.

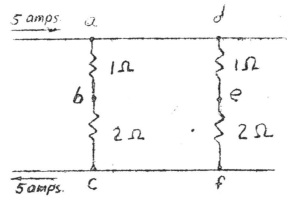

137

6. With reference to the diagram above, the current flowing through resistance ab is _____ amperes.
   A. 5   B. 4   C. 2½   D. 1½

6.____

7. With reference to the diagram above, the voltage difference between points b and e is _____ volt(s).
   A. 1   B. 10   C. 5   D. 0

7.____

8. The resistance of copper wire is _____ proportional to its _____.
   A. directly; cross-sectional area   B. directly; length
   C. inversely; length   D. inversely; diameter

8.____

9. The insulation resistance of 50 ft. of #12 BS rubber-covered wire, as compared to the insulation resistance of 100 ft. of this wire, is
   A. one-half as much   B. the same
   C. four times as much   D. twice as much

9.____

10. The resistance of a 150-scale voltmeter is 10,000 ohms. The power, in watts, consumed by this voltmeter when it is connected across a 100-volt circuit is
    A. 10   B. 5   C. 2.5   D. 1

10.____

11. A battery cell having an e.m.f. of 2.2 volts and an internal resistance of 0.2 ohm is connected to an external resistance 0.2 ohm. The current, in amperes, of the battery under this condition is *approximately*
    A. 15   B. 10   C. 2.5   D. 1

11.____

12. In reference to the preceding question, the efficiency, in percent, of the battery under this condition is *most nearly*
    A. 70   B. 80   C. 90   D. 100

12.____

13. During discharge, the internal resistance of a storage battery
    A. increases   B. remains the same
    C. decreases   D. is negative

13.____

14. The weight of a round copper bar is given by the formula, 3.14 R^2LK, where R is the radius, L is the length, and K for copper is .32 lbs. per cubic inch. The weight of a round copper bar 8'4" long and 2" in diameter is *approximately*
    A. 400 lbs.   B. 300 lbs.   C. 100 lbs.   D. 50 lbs.

14.____

15. Compound d.c. generators are usually wound so as to be somewhat over-compounded. The degree of compounding is *usually* regulated by
    A. shunting more or less current from the series field
    B. shunting more or less current from the shunt field
    C. connecting it short-shunt
    D. connecting it long-shunt

15.____

16. With reference to a shunt wound d.c. generator, if the resistance of the field   16.____
is increased to a value exceeding its critical field resistance, the generator
    A. output may exceed its name plate rating
    B. may burn out when loaded to its name plate rating
    C. output voltage will be less than its name plate rating
    D. cannot build up

17. The PROPER way to reverse the direction of rotation of a compound motor   17.____
is to interchange the
    A. line leads   B. armature connections
    C. shunt-field connections   D. series field connections

18. In the d.c. series motor, the field   18.____
    A. has comparatively few turns of wire
    B. has comparatively many turns of wire
    C. is connected across the armature
    D. current is less than the line current

19. In the d.c. series motor, when the load torque is *decreased*, the   19.____
    A. armature rotates at a lower speed
    B. armature rotates at a higher speed
    C. current through the field is increased
    D. current through the armature is increased

20. To fasten an outlet box to a concrete ceiling, you should use   20.____
    A. wooden plugs   B. toggle bolts
    C. mollys   D. expansion bolts

21. To fasten an outlet box to a finished hollow tile wall, it is BEST to use   21.____
    A. wooden plugs   B. toggle bolts
    C. through bolts and fishplates   D. expansion bolts

Questions 22-23.

DIRECTIONS: Questions 22 and 23 are to be answered in keeping with the statement below
and Figure I, which is an incomplete diagram of the connections of a
fluorescent lamp. The ballast and starter are not shown.

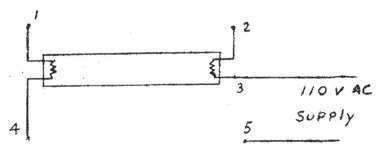

Figure I

The glow type starter used to operate a fluorescent lamp is designed to act as a time switch which will connect the two filament type electrodes in each end of the lamp in series with the ballast during the short preheating period when the lamp is first turned on. The starter will then open the circuit to establish the arc.

22. From the above statement, the competent electrician should know that the starter should be shown connected between points
   A. 4 and 3　　　　B. 1 and 2　　　C. 4 and 5　　　D. 3 and 5

22.____

23. From the above statement, the competent electrician should know that the choke of the ballast should be shown connected between points
   A. 4 and 3　　　　B. 1 and 2　　　C. 4 and 5　　　D. 3 and 5

23.____

24. A 6000-watt 3-phase heater composed of three resistance units in delta is connected to a 3-phase, 208-volt supply. The resistance, in ohms, of each resistance unit is *most nearly*
   A. 20.8　　　　B. 41.6　　　　C. 83.2　　　　D. 208

24.____

25. Based upon the data given in the preceding question, if the 3-heater resistance units are now connected in star (or wye) to a 3-phase, 208-volt supply, the power, in watts, consumed by this heater is *most nearly*
   A. 10,400　　　　B. 6,000　　　　C. 3,500　　　　D. 2,000

25.____

KEY (CORRECT ANSWERS)

1.	A		11.	B
2.	B		12.	C
3.	A		13.	A
4.	B		14.	C
5.	C		15.	A
6.	C		16.	D
7.	D		17.	B
8.	B		18.	A
9.	D		19.	B
10.	D		20.	D

21.	B
22.	B
23.	C
24.	A
25.	D

TEST 3

DIRECTIONS: Each question or incomplete statement is followed by several suggested answers or completions. Select the one that BEST answers the question or completes the statement. *PRINT THE LETTER OF THE CORRECT ANSWER IN THE SPACE AT THE RIGHT.*

Questions 1-3.

DIRECTIONS: Questions 1 through 3 are to be answered on the basis of the diagram below. The sketch is a lamp independently controlled from 3 points.

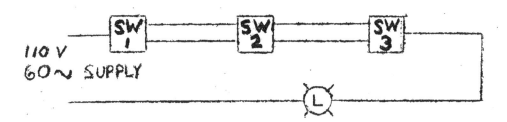

1.   The conductor running from the supply to switch No. 1 should be the _____ wire.   1._____
      A. blue   B. white   C. black   D. ground

2.   Switch No. 1 should be a _____ switch.   2._____
      A. single-pole   B. four-way   C. two-way   D. three-way

3.   Switch No. 2 should be a _____ switch.   3._____
      A. single-pole   B. two-way   C. four-way   D. three-way

Questions 4-15.

DIRECTIONS: Questions 4 through 15 refer to the material given on the next page. Column I lists descriptions of work to be done. Column II lists a tool or instrument for each description listed in Column I. For each description in Column I, select the instrument or tool from Column II which is used for the particular job and write the letter which appears in front of the name of the tool or instrument.

Column I	Column II	
4. Testing an armature for a shorted coil	A. Neon light	4.____
	B. Growler	
5. Measure of electrical pressure	C. Iron-vane Voltmeter	5.____
	D. Ohmmeter	
6. Measurement of electrical energy	E. Wattmeter	6.____
	F. Hot-wire Ammeter	
7. Measurement of electrical power	G. Megger	7.____
	H. Watthour Meter	
8. Direct measurement of electrical insulation resistance	J. Manometer	8.____
	K. Cable clamp pliers	
	L. Pair of test lamps	
9. Direct measurement of electrical resistance (1 ohm to 10,000 ohms)	M. Hack Saw	9.____
	N. Hydrometer	
	O. Electrician's blow torch	
10. Direct measurement of electrical current	P. American wire gage	10.____
	Q. Micrometer	
	R. Hygrometer	
11. Testing to find if supply is d.c. or a.c.	S. Rip Saw	11.____
12. Testing the electrolyte of battery		12.____
13. Cutting an iron bar		13.____
14. Soldering a rat-tail splice		14.____
15. A standard for checking the size of wire		15.____

16. To transmit power economically over considerable distances, it is necessary that the voltage be high. High voltages are *readily* obtainable with _____ current.   16.____
   A. d.c.   B. a.c.   C. rectified   D. carrier

17. With reference to the preceding question, the one *favorable* economic factor in the transmission of power by using high voltages is the   17.____.
   A. reduction of conductor cross section
   B. decreased amount of insulation required by the line
   C. increased I²R loss
   D. decreased size of generating stations

18. The electric meter NOT in itself capable of measuring both d.c. and a.c. voltages is the _____ voltmeter.   18.____
   A. D'Arsonval   B. electrodynamometer
   C. iron vane   D. inclined-coil

19. The hot wire voltmeter   19._____
     A. is a high precision instrument
     B. is used only for d.c. circuits
     C. reads equally well on d.c. and/or a.c. circuits
     D. is used only for a.c. circuits

Questions 20-22.

DIRECTIONS: Questions 20 through 22 are to be answered on the basis of the diagram
              below.

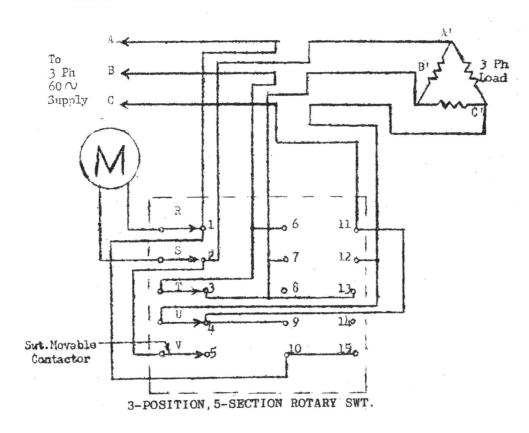

3-POSITION, 5-SECTION ROTARY SWT.

20. With switch movable contacts R, S, T, U and V in position 1, 2, 3, 4, and 5 as   20._____
     shown, Meter M is connected between points _____ and load is _____
     connected to supply.
     A. A-A'; improperly   B. A-A'; properly
     C. C-C'; improperly   D. C-C'; properly

21. With switch movable contactors R, S, T, U and V in position 6, 7, 8, 9 and 10,   21._____
     the function of Meter M is to measure the
     A. current in line B-B'   B. voltage in line B-B'
     C. power drawn by the load   D. power factor of the load

22. With switch movable contactors R, S, T, U and V in position 11, 12, 13, 14 and 15, Meter M is connected between points _____ and load is _____ connected to supply.
    A. A-A'; improperly
    B. A-A'; properly
    C. C-C'; improperly
    D. C-C'; properly
22.____

23. To increase the range of d.c. ammeters, you would use a(n)
    A. current transformer
    B. inductance
    C. condenser
    D. shunt
23.____

24. To increase the range of an a.c. ammeter, the one of the following which is MOST commonly used is a(n)
    A. current transformer
    B. inductance
    C. condenser
    D. straight shunt (not U-shaped)
24.____

25. In order to properly connect a single-phase wattmeter to a circuit, you should use two
    A. current and two potential leads
    B. current leads only
    C. potential leads only
    D. current leads and two power leads
25.____

KEY (CORRECT ANSWERS)

1.	C	11.	A
2.	D	12.	N
3.	C	13.	M
4.	B	14.	O
5.	C	15.	P
6.	H	16.	B
7.	E	17.	A
8.	G	18.	A
9.	D	19.	C
10.	F	20.	B

21.	A
22.	D
23.	D
24.	A
25.	A

TEST 4

DIRECTIONS: Each question or incomplete statement is followed by several suggested answers or completions. Select the one that BEST answers the question or completes the statement. *PRINT THE LETTER OF THE CORRECT ANSWER IN THE SPACE AT THE RIGHT.*

Questions 1-2.

DIRECTIONS: Questions 1 and 2 are to be answered on the basis of the following diagram.

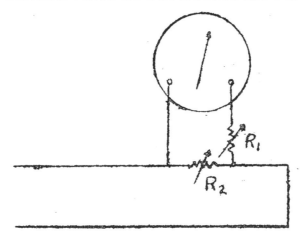

1. The above diagram represents the circuit of a d.c. ammeter. If the value of R_1 is increased while the value of R_2 remains unchanged, the
   A. deflection of the instrument is no longer proportional to the current
   B. range of the ammeter is decreased
   C. range of the ammeter remains the same
   D. range of the ammeter is increased

1.____

2. In reference to the above diagram, if the value of R_2 is decreased while the value of R_1 remains unchanged, the
   A. range of the ammeter is increased
   B. range of the ammeter is decreased
   C. range of the ammeter remains the same
   D. deflection of the instrument is no longer proportional to the current

2.____

3. In multiple-conductor armored cable construction, a color scheme is used for identifying purposes. The color-coding of a 3-conductor cable should be which one of the following?
   A. One white, one red, and one black
   B. Two black and one white
   C. Two white and one black
   D. One white, one black, and one blue

3.____

4. To properly make a short Western Union splice, the competent electrician   4.____
    should understand the common splicing rules. The one of the following which
    is NOT a common splicing rule is:
    A. Wires of the same size should be spliced together in line.
    B. A joint, or splice, must be as mechanically strong as the wire itself.
    C. A splice must provide a path for the electric current that will be as good as
        another wire.
    D. All splices must be mechanically and electrically secured by means of
        solder.

Question 5.

DIRECTIONS: Question 5 refers to the following statement.

The ampere-turns acting on a magnetic circuit are given by the product of the turns lined
by the amperes flowing through these turns. Magnetomotive force tends to drive the flux
through the circuit and corresponds to e.m.f. in the electric circuit. It is directly proportional
to the ampere-turns and only differs from the numerical value of the ampere-turns by the
constant factor 1.257, and the product of this factor and the ampere-turns equals the
magnetomotive force. This unit of m.m.f. is the gilbert.

5. One pole of a d.c. motor is wound with 500 turns of wire, through which a   5.____
    current of 2 amperes flows. Under these conditions, the m.m.f., in gilberts,
    acting on this magnetic circuit is *most nearly*
    A. 1,000   B. 1,257   C. 500   D. 628

6. The flux *commonly* used for soldering electrical wire is   6.____
    A. tin chloride   B. zinc chloride
    C. rosin   D. silver amalgam

7. The operation of electrical apparatus such as generators, motors, and   7.____
    transformers depends *fundamentally* on induced
    A. permeance   B. e.m.f.   C. reluctance   D. permeability

8. If an inductive circuit carrying current is short-circuited, the current in the 8.____
    circuit will
    A. cease to flow immediately
    B. continue to flow indefinitely
    C. continue to flow for an appreciable time after the instant of short circuit
    D. increase greatly

9. With reference to a.c. supply circuits, the waves of voltage and current   9.____
    ordinarily encountered in practice are _____ waves.
    A. sine   B. triangular   C. circular   D. rectangular

Questions 10-12.

DIRECTIONS: Questions 10 through 12 are to be answered on the basis of the following diagram.

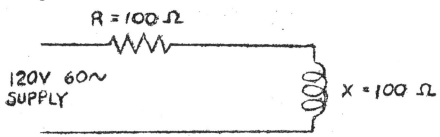

10.   The value of the impedance, in ohms, of the above circuit is *most nearly*   10._____
      A. 200   B. 50   C. 150   D. 140

11.   The current, in amperes, flowing in the above circuit is *most nearly*   11._____
      A. .6   B. 2.4   C. 1.2   D. .85

12.   The power, in watts, consumed in the above circuit is *most nearly*   12._____
      A. 72   B. 144   C. 576   D. 36

13.   The power, in watts, taken by a load connected to a three-phase circuit is   13._____
      generally expressed by
      A. EI P.F. $\sqrt{2}$ B. EI P.F.   C. $\sqrt{3}$ EI P.F.   D. EI/$\sqrt{3}$ P.F.

14.   Three 100-ohm resistances are connected in wye (Y) across a 208-volt,   14._____
      3-phase circuit. The line current, in amperes, is *approximately*
      A. 6.24   B. 3.6   C. 2.08   D. 1.2

15.   An a.c. ammeter is calibrated to read R.M.S. values. This also means that   15._____
      this meter is calibrated to read the _____ value.
      A. average   B. peak   C. effective   D. square

16.   An a.c. current of one ampere R.M.S. flowing through a resistance of 10 ohms   16._____
      has the same heating value as a d.c. current of _____ ampere(s) flowing
      through a _____ resistance.
      A. one; 10-ohm   B. one; 5-ohm   C. two; 10-ohm   D. five; 1-ohm

17.   In the common 3-phase, 4-wire supply system, the voltage (in volts) from   17._____
      line to neutral is *most nearly*
      A. 110   B. 120   C. 208   D. 220

18.   With reference to the preceding question, the neutral line   18._____
      A. does not carry current at any time
      B. carries current at all times
      C. has a potential difference with respect to ground of approximately zero volts
      D. has a potential difference with respect to ground of 208 volts

19. To *reverse* the direction of rotation of a repulsion motor you should
    A. move the brushes so that they cross the pole axis
    B. interchange the connection of either the main or auxiliary winding
    C. interchange the connections to the armature winding
    D. interchange the connections to the field winding
19.____

20. The ordinary direct current series motor does not operate satisfactorily with alternating current. One of the MAIN reasons for this is
    A. excessive heating due to eddy currents in the solid parts of the field structure
    B. that the armature current and field current are out of phase with each other
    C. that the field flux lags 120° in time phase with respect to the line voltage
    D. excessive heating due to the low voltage drop in the series field
20.____

21. If the full rating of a transformer is 90 KV at 90% power factor, then the KVA rating is
    A. 81   B. 90   C. 100   D. 141
21.____

22. A 10-ampere cartridge fuse provided with a navy blue label has a voltage rating, in volts, of
    A. 220   B. 250   C. 550   D. 600
22.____

23. The electrical code states that electrical metallic tubing shall not be used for interior wiring systems of more than 600 volts, nor for conductors *larger than* No.
    A. 6   B. 4   C. 2   D. 0
23.____

24. The diameter of one strand of an electrical conductor having 7 strands is .0305". The size of the conductor, in C.M., is *most nearly*
    A. 13090   B. 10380   C. 6510   D. 4107
24.____

25. To *properly* start a 15 HP d.c. compound motor, you should use a
    A. transformer   B. 4-point starting rheostat
    C. compensator   D. diverter
25.____

KEY (CORRECT ANSWERS)

1.	D		11.	D
2.	A		12.	A
3.	A		13.	C
4.	D		14.	D
5.	B		15.	C
6.	C		16.	A
7.	B		17.	B
8.	C		18.	C
9.	A		19.	A
10.	D		20.	A

21.	C
22.	B
23.	D
24.	C
25.	B

TEST 5

Questions 1-10.

DIRECTIONS: Questions 1 through 10 refer to the material given below. Column I lists definitions of terms used by the electrical code. Column II lists these terms. For each definition listed in Column I, select the term from Column II which it defines and write the letter which precedes the term.

COLUMN I	COLUMN II	
1. Current consuming equipment fixed or portable	A. Mains	1._____
	B. Switchboard	
	C. Fuse	
2. That portion of a wiring system extending beyond the final overcurrent device protecting the circuit	D. Outlet	2._____
	E. Service raceway	
	F. Feeder	
	G. Isolated	
3. Any conductors of a wiring system between the main switchboard or point of distribution and the branch circuit overcurrent device	H. Appliances	3._____
	J. Branch circuit	
	K. Fitting	
	L. Conductor	
	M. Enclosed	
4. Not readily accessible to persons unless special means for access are used	N. Surrounded	4._____
	O. Service drop	
5. A point on the wiring system at which current is taken to supply fixtures, lamps, heaters, motors and current consuming equipment		5._____
6. The rigid steel conduit that encloses service entrance conductors		6._____
7. That portion of overhead service conductors between the last line pole and the first point of attachment to the building		7._____
8. Conductors of a wiring system between the lines of the public utility company or other source of supply and the main switchboard or point of distribution		8._____

9. A wire or cable or other form of metal
   suitable for carrying electrical energy

9.____

10. Surrounded by a case which will prevent
    accidental contact with live parts

10.____

Questions 11-12.

DIRECTIONS: Questions 11 and 12 are to be answered on the basis of Figure I below.

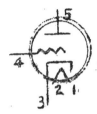

Figure I

11. The above diagram in Figure I is a *commonly* used symbol for a vacuum tube
    and represents which one of the following types of tubes?

11.____

   A. Triode   B. Tetrode   C. Pentode   D. Heptode

12. Tube element No. 5 is *usually* called the

12.____

   A. grid   B. plate   C. filament   D. cathode

Questions 13-14.

DIRECTIONS: Questions 13 and 14 are to be answered on the basis of Figure II below.

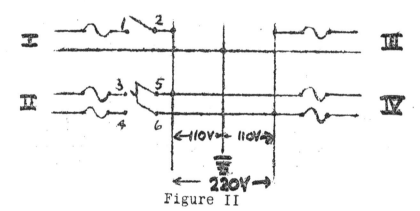

Figure II

13. Circuit No. I in the above diagram

13.____

   A. is not properly fused as it should have one fuse in each leg
   B. supplies 220 volts to the load
   C. is grounded if a pair of test lamps light when placed between point 2 and
       ground
   D. supplies 110 volts to the load at the board

14. Circuit No. II in the above diagram   14.____
    A. is not properly fused as it should have only one fuse in the hot leg
    B. supplies 110 volts to the load at the board
    C. is grounded if a pair of test lamps light up when placed between points 5
       and 6
    D. is grounded if, with the switch in the open position, test lamps light up
       when placed between points 3 and 5

15. To *properly* start a 15 HP, 3-phase induction motor, you should use a   15.____
    A. shunt   B. 4-point starting rheostat
    C. compensator   D. diverter

Questions 16-25.

DIRECTIONS: Questions 16 through 25 refer to the material given below. Column I lists items
              which are represented by symbols listed in Column II. For each item in Column
              I, select the appropriate symbol from Column II which it represents and write
              the letter which precedes the symbol.

COLUMN I   COLUMN II

16. Lighting panel   A.   16.____

17. Special purpose outlet B.   17.____

18. Floor outlet   C. S_3 18.____

19. Three-way switch   D.   19.____

20. Normally closed contact E.   20.____

21. Resistor   F.   21.____

22. Watt-hour meter   G.   22.____

23. Two-pole electrically operated H. 23.____
    contact with blowout coil   J.

24. Capacitor   24.____

25. Bell   K.   25.____

                            L.

                            M.

152

KEY (CORRECT ANSWERS)

1.	H		11.	A
2.	J		12.	B
3.	F		13.	D
4.	G		14.	D
5.	D		15.	C
6.	E		16.	B
7.	O		17.	D
8.	A		18.	E
9.	L		19.	C
10.	M		20.	F

21.	G
22.	K
23.	J
24.	H
25.	A

TEST 6

DIRECTIONS: Each question or incomplete statement is followed by several suggested answers or completions. Select the one that BEST answers the question or completes the statement. *PRINT THE LETTER OF THE CORRECT ANSWER IN THE SPACE AT THE RIGHT.*

Questions 1-8.

DIRECTIONS: Questions 1 through 8 are to be answered on the basis of the figures below. Each question gives the proper figure to use with that question.

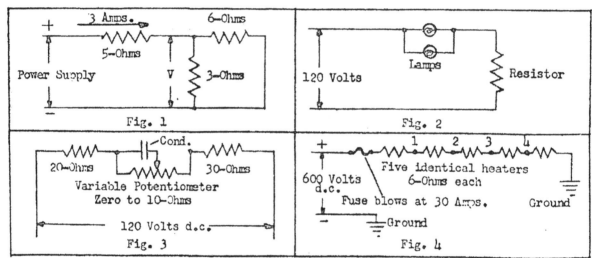

1. In Figure 1, the voltage V is _____ volts.
   A. 27   B. 9   C. 6   D. 3   1.____

2. In Figure 1, the current in the 6-ohm resistor is _____ ampere(s).   2.____
   A. 3   B. 2   C. 1.6   D. 1

3. In Figure 2, each lamp is to take 1 ampere at 20 volts. The resistor should   3.____
   be _____ ohms.
   A. 100   B. 80   C. 50   D. 40

4. In Figure 3, the MAXIMUM voltage which can be placed across the condenser   4.____
   by varying the potentiometer is _____ volts.
   A. 120   B. 60   C. 40   D. 20

5. In Figure 3, the MINIMUM voltage which can be placed across the condenser   5.____
   by varying the potentiometer is _____ volts.
   A. 60   B. 40   C. 20   D. zero

6. In Figure 4, the heater circuit is normally completed through the two ground 6.____
connections shown. If an accidental ground occurs at point 4, then the number
of heaters which will heat up is
   A. five   B. four   C. one   D. none

7. In Figure 4, the fuse will NOT blow with a ground at point 7.____
   A. 1   B. 2   C. 3   D. 4

8. In Figure 4, if a short occurs from point 2 to point 3, then the number of 8.____
heaters which will heat up is
   A. five   B. four   C. two   D. none

Questions 9-16.

DIRECTIONS: Questions 9 through 16 are to be answered on the basis of the wiring diagram
below. Refer to this diagram when answering these questions.

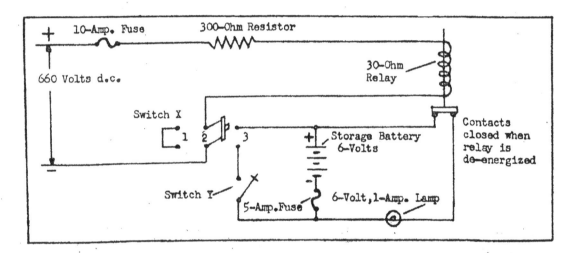

9. Throwing switch X to Position No. 1 will 9.____
   A. charge the battery   B. energize the lamp
   C. energize the relay   D. blow the 5-ampere fuse

10. With switch X in Position No. 1, the 10-ampere fuse will blow if a dead short 10.____
occurs across the
   A. 300-ohm resistor   B. relay coil
   C. battery   D. lamp

11. With switch X in Position No. 2, the current through the 300-ohm resistor 11.____
will be
   A. zero   B. 2 amperes   C. 2.2 amperes   D. 10 amperes

12. With switch X in Position No. 3 and switch Y open, the current taken from
the battery will be
    A. zero   B. 1 ampere   C. 5 amperes   D. 10 amperes

12._____

13. With switch Y in the open position and the relay contacts open, the
    A. lamp will be lit   B. lamp will be dark
    C. battery will be discharging   D. 5-ampere fuse will be overloaded

13._____

14. The battery will charge with switch X in Position No. _____ and switch Y
_____.
    A. 3; closed   B. 3; open   C. 1; closed   D. 1; open

14._____

15. With the relay contacts closed, a dead short across the lamp will
    A. blow the 10-ampere fuse   B. blow the 5-ampere fuse
    C. not blow any fuses   D. cause the battery to charge

15._____

16. When the switches are set to the positions which will charge the battery,
the charging current will be *approximately* _____ ampere(s).
    A. ½   B. 2   C. 5   D. 10

16._____

17. The MOST important reason for NOT having a power line splice in a conduit
run between boxes is that
    A. it will be impossible to pull the wires through
    B. this would be an unsafe practice
    C. the splice will heat up
    D. the splice would be hard to repair

17._____

18. Goggles would be LEAST necessary when
    A. recharging soda-acid fire extinguishers
    B. chipping stones
    C. putting electrolyte into an Edison battery
    D. scraping rubber insulation from a wire

18._____

19. A commutator and brushes will be found on a(n)
    A. alternator   B. rotary converter
    C. squirrel-cage induction motor   D. wound-rotor induction motor

19._____

20. In a house bell circuit, the pushbutton for ringing the bell is generally
connected in the secondary of the transformer feeding the bell. One reason for
this is to
    A. save power
    B. keep line voltage out of the pushbutton circuit
    C. prevent the bell from burning out
    D. prevent arcing of the vibrator contact points in the bell

20._____

KEY (CORRECT ANSWERS)

1.	C	11.	A
2.	D	12.	B
3.	C	13.	B
4.	D	14.	A
5.	D	15.	B
6.	B	16.	B
7.	D	17.	B
8.	B	18.	D
9.	C	19.	B
10.	A	20.	B

ELECTRICITY
EXAMINATION SECTION
TEST 1

DIRECTIONS: Each question or incomplete statement is followed by several suggested answers or completions. Select the one that BEST answers the question or completes the statement. *PRINT THE LETTER OF THE CORRECT ANSWER IN THE SPACE AT THE RIGHT.*

1. A unit of inductance is the
   A. microfarad   B. milliohm   C. millihenry   D. micromho

   1._____

2. The resistance which is equivalent to 10 megohms is
   A. 1×10^8 ohms   B. 1×10^7 ohms
   C. 1×10^6 ohms   D. 1×10^5 ohms

   2._____

3. A two-microfarad capacitor is connected in parallel with an eight-microfarad capacitor. The TOTAL capacitance of this combination is
   A. 0.25 microfarad   B. 0.5 microfarad
   C. 1.6 microfarads   D. 10 microfarads

   3._____

4. A current of 10 milliamperes is
   A. 0.0001 amperes   B. 0.001 amperes
   C. 0.01 amperes   D. 0.1 amperes

   4._____

5. If 120 volts are impressed across a resistance of 300 ohms, 5. the power dissipated by the resistance is
   A. 0.4 watt   B. 2.5 watts   C. 36 watts   D. 48 watts

   5._____

6. The number of circular mils in a conductor 0.04 inch in diameter is
   A. 1600 circular mils   B. 1260 circular mils
   C. 126 circular mils   D. 40 circular mils

   6._____

7. When an electrical device is connected across a 208-volt, 60-Hertz, A.C. supply, the peak voltage across the device is, most nearly,
   A. 208 volts   B. 295 volts   C. 360 volts   D. 416 volts

   7._____

8. The colors of the three conductors in a 3-conductor cable DS for a 120/208-volt system should be
   A. white, black and green   B. white, red and blue
   C. white, blue and black   D. white, black and red

   8._____

9. A 15-ohm resistor is connected in parallel with a 10-ohm resistor. This combination of resistors are in turn connected in series with a 4-ohm resistor. The TOTAL resistance of this combination of three resistors is
   A. 29.0 ohms   B. 10.0 ohms   C. 6.0 ohms   D. 4.2 ohms

   9._____

10. The insulation resistance of a certain conductor is 16 megohms. If the conductor is cut into two equal lengths, the insulation resistance of each length is
    A. 32 megohms   B. 16 megohms   C. 8 megohms   D. 4 megohms

    10._____

11. A certain circuit consists of a reactance with a value of 18 ohms at 60 Hertz connected in series with a 6-ohm resistance. When this circuit is connected to a 120-volt, 60-Hertz, A.C. supply, the current in the circuit is
    A. 20 amperes   B. 15 amperes   C. 12 amperes   D. 10 amperes
11._____

12. A resistance of 2.5 ohms is connected across the terminals of a battery which has an open circuit voltage of 12 volts and an internal resistance of 0.5 ohms. The current in this circuit is, most nearly,
    A. 4.0 amperes   B. 4.8 amperes   C. 6.0 amperes   D. 24 amperes
12._____

13. Assuming that the resistance of a No. 10 (AWG) conductor at 68°F is approximately 1 ohm per 1000 ft., the resistance of 1000 ft., of a No. 13 (AWG) conductor at 68°F is, approximately,
    A. 0.5 ohm   B. 1.26 ohms   C. 2.0 ohms   D. 3.0 ohms
13._____

14. Suppose that the line voltage of a 3-phase circuit is E, the line current, in amperes, is I and the power factor is P.F. The formula for the power consumed, in watts, in this circuit is
    A. $\sqrt{3}$ EI P.F.   B. EI P.F.   C. 3 EI P.F.   D. $\sqrt{2}$ EI P.F.
14._____

15. Assume that a current density of 1000 amperes per square inch is allowable for bus bars. A certain bus bar which has a circular cross section is 1.5 inches in diameter and is 3 feet long. The MAXIMUM allowable current for this bus bar is, most nearly,
    A. 400 amperes   B. 1500 amperes
    C. 1800 amperes   D. 7200 amperes
15._____

16. The color of the label on a 600-volt fuse should be.
    A. blue   B. green   C. red   D. yellow
16._____

17. Of the following, the colors of the three conductors of a 3-conductor cable for a 277/490-volt system used to supply 277-volt fluorescent lights should be
    A. white, brown, and yellow   B. white, black, and yellow
    C. white, red, and orange   D. white, blue, and orange
17._____

18. Although all fuses on a panel are good, the clips on the fuse in circuit No. 1 are much hotter than the clips of the other fuses. The most likely cause of this condition is that
    A. circuit No. 1 is greatly over-loaded
    B. circuit No. 1 is carrying much less than rated load
    C. the fuse of circuit No. 1 is very loose in its clips
    D. the room temperature is abnormally high
18._____

19. Of the following colors, the one that may be used for the 19. ground wire for a piece of portable equipment is
    A. gray   B. green   C. white   D. black
19._____

20. Fixture wire should NOT be smaller than
    A. No. 14   B. No. 16   C. No. 18   D. No. 20
20._____

KEY (CORRECT ANSWERS)

1.	C	11.	C
2.	B	12.	A
3.	D	13.	C
4.	C	14.	A
5.	D	15.	C
6.	A	16.	C
7.	B	17.	A
8.	D	18.	C
9.	B	19.	B
10.	A	20.	C

TEST 2

DIRECTIONS: Each question or incomplete statement is followed by several suggested answers or completions. Select the one that BEST answers the question or completes the statement. *PRINT THE LETTER OF THE CORRECT ANSWER IN THE SPACE AT THE RIGHT.*

1. An example of an adjustable wrench is the   1._____
   A. Bristol wrench   B. Crescent wrench
   C. Allen wrench   D. box wrench

2. The term which is defined by the electrical code as a set of conductors originating at a   2._____
   distribution center other than the main distribution center, and supplying one or more
   branch circuit distribution centers, is a
   A. raceway   B. main   C. sub-feeder   D. service

3. When three No. 10-type R wires are run in the same conduit, 3. the allowable current-   3._____
   carrying capacity of each wire is
   A. 15 amperes   B. 20 amperes   C. 25 amperes   D. 30 amperes

4. Two No. 12-type R conductors in a 3/4-inch conduit are carrying the maximum allowable   4._____
   current to an appliance. It is desired to double the load. Of the following, the BEST way
   to supply this new load is to
   A. run two more No. 12-type R conductors in multiple with the existing conductors
   B. remove the existing conductors and run two No. 10-type R conductors in the conduit
   C. replace the existing conduit and conductors with a 1-inch conduit and two No. 10-type
       R conductors
   D. remove the existing conductors and run two No. 8-type R conductors in the conduit

5. According to the electrical code, No. 1/0 copper conductors in vertical raceways should   5._____
   be supported at intervals of not greater than
   A. 100 feet   B. 80 feet   C. 60 feet   D. 50 feet

6. A universal motor is also a   6._____
   A. squirrel-cage motor   B. synchronous motor
   C. series motor   D. wound-rotor motor

7. In a run of non-metallic conduit between two outlets, the MAXIMUM number of equivalent   7._____
   quarter bends permitted is
   A. 2   B. 3   C. 4   D. 5

8. The MINIMUM number of wattmeters required to measure the power in an unbalanced   8._____
   3-phase, 4-wire system, is
   A. 1   B. 2   C. 3   D. 4

9. An A.C. ammeter which reads 5 amperes full scale and a voltmeter which reads 150 volts   9._____
   full scale are properly connected, without instrument transformers, to various loads on a
   120-volt A.C. circuit. The MAXIMUM load that can be safely measured under these condit-
   ions is
   A. 750 watts at 80% leading power factor
   B. 750 watts at unity power factor
   C. 600 watts at 80% lagging power factor
   D. 600 watts at unity power factor

10. In a single-phase A.C. circuit, the voltage is E, the current is I, the resistance is R, and   10._____
the wattage is W. A formula which will give the power factor of the circuit is:
   A. E I ÷ RB.   B. $I^2 ÷ R$ C. W ÷ E I   D. E I ÷ W

11. A single-phase 100-ampere load is fed from a 120-volt panel board 500 feet away by   11._____
means of two conductors. Each conductor has a resistivity of 10.5 ohms per circular-
mil-foot. The size of conductor that will cause the voltage drop to the load to be most
nearly 2 ½ %, is
   A. 148,000 C M   B. 175,000 C M
   C. 350,000 C M   D. 420,000 C M

12. The method of motor control which is called jogging is the   12._____
   A. quick reversal of the direction of rotation of a motor
   B. repeated closing of the circuit to start a motor from rest in order to get a small
       movement
   C. using up of the energy in a motor by making it act as a generator with a resistive
       load
   D. slowing of a motor by using it as a generator to return energy to the power supply
       system

13. When the armature current drawn by a certain D.C. series motor is 10 amperes-, the   13._____
torque is 10 pound-feet. If the current is increased to 20 amperes, the torque is
   A. 5 pound-feet   B. 15 pound-feet
   C. 20 pound-feet   D. 40 pound-feet

14. The proper way to reverse the direction of rotation of a repulsion motor is to   14._____
   A. reverse the connections to the auxiliary field winding
   B. move the brushes to the opposite side of the pole axis
   C. interchange the line leads
   D. interchange the main field connections

15. A D.C. series motor is running at rated load and rated speed. If the entire load is sud-   15._____
denly removed, the
   A. field strength will increase
   B. armature current will increase
   C. efficiency will increase
   D. motor will start to "race"

16. One way of distinguishing an A.C. series motor from aD.C. series motor of the same   16._____
horsepower and voltage rating is that the A.C. motor has
   A. relatively fewer poles
   B. a larger armature
   C. more turns of the same size wire in the field
   D. fewer turns of the same size wire in the armature

17. The proper way to reverse the direction of rotation of a cumulative compound motor   17._____
without changing its operating characteristics is to
   A. interchange the connections to the armature
   B. reverse the polarity of the supply
   C. interchange the connections to the shunt field
   D. interchange the connections to the series field

18. A certain ideal transformer has a primary voltage of 2200 volts and a secondary voltage of 110 volts. The primary-to-secondary-turns ratio of this transformer is
    A. 22 to 1   B. 20 to 1   C. 1 to 11   D. 1 to 20   18._____

19. A light is to be controlled independently from six separate locations. Of the following, the group of switches required to do this is
    A. two 3-way, two S.P.S.T. and two 4-way
    B. three 3-way and three 4-way
    C. four 3-way and two 4-way
    D. two 3-way and four 4-way   19._____

20. A D.C. motor operating at 110 volts and drawing 40 amperes has an efficiency of 80%. The horsepower output of this motor is, most nearly,
    A. 1   B. 3   C. 5   D. 7   20._____

KEY (CORRECT ANSWERS)

1. B	11. C
2. C	12. B
3. D	13. D
4. D	14. B
5. A	15. D
6. C	16. B
7. C	17. A
8. C	18. B
9. D	19. D
10. C	20. C

TEST 3

DIRECTIONS: Each question or incomplete statement is followed by several suggested answers or completions. Select the one that BEST answers the question or completes the statement. *PRINT THE LETTER OF THE CORRECT ANSWER IN THE SPACE AT THE RIGHT.*

1. The instrument which should be used to measure the insulation resistance of a motor is a (n)   1._____
   A. ohmmeter   B. megger
   C. ammeter   D. varmeter

2. Of the following, the piece of equipment which should be used to locate a shorted coil in the armature of a D.C. motor is a   2._____
   A. permeameter   B. varley loop growler
   C. fluxmeter   D. growler

3. Braking a motor by reversing the line polarity is called   3._____
   A. plugging   B. resistance braking
   C. inching   D. regenerative braking

4. The full load-speed of a 120-volt, 60-Hertz, four-pole squirrel cage motor, which has a slip of 6% at full load, is, most nearly,   4._____
   A. 1600 rpm   B. 1700 rpm   C. 1800 rpm   D. rpm

5. The formula for the resistance of one branch of a delta which is equivalent to a given wye   5._____

   is RAB = $\frac{ab+bc+ca}{c}$ If a = b = c = 2 ohms, the value of RAB is, most nearly,
   A. 3 ohms   B. 6 ohms   C. 9 ohms   D. 12 ohms

6. A 3-phase wound-rotor induction motor is running hot and is slower than usual for the load. When stopped, the motor hums and fails to start up again. A possible cause of this condition is that   6._____
   A. the resistance in the rheostat is too low
   B. the brush tension is too great
   C. one phase of the stator is open
   D. the frequency of the supply is too high

7. A 208-volt, 3-phase, A.C. supply is connected to the stator of a motor. D.C. is supplied to its rotor by a small generator directly connected to the end of the motor's shaft. Of the following, it is most likely that this motor is a   7._____
   A. squirrel-cage motor   B. wound-rotor motor
   C. repulsion motor   D. synchronous motor

8. Assume that two single-phase wattmeters are properly connected to measure the power consumed by a 3-phase, 3-wire system. The wattmeters read 1000 watts and 0 watts, respectively. The power factor of the system is   8._____
   A. 0   B. 0.5   C. 0.8   D. 1.0

9. The range of a D.C. ammeter is most often increased by the use of a   9._____
   A. multiplier   B. current transformer
   C. shunt   D. potential transformer

10. According to the electrical code, three-way and four-way switches should be classed as   10._____
    A. D.P. D.T. switches   B. single-pole switches
    C. D.P. S.T. switches   D. three-pole switches

11. The definition of a trip-free circuit breaker is one that is designed   11._____
    A. for remote control from any desired location
    B. to be free from damage by "chattering" of the contacts
    C. to be free from damage of the contacts by arcing
    D. so that it will open even if the handle is manually held down

12. Of the following, the BEST hacksaw blade to use to cut EMT is one having   12._____
    A. 32 teeth per inch   B. 14 teeth per inch
    C. 12 teeth per inch   D. 10 teeth per inch

13. The one of the following fasteners that is BEST to use to secure an outlet box to a brick wall is   13._____
    A. toggle bolts   B. lead expansion anchors
    C. wooden plugs   D. steel masonry nails

14. Of the following, the usual way of extending the range of an A.C. ammeter is to use a   14._____
    A. straight shunt   B. series resistance
    C. current transformer   D. diode

15. In variable-speed induction motors, the phases should be connected in   15._____
    A. series delta for high speed and parallel star for low speed in constant torque motors
    B. parallel star for high speed and series delta for low speed in constant torque motors
    C. parallel star for high speed and series delta for low speed in constant horsepower motors
    D. series star for high speed and parallel star for low speed in constant horsepower motors

16. Of the following, the type of fire extinguisher which is suitable for use on fires in or near electrical equipment is the   16._____
    A. soda-acid fire extinguisher
    B. stored pressure water fire extinguisher
    C. foam fire extinguisher
    D. carbon dioxide fire extinguisher

17. A portable drill is marked with the symbol ▢.This means that it   17._____
    A. should be used for high voltage circuits
    B. can properly operate at 25-Hertz A.C.
    C. has double insulation
    D. is a D.C. drill

18. Conductors with lead sheaths are run in a 1-inch nonmetallic conduit. The code requires that the minimum radius of the curve to the inner edge of a field bend of this conduit should be   18._____
    A. 6 inches   B. 11 inches
    C. 16 inches   D. 21 inches

19. The minimum permissible radius of the curve of the inner edge of any bend in armored   19._____
cable is   the diameter of the cable.
   A. four times   B. five times
   C. six times   D. eight times

20. Connectors of the "visible type" (i.e., having peep holes) are required when making   20._____
connections between outlet boxes and
   A. flexible conduit   B. electric metallic tubing
   C. armored cable   D. rigid iron conduit

KEY (CORRECT ANSWERS)

1. B		11. D
2. D		12. A
3. A		13. B
4. B		14. C
5. B		15. B
6. C		16. D
7. D		17. C
8. B		18. B
9. C		19. B
10. B		20. C

TEST 4

DIRECTIONS: Each question or incomplete statement is followed by several suggested answers or completions. Select the one that BEST answers the question or completes the statement. *PRINT THE LETTER OF THE CORRECT ANSWER IN THE SPACE AT THE RIGHT.*

1. The MAXIMUM spacing permitted between the supports of 1-inch rigid nonmetallic Conduit containing RHH wire is   1._____
   A. 2 1/2 feet   B. 3 1/2 feet
   C. 4 feet   D. 5 feet

2. The MINIMUM permitted size of flexible metal conduit containing leads to recessed light   2._____
   fixtures is
   A. 1/4 inch   B. 3/8 inch
   C. 1/2 inch   D. 5/8 inch

3. A 16-foot extension ladder is to be placed against a vertical wall. According to most safety   3._____
   manuals, the distance between the foot of the ladder and the base of the wall should be
   A. less than 1' 0"
   B. exactly l' 6"
   C. 1/12 the length of the ladder
   D, 1/4 the length of the ladder

4. The MAXIMUM voltage defined as low potential is   4._____
   A. 208 volts B. 477 volts C. 600 volts D. 1100 volts

5. In which one of the following locations are types NM and NMC cables permitted?   5._____
   A. Hoistways   B. Battery rooms
   C. Unfinished basements   D. Commercial garages

6. A bank of three single-phase transformers, each having a ratio of 20 to 1, are connec-   6._____
   ted with their primaries in delta and their secondaries in wye. If the low-voltage windings are used as the secondaries, and the line voltage on the secondary side is 480
   volts, the line voltage on the primary side is
   A. 3,200 volts   B. 5,540 volts
   C. 9,600 volts   D. 16,600 volts

7. Of the following tools, the proper one to use to make a hole in a brick wall is a   7._____
   A. carbon steel drill   B. cold chisel
   C. diamond point chisel   D. star drill

8. A light-and-power circuit consists of four wires colored white, black, blue and red, resp-   8._____
   ectively. In order to properly de-energize this circuit, it is necessary to install a switch
   which simultaneously opens the
   A. blue, black, and white wires
   B. black, red, and white wires
   C. red, black, and blue wires
   D. red, white, and blue wires

9. A heavy object should be lifted by first crouching and firmly grasping the object to be lifted.   9._____
    Then, the worker should lift
    A. using his back muscles and keeping his legs bent
    B. by straightening his legs and keeping his back as straight as possible
    C. using his arm muscles and keeping his back nearly horizontal
    D. using his arm muscles and keeping his feet close together

10. When mouth-to-mouth resuscitation is administered to an adult, the recommended   10._____
    breathing-rate of the rescuer is
    A. 4 breaths per minute
    B. 12 breaths per minute
    C. 25 breaths per minute
    D. 35 breaths per minute

11. The standard number of threads per inch on 1-inch rigid-steel conduit is   11._____
    A. 16 threads per inch
    B. 14 threads per inch
    C. 11 1/2 threads per inch
    D. 8 threads per inch

12. An example of type S fuse is a   12._____
    A. standard ferrule contact cartridge fuse of the renewable type
    B. standard knife-blade contact one-time fuse
    C. dual element time-delay type of standard screw base plug fuse
    D. tamper-resistant type of time-delay plug fuse

13. The method of wiring known as concealed knob-and-tube work   13._____
    A. should not be used in the hollow spaces of walls and ceilings of any building
    B. may be used in the hollow spaces of walls and ceilings of residences
    C. Test 4/KEYS
    D. may be used in the hollow spaces of walls and ceilings of commercial garages
    E. should not be used in the hollow spaces of walls and ceilings of offices

14. The one of the following which is BEST to use to keep a commutator smooth is   14._____
    A. No. 1/0 emery cloth
    B. No. 00 sandpaper
    C. No. 2 steel wool
    D. a wire brush

15. A photoelectric relay used in conjunction with the controls for boiler room equipment uses   15._____
    a pentode amplifier.
    The one of the following elements of the pentode which receives the signal is the
    A. plate   B. screen grid
    C. control grid   D. suppressor grid

16. A pair of wires which can be run in multiple is one   16._____
    A. No. 2 type R and one No. 1 type R, each 100 ft. long
    B. one No. 1/0 type R and one No. 1/0 type AA, each 100 ft. long
    C. two No. 2 type AA, each 200 ft. long
    D. two No. 1/0 type R, each 100 ft. long

17. Knobs used in knob-and-tube work are usually made of   17._____
    A. molded asbestos
    B. wood
    C. porcelain
    D. steatite

18. As the speed of a fractional-horsepower, split-phase, single-phase, induction motor of   18._____
    the capacitor-start, induction-run type, increases and approaches full-load speed, the
    auxiliary winding circuit is
    A. closed by a thermal switch
    B. opened by a thermal switch
    C. closed by a centrifugal switch
    D. opened by a centrifugal switch

19. The SMALLEST size of wire which is required to have stranded conductors is   19._____
    A. No. 10   B. No. 8   C. No. 6   D. No. 4

20. The MAIN purpose of the electrical code is   20._____
    A. economy   B. neatness   C. efficiency   D. safety

_____

KEY (CORRECT ANSWERS)

1. A	11. C
2. B	12. D
3. D	13. B
4. C	14. B
5. C	15. C
6. B	16. D
7. D	17. C
8. C	18. D
9. B	19. C
10. B	20. D

_____

BASIC FUNDAMENTALS OF ELECTRICITY

CONTENTS

———

BASIC FUNDAMENTALS OF ELECTRICITY

Electricity
Unit 1

When you use a small hand drill, the energy that turns the drill comes from your body. When you snap the switch on an electric drill, another form of energy spins the bit of the drill. We call this form of energy *electricity*. Electrical energy plays a vital part in our environment. It lights our houses, cooks our food, runs our factories, and carries messages for us.

Like other forms of energy, electricity is something that we cannot create. We get it by converting another form of energy into electrical energy. The energy in running water is often used to produce, or *generate*, electricity. Waterpower can be used to turn a generator, which converts the energy in running water into electrical energy. Plants which use this process are called *hydroelectric* plants.

In the United States most of our electricity is produced by changing heat energy into electrical energy. A plant which uses this process is called a thermoelectric plant. In a *thermoelectric* plant, heat energy is first changed into mechanical energy. A steam turbine is often used for this purpose. Then the mechanical energy, produced by the turbine, is changed into electrical energy by a large *generator*. Today we produce some electricity also by changing atomic energy into electric energy.

Electrical Charges

Electricity is a form of energy produced when an electrical charge moves along a wire. Let us try to explain what an electrical charge is. If you lift a brick into the air, the brick acquires potential energy. You have separated the brick from the ground by using energy in your body. If you drop the brick, it will move to the ground, expending the energy it picked up when it was lifted. If the brick strikes a pane of glass on the way down, the energy in the brick will break the glass. The moving brick has kinetic energy; it will do work.

Electricity depends on this same principle. Inside the atom the tiny particles called *protons and electrons* are attracted to one another just as the brick is attracted to the ground. The proton and electron are called *charged particles*. The proton carries a *positive* charge. The electron carries a *negative* charge. They attract one another. If we force them apart, we must use energy, just as we use energy to raise a brick. When we release them, the electrons and protons move back together. While they are moving they can do work. For convenience sake, we say that the electrons move toward the protons.

Whenever electrons are moving, electricity is present. As they move, electrons can do work. They have energy. The reason they have energy is the same as the reason the brick has energy. Work must be done to separate electrons and protons. When they come back together, the energy they picked up is released.

Eletrical Energy

Let's take a simple example. Suppose we have a small heap of protons and electrons. We take all the electrons in one hand, and all the protons in the other hand. Then we pull them apart. Since they attract each other, we must use energy when we pull them apart. The electrons and protons then have potential energy. If they can, they will move back together again.

If we connect the two piles with a wire, the electrons will move along the wire and return to the protons. Like the falling brick, the electrons have energy as they move back to the protons. If we put a glass pane under the brick, we can make the brick use some of its energy to break the glass.

If we put a hurdle in front of the electrons, we can make them work as they move back toward the protons. That is the basis of all electricity-powered equipment. Electrons are made to use some of their energy as they try to return to the protons.

Suppose we connect electrons and protons by a wire, but we put in a high hurdle that the electrons must cross. As the electrons move over the hurdle, they release some of their energy. The electron must use energy to jump the hurdle just as we do. This energy is not destroyed. It is converted into heat. A "hot spot" will appear in the wire at the hurdle we placed in the road. If we put the resistance inside a glass bulb, and take out most of the air, the spot will glow white. We will have made an electric light bulb. By making the electrons work as they returned to the protons, we have created a light that we can use.

Electron flow

This illustration is a little too simple. But all electricity works on this general principle. Actually, one electron usually does not move the whole length of a wire. It moves only a short distance. The effect is like one billiard ball striking a long row of billiard balls. The shock is passed from one ball to the next, but each ball does not move very far. Another example is the way a shock runs through a long train when the engine stops. In any electric wire there are millions and millions of electrons that pass the movement along. This is called electron flow. The flow of electrons is the form of energy we call electricity.

The flow of electrons along a wire depends upon the way electrons are placed in an atom. You remember that electrons are arranged in shells around the nucleus of the atom. The nucleus has a positive charge. The electrons have a negative charge. In some atoms the electrons in the outer shell can be knocked loose very easily. Loose electrons are called *free electrons*, and they are the carriers of electrical energy. When the wire connects a supply of protons and a supply of electrons, these free electrons move along the wire-or drift-toward the protons. This movement produces an *electric current*.

Conductors and Insulators

If there are no free electrons, no electric current can be produced. Some materials produce hirge numbers of free electrons. They can carry an electric current very easily. These materials are called *conductors* because they conduct electricity. Other materials contain few free electrons. Little or, no electricity can flow through them. They are called *insulators*. They do not conduct electricity. Materials like silver, copper, aluminum, and gold possess many free electrons. They are good electrical conductors. Because copper is inexpensive, it is used most often for electrical wire. Materials like glass, rubber, wood, air, and paper are *insulators*. They do not carry electricity because they have few free electrons.

Measuring Electricity

When electrons flow along a conductor, we have electrical energy. Energy passes along the wire at the same speed as light, 186,000 miles each second. But how much electrical energy is passing through the wire? How much work can the electricity do? To answer these questions, we must measure electricity. To measure, we must have standards.

To find out how much electricity we have, we need only count the number of electrons available. If there are 6¼ billion billion electrons separated from protons, we have one *coulomb* of electrical charge. This sounds like a large number of electrons. But it is only a small amount of electricity.

A second question we must answer is, "How hard are the electrons trying to get back to the protons? How much pressure do they exert?" If we have electrons in one hand and protons in the other, how hard do they pull? The standard unit used by science to measure electrical pressure is based on the coulomb. If one coulomb of electrons is available, the amount of pressure they produce is defined as one *volt*. This is our standard for electrical pressure. If we have five coulombs of electrons in one hand, they will exert five volts of pressure trying to return to the protons. The volt is often called an *electromotive* force, and abbreviated as *emf*, or just a capital *E*. In our formulas, we will always abbreviate volts as *E*.

The coulomb and the volt measure potential energy. They tell us how many electrons we are holding. This is like weighing a rock we have lifted off the ground. But we would also like to know about electricity when it is in action. How fast are the electrons moving in our wire? To find this, we simply measure the number of electrons that pass one point in one second. If one coulomb of electrons flows past in one second, we say that one *ampere* of electric current is flowing in the wire. In other words, if one coulomb of electronsmoves past a point in one second, one ampere of electricity is flowing.

Notice that all of these definitions are tied together. One coulomb is equal to 6¼ billion billion electrons. This number of electrons produces one volt of pressure. If one coulomb of electrons flows each second, the current is called one ampere. Of course, electricity will flow only when two points are connected. It will flow only if there is some separation of electrons and protons. If the number of electrons and the number of protons are equal at the same ends of a wire, no electricity will flow.

Resistance

When you apply energy to a machine like the wheel and axle, you lose some of the energy inside the machine because of friction. If you apply electrical energy to a wire, you also lose some energy in the wire. This loss is due to the *resistance* of the wire. The wire must have free electrons to carry electrical energy through the wire. But the electrons are tied to the nucleus of the atom by a small force. This force must be overcome before the electrons are free. The energy to free the electrons must be supplied from the energy in the electrons moving into the wire.

In a machine we must know how much energy we lose to friction to know the efficiency of the machine. We also measure the amount of loss in an electrical conductor. To do this, we measure the resistance of the conductor. Now, we know that the energy lost was used to pull electrons loose from their shells. And we know that this energy is converted into heat. So if we measure the amount of heat generated in a conductor, we know how much energy we have lost.

The standard unit used to measure resistance is called the ohm. This is the amount of resistance that generates 0.24 calories of heat when one ampere of electrical current flows through a wire. In other words, we run one ampere of current through a wire and measure the heat that is produced. If the heat equals 0.24 calories, then the resistance of the wire is one ohm. This definition of the unit of resistance ties it to all the other measuring standards in electricity. Look at the following table.

NAME OF UNIT	MEANING	UNINT	ABBREVIATION
Voltage	Pressure, or potential difference	Volt	*E*
Current	Flow of Electrons	Ampere	*I*
Resistance	Opposition to the flow of electrons	Ohm	*R*

Ohm's Law

If we separate electrons and protons and keep them separated, we have a potential difference between them. If we connect these two points with a conductor, we have an *electrical circuit*. When the two points are connected, electrons will flow through the conductor. We can find the voltage, the current, and the resistance in any electrical circuit by using a simple formula called *Ohm's Law*. This is one of the basic laws in all electricity, and you should learn it thoroughly. Ohm said that in any electrical circuit:
1. The current flowing is equal to the voltage divided by the resistance.
2. The resistance is equal to the voltage divided by the current.

3. The voltage is equal to the resistance multiplied by the current.

These three rules apply simply because they are defined that way. We know that one volt of electricity will push one ampere of current across a resistance of one ohm. Ohm produced his three rules by combining the definitions into one general rule. The formula is:

$$\text{Current}(I)\,\frac{(E)\text{voltage}}{(R)\text{ resistance}}$$

We can write this in three ways:

1. $I=\dfrac{E}{R}$ 　　　 2. $E=I\times R$ 　　 3. $R\,\dfrac{E}{R}$

Learn all three forms of Ohm's Law thoroughly.

Using Ohm's Law
In the United States most of our houses are wired for 110 volts of electricity. Suppose you had a heater that had a resistance of eleven ohms. But you did not know how many amperes of current the heater used. Ohm's Law could tell you the answer easily. You know the voltage and resistance. You want to know the current. Using formula 1 above:

$$I=\frac{E}{R} \qquad I=\frac{110}{11} \qquad I=10 \text{ amperes}$$

Your heater would need a ten ampere fuse. You can solve any other problems of this type using the same formula.

Power
If we know the voltage, current, and resistance in an electrical current, we still do not know how much energy the circuit is using. This can be a serious problem when we want to figure out our own electricity bills.

The unit of electrical power is the watt. This is the amount of work done in one second when one volt of electricity moves one ampere of current through a circuit. In other words, if we have one volt of pressure and it moves one ampere of current through the circuit, we are using one watt of electrical energy. When larger units are needed, we use the unit called the kilowatt which is equal to one thousand watts.

To find the power (in watts) used in a circuit, simply multiply the voltage of the circuit by the current flowing through a circuit. The power formula is written:

Power (*W*) = (*E*) Voltage X (*I*) Current

Almost every electrical problem can be solved by using the power formula, or combining the power formula with Ohm's Law.

Examples
1. An air conditioner has a tag which states that the unit uses 2,200 watts of power. The unit plugs into 110 volt electricity. How large must the fuse be in the line?

a. $W = E \times I$ or $2,200 = 110 \times I$

b. $I=\dfrac{2,200}{110}$ or $I = 20$ ampers

The air conditioner will use a twenty ampere fuse. This is a very heavy load for house wiring, and the wiring should be checked before adding this much current to a line.

2. You have just bought a new electric heater. It operates on 110 volt electricity, and it has a resistance of ten ohms. You pay five cents for each kilowatt of electricity. How much will it cost to run the heater for thirty days?

a. First, you must use Ohm's Law to find the current that flows through the heater:

$$I = \frac{E}{R} \qquad\qquad I = \frac{110}{10} \qquad\qquad I = 11 \text{ amperes}$$

b. Then you find the number of watts the heater uses, using the power formula:

$$W = E \times I \qquad\qquad W = 110 \times 11 \qquad\qquad W = 1{,}210 \text{ watts}$$

c. Now you know that the heater uses 1.21 kilowatts every hour. This electricity costs five cents for each kilowatt hour. You can figure that the heater will cost about six cents per hour to run. If it ran day and night for thirty days, the total cost would be approximately forty-three dollars ($43.56, to be exact). This is the way you can use the two formulas to work out electrical problems in the home.

Words Used in Unit 1

abbreviated (ə brē´vĭ āt əd), shortened
convenience (kən vēn´ yəns), saving of trouble
electron (ĭ lĕk´trŏn), a tiny particle carrying one unit of negative electricity
expending (ĕks pĕnd´ĭng), i using up
hurdle (hər´ dəl), an obstacle in one's way
illustration (ĭl əs trā´shən), story, example
proton (prō´tŏn), tiny particle carrying one unit of positive electricity
thermoelectric (thər mō ĭ lĕk´trĭk), having to do with electricity produced by heat

Magnetism
Unit 2

If you take a small piece of the mineral magnetite and hold it near some iron filings, the iron filings will cling to the magnetite. This material is called a *natural magnet.* Since this magnet actually pulls the iron filings toward it, we know that it can do work. So we know that a magnet contains energy of some sort.

We can make a magnet with electricity, too. If we wrap some wire around an iron spike and run an electric current through the wire, the spike will also attract iron filings. But the spike will attract iron only while the electric current is flowing. When the current is shut off, the spike loses its magnetism. Such a magnet is called an electromagnet.

What is this mysterious force that draws the iron to the magnet? We know that it is related to electricity because we can produce magnetism by electricity.

What's a Magnet?

Like most basic questions about our universe, this isa hard question to answer. We know that the molecules inside a magnet are organized. They are so arranged that there is potential difference between the two ends of the magnet. That is, one end has a positive charge and the other end has a negative charge. We know that energy must have been used to make this arrangement. Each end of the magnet is called a pole. We say that one pole is positive and the other is negative. The two poles act like electrons and protons. That is, likes repel each other; opposites attract. Two positive poles repel each other, and two negative poles repel each other. But a positive· pole and a negative pole will attract one another.

The charges at the poles of a magnet are probably due to the movement of electrons inside the magnet. We are not exactly certain what bring this about. But we do know a great deal about the way magnets work. And we know many of the relations between magnetism and electricity. These are the things we will study in this unit.

Magnetic fields

A magnet attracts an iron filing *before* it touches the filing. The area around a magnet is charged, and the charge around the magnet pulls the iron toward the magnet. This charged area is called a magnetic field. Without these magnetic fields there could be no electricity as we know it.

The magnetic field increases in strength as we move closer to the surface of the magnet. If we place a magnet beneath a sheet of paper, and sprinkle tiny iron particles on the paper, the iron particles will arrange themselves along field lines of the magnet. Notice the pattern the lines form. Near the poles the lines are close together. The field is very strong here. At the center point between the poles, the lines are spread apart. The field is weakest here.

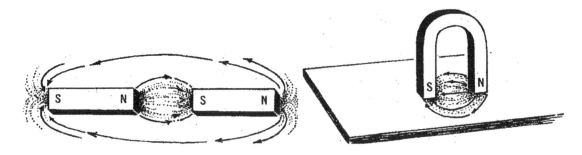

Fig. 1 a

Fig. 1 b

Figures 1a, 1 b Magnetic Lines of Force-Bar Magnet and Horseshoe Magnet.

The strength of the magnet determines the strength of the field. If we place a pieee of iron in the field, it concentrates the lines of force and increases the strength of the field. A magnetic field can attract certain objects through solid wood and some other materials. It can exert force through a perfect vacuum. Every magnet or electromagnet produces a magnetic field.

Induction

We have the whole science of electronics because a magnet produces a magnetic field. Yet we cannot really explain magnetism very well. We can only say how magnetism works, not why it works. One property of a magnetic field is of outstanding importance. If a small piece of wire is moved across the lines of force of a magnetic field, a small electric current flows in the wire. The kinetic energy of the moving wire is changed into electrical energy. The wire does not have to touch the magnet. All it must do is cut *across* the lines of force. The faster the wire moves the more electrical current runs in the wire. The more lines of force the wire cuts, the more electric current runs in the wire. This principle is called *induction*. An electric current is *induced* in the moving wire. Actually, the magnetic field is able to change mechanical energy into elctrical energy. Every electric motor, every electric generator, and every transformer depends upon this principle of induction.

REMEMBER

> ➤ A moving wire cutting the lines of force in a magnetic field produces an electric current in the wire.

> ➤ The more lines of force the wire cuts, the more current generated.

> ➤ The faster the wires move, the more electric current generated.

Electromagnetism

If a wire is passed through a magnetic field, an electric current is produced. To reverse the process, if an electric current is run through a wire, a magnetic field is produced. This is called an electromagnet. You can test this principle by connecting the two terminals on a small battery with a bare wire. The wire will pick up iron filings while it is connected. If the wire is shaped into a loop, the shape of the magnetic field changes. Figure100 (A) shows the effect of the loop. Th lines of force are increased inside the loop. If more loops are added, the magnetic field grows stronger. A coiled wire carrying electricity that has more than one loop is usually called a *solenoid, or coil*. The coil will act like any other magnet. One end of the coil is positive; the other end is negative. Because the coil has two poles, we say that it shows *polarity*.

A solenoid acts just like a bar magnet. The strength of the magnet depends upon the size of the wire, the number of turns of wire, and the amount of electrical current running through the wire. An increase in any of these factors makes the magnet stronger. If an iron bar is placed inside the coiled wire, it concentrates the lines of force and makes the magnet much stronger. Most electromagnets have an Iron core.

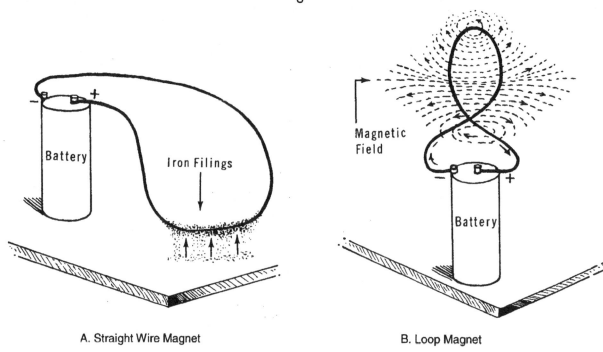

A. Straight Wire Magnet   B. Loop Magnet

FIGURE 2

Making Electricity

When electrons flow through wire, an electric current is present. That is what we mean by electricity. Before electrons will flow, there must be an excess of electrons in one place, separated from an excess of protons. This makes a potential difference between the two points. To make electricity we must create a potential difference between two points. We can do this with a magnet and a length of WIre.

Let us place a large U-shaped magnet in a vice. Then we take a piece of copper wire and attach the wire to a sensitive meter that measures electric current. Now we move the wire down between the poles of the magnet. We have cut the lines of force, and we have created a potential difference inside the wire. For electrons will move from one end of the wire to the other. An electric current flows in the wire. If we move the wire back up between the poles of the magnet, the electrons flow back in the other direction. The magnetic field holds the electrons in position. When the wire moves, the electrons are strained apart. This produces the potential difference that causes electrical current to flow. And this is the way we change the mechanical energy of the moving wire into electrical energy.

The Alternating Current Generator

Now let us put this principle to work. In figure 101, a simple electric generator is shown. There is a large magnet, with a loop of wire that rotates between the poles of the magnet. We must have some source of energy to spin the wire loop. The energy that spins the loop is converted into electrical energy by the generator. The generator is called an *alternating current generator*. The electrons flow first in one direction along the wire and then in the reverse direction.

Each complete turn of the wire loop is called one *cycle*. As the loop turns, the amount of electric current flowing in the wire varies in a regular pattern. If we follow the wire loop through one complete turn, or cycle, we can see how this change takes place.

In position A the wire loop is horizontal. It is not cutting any lines of force in the magnetic field. Therefore no electric current is flowing in the wire. As the loop turns from A to B, it begins to cut lines of force. More and more electric current flows in the wiare. When the loop reaches position

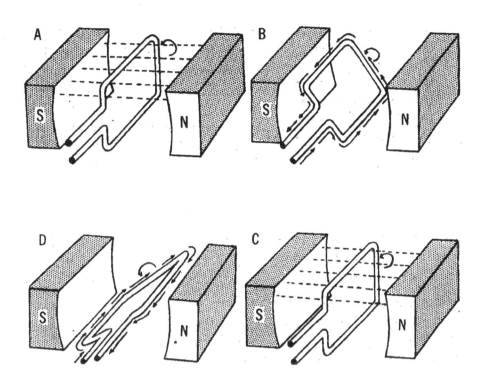

FIGURE 3. Loop Generator-Four Positions.

B, it is cutting all of the lines of force, and the current in the wire reaches a peak. Moving from B to C, the amount of current in the wire drops away to zero. The number of lines of force cut by the wire drops away to zero. When the wire is in position C, no current is flowing in the wire

The wire loop continues to turn from position C to position D. But this time the wires are reversed, and the current is flowing in the opposite direction. The amount of current increases once again to a peak at position D, but the current is flowing in the opposite direction in the wire. From position D back to position A, the current drops off once again. Back at position A, the current in the wire is zero, and one full cycle is complete.

Tile Current Cycle
We can draw a graph to show the amount of current flowing in the wire loop at different parts of the cycle. This graph is shown in figure 102. The graph begins at position A in figure 101. Each quarter turn of the loop is marked. Notice that the current reaches a peak after one quarter turn, and then returns to zero. In the next quarter turn, it reaches a second peak--*in the opposite direction*. Then it returns again to zero. Alternating current always has peaks in both directions because the current flows in both directions in the wire loop. The graph in figure 102 is called a sine wave. It shows one full cycle of electric current, produced by an alternating current generator.

The number of cycles of current produced each second is called the *frequency* of the electricity. In the United States most generators produce sixty full cycles of current each second. This is written sixty cps. For radio broadcasting, much higher frequencies are used. The radio

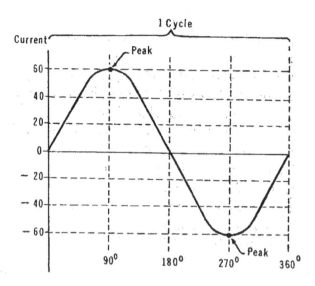

FIGURE 4. Graph: Sine Wave.

broadcasting band begins at 550 kilocycles, or 550,000 cycles per second. One kilocycle is equal to one thousand cycles. For special types of radio, a unit of one million cycles is used. This is called a *megacycle*. The human ear cannot hear these electrical frequencies. Our ears can be stimulated by mechanical energy only. Electrical energy has no effect on the ear.

The Electric Generator

An electric motor and electric generator are nearly the same. The electric generator converts mechanical energy into electrical energy. An electric motor converts electrical energy into mechanical energy. Actually, electricity is not very useful until it is changed into another form. But it is easy to transport and store, and cheap to produce. This makes it an ideal form of energy for many purposes.

The magnetic field in an electric generator is supplied by an electromagnet called the field coil. This coil lies just inside the housing of the generator. The moving part of the generator (the loop) is called the *armature*. The armature is wound with many loops of wire. Some wire is always cutting the lines of force of the magnetic field and producing electric current. The ends of the loop of wire wound on the armature are attached to two *slip rings*. The electric current generated in the generator is taken off the armature from these two rings. They are in contact with two *brushes* which carry the current away from the rings. When the generator is used to produce *direct current*, which flows in only one direction, a device is used to reverse the connections after each half turn of the armature. This device is called a *commutator*.

The generator cannot produce energy. It can only convert mechanical energy into electrical energy. Some outside power must turn the armature. In large electric plants a steam turbine is used to turn the armature in a very heavy generator. In an automobile, the small generator is attached to the drive shaft of the car.

The Electric Motor

The electric generator changes mechanical energy into electrical energy. The electric motor changes electrical energy into mechanical energy. The parts in a motor and a generator are nearly the same. But an electric motor depends on a different principle. A pole that has a positive charge is attracted to a pole with a negative charge. But it is repelled by another positive pole. This is the principle that runs an electric motor.

In an electric motor, electricity is fed into the field coil and into the winding of the armature. This creates two electromagnets, each with a positive pole and a negative pole. When the electricity is connected, the positive pole of the armature moves toward the negative pole of the field coil. This turns the armature. But the turning would stop as soon as the positive armature pole reached the negative field coil pole. So, when the positive pole has nearly reached its goal, the commutator on the motor reverses the current.

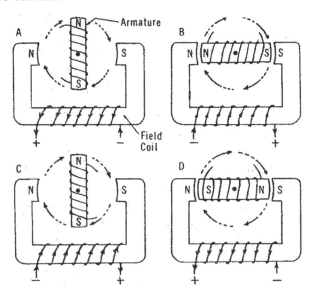

FIGURE 5.   Electric Motor Showing Rotation

The positive pole on the armature is now facing a positive pole and is pushed away toward the negative pole. Again, just as it reaches its goal, the commutator reverses the connections. Again the armature pole is shoved away. So the armature keeps turning, trying to bring a positive and negative pole together. Because of the commutator it never succeeds. The pole on the armature is like a dog chasing a mechanical rabbit at a race track. Just as the dog reaches the rabbit, the rabbit's speed is increased and the dog falls bechind. The turning armature of the motor produces mechanical energy which can be used to do work.

Transformers

The electric line that passes your house carries about eighteen thousand volts. But inside the house it is a safe 110 volts. This voltage is produced by a transformer. A transformer also uses the principle of induction. But it uses it to move electricity from one wire to another even though the two wires are not touching. Inside a transformer there are two solenoids or coils. They are often wound around the same center.

One solenoid is connected to a source of alternating current. As the current moves through the coil, it produces an electric field around the coil. The electric field passes through the second coil nearby. As the current moving through the coil rises and falls with each cycle, the magnetic field

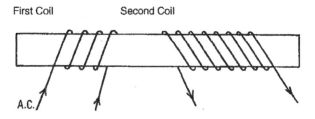

FIGURE 6. Principle of the Transformer.

around the coil also rises and falls. This produces an electric current in the second coil which is an exact duplicate of the electric current in the first coil. Although neither of the coils moves, the lines of force move as the field expands and collapses. As the lines of force cut across the wire in the second coil, they induce an electric current in the second coil.

The voltage in the second coil depends upon the number of turns of wire used in each coil. If there is the same number of turns in each coil, the voltage will not change as it moves from one to the other. If the second coil has ten times as many turns as the first coil, the voltage will be increased ten times. This is called a *step-up* transformer. If the number of turns in the second coil is 1/10 as large as the number in the first coil, only 1/10 as much voltage will be produced in the second coil. This is called a *step-down* transformer. Transformers can be used any time the voltage must be changed in an electric circuit. They are manufactured in a wide variety of sizes for different types of voltage changes.

Words Used in Unit 2

armature (ăr´məchər), the moving part of a generator
arranged (ərănjd´), put into proper order
collapses (kə lăps´əz), shrinks together
commutator (kŏm´ū tă tər), device which reverses the direction of flow of electricity
concentrates (kŏn´sən trăts) , brings together to one place
induced (in dūst´), produced, caused to appear
organized (ŏr´gən īzd), put into working order
repel (rĭ pĕl´), force back, move away from
terminals (tər´mə nəlz), the ends of a battery where an electrical connection is made

Batteries

Unit 3

Science is full of surprises. We learned in the last unit that a spinning loop of wire in a magnetic field can produce electricity. It does this by separating electrons and protons to produce an electrical potential in the spinning wire. No liquids are used. No chemical reaction takes place. Yet electricity is produced. This seems to be a long way from the chemist's laboratory. Yet the chemist only smiles to himself. He fills a glass with a few chemicals dissolved in water. He places a rod of carbon and a rod of zinc in the water and attaches a wire to each rod. When the two wires are connected, an electric current flows through the wires. The chemist too can produce electricity.

There is a useful lesson in this for anyone who studies science. The chemist and the physicist start from different points. But they both deal with electricity, even though they use different approaches. You see nature is not divided into only chemistry and physics. Our environment is all one. We have divided our world into physical and chemical things. But electricity is only the flow of electrons along a wire. It does not matter how you cause the electrons to flow. The physicist does it one way; the chemist does it another. Both men produce electricity.

The Voltaic Cell

When you start your car, you must use a battery to turn the engine over until the small electrical generator gets going. This battery produces electricity by a chemical reaction. We know that electricity is produced when there is a potential difference between two points. This occurs when electrons and protons, or positive and negative charges, are separated. The chemist separates his charges in a unit called the *voltaic cell*. All batteries are a variation of this basic unit.

The voltaic cell consists of three parts:

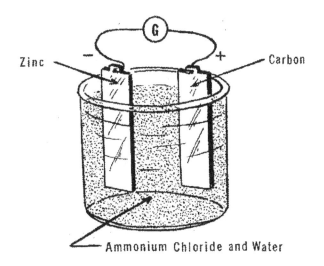

FIGURE 7. Voltaic cell

(1) a container made of insulating material-some material that will not conduct electricity; (2) a chemical solution called an electrolyte; and (3) two metal plates, called electrodes, which are placed in the solution. The electrodes must be conductors of electricity. When the electrodes are joined by a wire, electrons will flow along the wire. The voltaic cell will produce an electric current.

What happens inside the cell to produce electricity? One of the electrodes is made of the metal zinc. The other is made of pure carbon. The electrolyte is usually a mixture of water and sulfuric acid. Water is not a good electrical conductorthe sulfuric acid makes the solution a conducting material.

Chemical Action in Cell

When the electrodes are placed in the electrolyte, the zinc plate dissolves. It forms charged particles called irns. Ions can be either positively charged or negatively charged. If there is a surplus of eleetrons on the ion, it is negatively charged. If there is a shortage of electrons on the ion, it is positively charged. You can probably see the connection already. Electricity is produced by a flow of surplus electrons. Anyhow, the zinc forms ions with a surplus of electrons. These surplns electrons gather on the zinc electrode. This gives the zinc electrode a negative charge.

The electrons taken from zinc are added to the zinc strip. So the zinc electrode acquires a surplus of electrons. There is still one more step. The water in the electrolyte produces hydrogen ions, or negative charges. These hydrogen ions move to the carbon rod and collect electrons from it. So the carbon rod gets a surplus of protons, or positive charges.

By chemical action we thus produce a positive charge on the carbon rod and a negative charge on the zinc rod. The zinc rod has an excess of electrons. And so there is a potential difference between the carbon rod and the zinc rod. If we conned these two points, electrons will flow from the zinc rod to the carbon rod. An electric current will be produced in the wire. As the electrons move from the zinc plate, more zinc dissolves and the potential difference is maintained. Eleetric current will flow from zinc to carbon until the zinc has completely dissolved. Then the voltaic cell will be worn out. A new zinc rod must be added to make it work again.

This is the basic method which the chemist uses to produce electricity. He dissolves zinc and uses the energy to produce electricity. Many kinds of material can be used to make a voltaic cell. Usually electrodes are made of zinc and carbon because both minerals are cheap. The electrolyte is often a compound of ammonia and chlorine called *ammonium chloride.*

Primary Cells and Secondary Cells

When the zinc in the voltaic cell is used up, the battery is dead. A cell of this sort is called a *primary cell.* The chemical action inside the battery moves only in one direction. When the cell is unable to produce more electricity, nothing can be done to make the battery useful again.

There is another type of battery, however, which can solve this problem. The chemical action inside this battery cell can be reversed. When the cell is producing electricity, a chemical reaction takes place.

When the cell runs down, the chemical action can be reversed. We say that the battery is *discharging* when it is producing electricity. When the process is reversed, the cell is being charged. This type of battery is called a *secondary cell.* We know many examples of both batteries. A flashlight battery is a primary cell. When it is used up, we throw it away. An automobile battery is a secondary cell. It can be recharged again and again before it must be thrown away.

The Primary Cell --- A Dry Cell Battery

The most common primary cell is the small battery we use in a flashlight. Usually it is made in the shape of a small cylinder. The outer shell of the battery is a small can made of zinc. This is the negative electrode of the battery. The positive electrode is a solid carbon rod suspended in the can. The carbon rod is insulated from the zinc can-they do not touch. Inside the can there is a damp paste of ammonium chloride and water. The cell is not completely dry, but it can be turned upside down without spilling. The top of the can is sealed with some plastic insulating material. This separates the carbon rod from the zinc can and holds in the electrolyte.

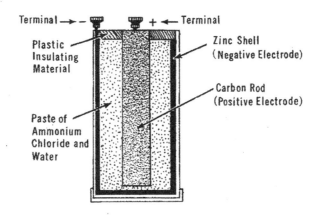

FIGURE 8. Dry Cell Battery

The dry cell works just like the voltaic cell. The zinc dissolves, and excess electrons form on the zinc can, and hydrogen ions take electrons from the carbon rod, creating a shortage of electrons on the rod. This produces a potential difference between the two points. When they are connected, electricity is produced in the connecting wire. When all of the zinc has dissolved, the cell is used up. These cells produce about one volt of electrical pressure and a small amount of electrical current.

Electrolysis

The secondary battery cell is based on another principle. When an electric current is passed through a solution of water, the process is called *electrolysis.* The results of *electrolysis* depend on the dissolved materials in the solution. If the solution is a mixture of water and sulfuric acid, electrolysis produces hydrogen at one electrode and oxygen at the other electrode. In other words, electrolysis separates water into hydrogen and oxygen molecules. If the solution contains copper sulfate, electrolysis will produce pure copper on the negative electrode. The electric current separates the dissolved materials so they have an electrical charge. They then move toward the terminal of the opposite polarity, or opposite charge.

Because electrolysis will separate dissolved materials, it is often used to place a thin metal coating on a metal base. Silver plating and chromium plating are done by electrolysis. This is called *electroplating.* Let us look at one example of the process. When electricity is passed through a solution of copper sulfate, copper ions and sulfate ions are formed. The copper ions have a positive charge; the sulfate ions have a negative charge. The positive copper ions move to the negative plate, and the negative sulfate ions move to the positive plate. This movement takes place when electric current is flowing.

Direct current must always be used for electrolysis to keep the current moving in just one direction. If the negative plate in the tank is a piece of metal, a layer of pure copper will be deposited on the plate. Because the ions of copper are pure, this is a good method for separating copper from any impurities it may contain. So electrolysis is widely used in the copper industry to produce pure metal.

The Storage Battery

The principle of electrolysis is used by the secondary cell to produce electricity. Electrolysis is made to produce a chemical change in a battery. When this chemical change is reversed, electricity is produced by the battery. Actually, the battery gives up the energy that caused the first chemical change. That is why it is often called a storage battery. It "stores" the electrical energy until its chemical process is reversed. Then it releases the energy.

How is this done? Let us take the automobile battery as an example. This is called a lead-acid battery because its main parts are lead and acid. This battery is an insulated case, containing an electrolyte and two plates. Both plates are made of the same material-lead. The electrolyte is a mixture of sulfuric acid and water.

Now, when the battery is made, both terminals are attached to lead plates. There is no potential difference between the two plates, and no electricity can be produced by the cell. Before the cell will produce electricity, it must go through electrolysis. A direct current is run through the battery. This causes a chemical change in one of the lead plates. It creates a potential difference between the two plates. This potential difference will produce electricity when the chemical re-action is reversed. Electrolysis is called *charging the battery*.

Grouping Battery Cells

A single battery cell provides a small voltage and a little current. A commercial battery usually contains several separate cells, tied together into one unit. There are various ways to tie the batteries together. Each method gives different voltage and current ratings for the battery. If all the positive terminals and all the negative terminals are tied together, the connection is called a *parallel* connection. If the positive terminal of one cell is tied to the negative terminal of the next cell, the connection is called a *series* connection. If a combination of the two eonncctions is used, it is called a *series-parallel* connection. Each method has advantages and disadvantages. In general, a parallel circuit supplies high current rating, but no increase in voltage. A series circuit supplies high voltage and low current ratings. A series-parallel circuit can combine the advantages of both types of connection.

Batteries

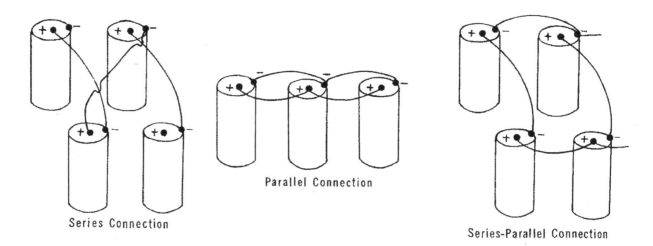

FIGURE 9. Series, Parallel, and Series-Parallel Connections.

Words Used in Unit 3

approaches (əprōch´əz), ways of getting to something
commercial (kə məer´shăl), made to be sold
electrolysis (ĭ lĕktr´ōlə sĭs), the passing of an electric current through a solution of water
ions (ī´ənz), electrically charged particles
laboratory (lăb´rə tŏ rĭ), place equipped for scientists to work
surplus (sər´pləs), amount over and above what is needed
voltaic (vŏl tā´ĭk), basic type of battery

Using Electricity

Unit 4

Electricity is energy. It can be used to do work. Electricity is probably the most convenient form of energy we have. It can be produced easily and cheaply. It can be transported from place to place rapidly and. economically. It can be changed into mechanical energy by a simple and inexpensive electric motor. Electric heat is clean and quickly produced. In many ways electricity is an ideal form of energy.

Producing Electricity

Every year the United States uses about 600 billion kilowatt-hours of electricity. One kilowatt-hour is the amount of electricity needed to burn a thousand watt bulb for one full hour. Some of our electricity is produced by converting water power into electric power. Running or falling water is used to spin a large turbine. A generator converts this spinning energy into electrical energy.

Most of the electricity used in the United States is produced by burning coal. In the last few years, we have begun to use atomic power to produce electricity. Most atomic plants use the heat energy in a nuclear reactor to produce steam. The steam is used in a turbine, and the turbine spins a large generator. The generators used to make electricity commercially are very large and heavy. The armature may weigh thousands of pounds. The coils are made of thick heavy wire. A large generator can produce thousands of amperes of electric current under a pressure of ten thousand to fifteen thousand volts.

Transporting Electricity

When electricity is transmitted for long distances, the voltage is always increased. The electricity is run through a step-up transformer. Then high voltage electricity is sent along heavy wires. This reduces the loss of energy in the transmission lines.

Electricity can also be transmitted without wires. But air has a very high resistance to electricity, and the losses are high. Wireless transmission of electric power is not yet practical. Radio waves are really electrical energy moving through air. But they must be produced at high frequencies. And the amount of energy that reaches a radio reeeiver is very small.

Long-distance electric power lines usually carry electricity at about 300,000 volts pressure. This high pressure cuts down losses. But it is too dangerous to use in the home. Three hundred thousand volts of pressure can force electricity through several inches of air, and cause an arc. This can be very dangerous. So the voltage is dropped for home use to 110 volts or 220 volts. Heavy appliances like stoves use 220 volt electricity because this reduces the relative amount of current flowing in the wires of the house. If a stove needs twenty amperes of 110 volt electricity, it needs only ten amperes of 220 volt electricity to produce the same energy. You can prove this by looking at Ohm's Law again. When the voltage is doubled, the current needed to produce the same power is cut in half. This makes for safer electrical operation.

Heating with Electricity

Electricity is produced when electrons flow through a wire. The electrons are carrying energy, and they can do work as they flow. If we place a high resistance in the path of the electrons, they will work hard to get past it. This work generates heat. This is the basic principle behind all electrical heating systems. The higher the resistance, the more work the electrons must do to pass. This produces more heat. An English physicist named Joule studied the relation between resistance and heating power in electricity. He discovered three basic laws that seem to explain what happens when we heat by electricity. The three laws are:
- ❖ The amount of heat produced is directly proportional to resistance.
  - o If one ohm of resistance in a cir- cuit produces one joule of heat, ten ohms of resistance will produce ten joules of heat. One joule is equal to 0.24 calories.

❖ The amount of heat produced is directly proportional to the time the current flows.
  o If one joule of heat is produced in one second, ten joules of heat will be produced in ten seconds.
❖ Heat produced in a circuit is directly proportional to the square of the current flowing in the circuit.
  o If two amperes of current produce four joules of heat, three amperes of current will produce nine joules of heat.

These three laws tell us that we can increase the amount of heat that is produced by an electrical circuit if we:
1. increase the resistance in the circuit.
2. increase the current in the circuit.
3. increase the time that current flows in the circuit.

Notice that an increase in current causes the greatest change in the amount of heat produced. That is why 220 volt electricity is used for heavy appliances. It reduces the current in the house wiring and reduces the amount of heat produced in the wires. This cuts down the danger of fire in the house.

Lighting
The electric light bulb was invented by an American, Thomas A. Edison. A light bulb is simply a piece of wire with a very high resistance and a high melting point which is placed inside an evacuated glass bulb. When electrons pass through the wire, they heat it white hot. The material must have a high resistance to produce the white heat. So it must have a high melting point too, or it will melt in the high temperature. Most light bulb filaments are made of tungsten wire. The filament is placed in a glass bulb, and most of the air is pumped out of the bulb. If the air remained in the bulb, the oxygen would burn the hot filament. Usually some inert gas like argon or nitrogen is placed in the bulb. This saves the filament and allows the use of higher temperatures.
Inert Gas

Filament   Inert Gas

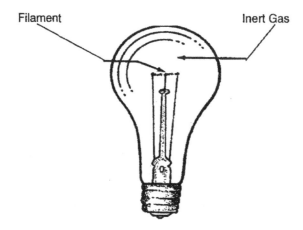

FIGURE 10. Light Bulb.

The Telegraph

Electricity travels at the speed of light --186,000 miles per second. This makes it an ideal carrier for messages. The first method of using electricity to carry messages was invented by Samuel F. B. Morse in 1837. Morse called his invention the *telegraph*. It uses the principle of an electromagnet. When an electric current flows through a coil of wire, the coil becomes a magnet, and it will attract metal. When the current is shut off, the magnet stops working. Morse used this simple principle to send his messages along electric wires.

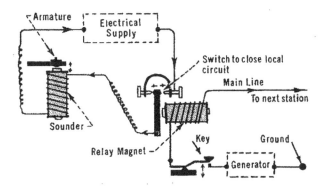

FIGURE 11. Simplified Telegraph with Key.

The main parts of a telegraph system are the key, the sounder, the wires, and a supply of electricity. These parts are shown in figure 109. When the key is pushed down, electricity flows through the wires and produces an electromagnet in the coil. This draws the sounder down with a sharp click. When the key is released, the magnet releases the sounder. By spacing the sounds made on the sounder, we can send messages. Morse also invented an alphabet made of long and short signals which is called the *Morse Code*. Using this code, we can send messages from one place to another. Of course, both the sender and the receiver must understand the Morse Oode-but it can be learned in a short time.

The old key and sounder system is not used much today. Instead, we use a machine that looks like a typewriter to send and receive messages. Each key of the machine sends a special signal along the wire. When that signal is received, the receiving machine types out the same message. These machines are called *teletype* machines. They are much faster and more accuurate than a key and sounder. They are used by the Armed Forces, police, news services, and many other organizations.

The Telephone
The telephone is more complex than the telegraph. The telegraph works by changing the *amount* of energy sent over a wire. The telephone must do more than this. First, it must change mechanical energy, produced by the voice, into electrical energy. Then the electrical energy is transmitted over a wire. Finally, the telephone must change the electrical energy back to mechanical energy that our ears can hear.

The principle that a telephone uses to change mechanical energy into electrical energy is a simple one. According to Ohm's Law, when the resistance in a circuit changes, the amount of current flowing through the circuit changes. A telephone transmitter uses the mechanical energy in sound to change the electrical resistance in a circuit. The method is quite simple.

A round disc, or diaphragm, is attached to a small box filled with carbon particles. Carbon is a resistor, and it is part of the electrical circuit of the telephone. When the sound waves strike the disc, it vibrates. This compresses the particles of carbon. As the carbon particles are pressed together, the resistance in the circuit drops. When the pressure is released, the resistance in the circuit rises. This causes changes in the current flowing in the circuit. They follow the same pattern as the vibrations of the disc

The telephone receiver must change the electrical energy carried by the electric current into mechanical energy. We cannot hear electrical waves. Our ears respond only to mechanical waves in the air. The telephone receiver uses the principle of the electromagnet. The variations in electric current produced by the transmitter cause variations in the strength of the electromagnet in the receiver.

In a telephone receiver there is a small electromagnet. This magnet holds the thin disc in place. As the strength of the magnet varies, the disc vibrates. Since the strength of the magnet is varied by the electric current produced by the vibrating disc in the transmitter, the disc in the receiver vibrates in exactly the same way. These vibrations produce mechanical sound waves exactly like those that activated the transmitter. Electrical energy is changed into mechanical energy, and our ears hear the sound coming from the receiver.

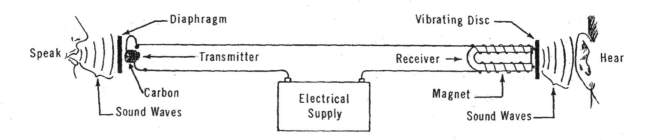

FIGURE 12 Simplified Telephone Circuit

Arc Welding

There are so many possible uses of electricity that we can cover only a very few of them. In this unit we are looking at a few nonelectronic uses of electricity. One of the most important of these uses is arc welding. In modern industry arc welding is a very important process. It is employed to build auto bodies, airplanes, and thousands of other things that we use every day.

Electric welding works on the same principle as the electric arc light. High voltage and very heavy electric currents are needed for welding. Usually this requires a special transformer and a special electric line into the building. One end of the electric line is attached to the material to be welded. The other end is run through a special tip or rod made of high resistance metal. This rod is held by the man who does the welding.

There are different kinds of welding rods for each type of welding, depending upon the material to be welded. The composition of the tip or rod determines the strength of the joint and the temperature at the arc. A skilled welder chooses the rod that will best do the particular job. When the metal rod is touched against the material to be welded, the electric circuit is closed and electric current runs through the rod. The high resistance produces a high temperature, and the material in the rod is vaporized. This produces a trail of metal vapor between the rod and the material being welded. The heavy electric current runs through this vapor arc, producing a white heat.

As in the carbon arc light, the metal tip keeps melting as electricity flows along the rod. The vaporized metal forms a solid deposit on the joint, called a "bead." The tip of the rod must be kept an even distance from the material to produce a smooth, even joint. This takes experience and a steady hand. When the metal hardens and cools, it produces a joint that is very strong. In fact, the welded part of a joint is often stronger than the metal that is joined together.

Other Uses of Electricity

Some of the special uses of electricity are often overlooked. It can be used to reduce smoke in cities, for example. If an electric device is placed inside a large chimney, it can be used to charge dirt particles as they move up the chimney. A collector higher up the chimney that has an opposite charge will collect the particles as they pass by. The amount of smoke and dirt that leaves the chimney is, thus, cut to a minimum. The collector must be emptied from time to time.

Electricity is very useful in the field of medicine. Special light bulbs are used to kill germs in hospitals. These lights produce energy of a particular frequency that is deadly to germs. Electric energy is used to provide heating for therapy machines, used to ease the pain when bones or muscles are seriously injured. There is even an electric knife that seals as it cut, thus eliminating the need for sewing. It is an excellent instrument for certain kinds of operations.

Radar and television, calculating machines, and weather satellites all come under the area of *electronics.* Yet all of these complex machines are built upon the same principles that are stated in Ohm's Law. The study of electronics is based on our study of electricity. The one great difference between electricity and electronics lies in making use of the effect that can be produced by a vacuum tube. But all electricity, whether it is passed through a vacuum tube or not, must obey the same general law.

Words Used in Unit 4

economically (ē kə nŏm´ĭk lĭ), inexpensively
evacuated (ĭ văk´ū ăt əd), emptied
filament (fil´ə mənt) , the wire in a light bulb
inert (ĭn ərt´) , not active
reduces (rĭ dūs´əs), makes less
transformer (trăns form´ər), an apparatus for increasing or decreasing voltage
vaporized (vă´pər ĭzd) , changed into vapor, or a gas
welded (wĕld´əd), joined together by pressing while soft and hot

———

BASIC ELECTRICITY

FUNDAMENTAL CONCEPTS OF ELECTRICITY
What is Electricity?

The word "electric" is actually a Greek-derived word meaning AMBER. Amber is a translucent (semitransparent) yellowish mineral, which, in the natural form, is composed of fossilized resin. The ancient Greeks used the words "electric force" in referring to the mysterious forces of attraction and repulsion exhibited by amber when it was rubbed with a cloth. They did not understand the fundamental nature of this force. They could not answer the seemingly simple question, "What is electricity?". This question is still unanswered. Though you might define electricity as "that force which moves electrons," this would be the same as defining an engine as "that force which moves an automobile." You would have described the effect, not the force.

We presently know little more than the ancient Greeks knew about the fundamental nature of electricity, but tremendous strides have been made in harnessing and using it. Elaborate theories concerning the nature and behavior of electricity have been advanced, and have gained wide acceptance because of their apparent truth and demonstrated workability.

From time to time various scientists have found that electricity seems to behave in a constant and predictable manner in given situations, or when subjected to given conditions. These scientists, such as Faraday, Ohm, Lenz, and Kirchhoff, to name only a few, observed and described the predictable characteristics of electricity and electric current in the form of certain rules. These rules are often referred to as "laws." Thus, though electricity itself has never been clearly defined, its predictable nature and easily used form of energy has made it one of the most widely used power sources in modern time. By learning the rules, or laws, applying to the behavior of electricity, and by learning the methods of producing, controlling, and using it, you will have "learned" electricity without ever having determined its fundamental identity.

THE MOLECULE

One of the oldest, and probably the most generally accepted, theories concerning electric current flow is that it is comprised of moving electrons. This is the ELECTRON THEORY. Electrons are extremely tiny parts, or particles, of matter. To study the electron, you must therefore study the structural nature of matter itself. (Anything having mass and inertia, and which occupies any amount of space, is composed of matter.) To study the fundamental structure or composition of any type of matter, it must be reduced to its fundamental fractions. Assume the drop of water in figure 1-1 (A) was halved again and again. By continuing the process long enough, you would eventually obtain the smallest particle of water possible-the molecule. All molecules are composed of atoms.

A molecule of water (H_2O) is composed of one atom of oxygen and two atoms of hydrogen, as represented in figure 1-1 (B). If the molecule of water were further subdivided, there would remain only unrelated atoms of oxygen and hydrogen, and the water would no longer exist as such. This example illustrates the following fact-the molecule is the smallest particle to which a substance can be reduced and still be called by the same name. This applies to all substances-liquids, solids, and gases.

When whole molecules are combined or separated from one another, the change is generally referred to as a PHYSICAL change. In a CHEMICAL change the molecules of the substance are altered such that

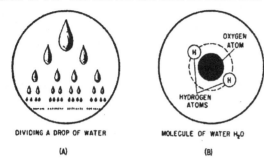

Figure 1-1.—Matter is made up of molecules.
new molecules result. Most chemical changes Involve positive and negative ions and thus are electrical in nature. All matter is said to be essentially electrical in nature.

THE ATOM

In the study of chemistry it soon becomes apparent that the molecule is far from being the ultimate particle into which matter may be subdivided. The salt molecule may be decomposed into radically different substancessodium and chlorine. These particles that make up molecules can be isolated and studied separately. They are called ATOMS.

The atom is the smallest particle that makes up that type of material called an ELEMENT. The element retains its characteristics when subdivided into atoms. More than 100 elements have been identified. They can be arranged into a table of increasing weight, and can be grouped into families of material having similar properties. This arrangement is called the PERIODIC TABLE OF THE ELEMENTS.

The idea that all matter is composed of atoms dates back more than 2,000 years to the Greeks. Many centuries passedbefore the study of matter proved that the basic idea of atomic structure was correct. Physicists have explored the interior of the atom and discovered many subdivisions in it. The core of the atom is called the NUCLEUS. Most of the mass of the atom is concentrated in the nucleus. It is comparable to the sun in the solar system, around which the planets revolve. The nucleus contains PROTONS (positively charged particles) and NEUTRONS which are electrically neutral.

Most of the weight of the atom is in the protons and neutrons of the nucleus. Whirling around the nucleus are one or more smaller particles of negative electric charge. THESE ARE THE ELECTRONS. Normally there is one proton for each electron in the entire atom so that the net positive charge of the nucleus is balanced by the net negative charge of the electrons whirling around the nucleus. THUS THE ATOM IS ELECTRICALLY NEUTRAL.

The electrons do not fall into the nucleus even though they are attracted strongly to it. Their motion prevents it, as the planets are prevented from falling into the sun because of their centrifugal force of revolution.

The number of protons, which is usually the same as the number of electrons, determines the kind of element in question. Figure 1-2 shows a simplified picture of several atoms of different materials based on the conception of planetary electrons describing orbits about the nucleus. For example, hydrogen has a nucleus consisting of 1 proton, around which rotates 1 electron. The helium atom has a nucleus containing 2 protons and 2 neutrons with 2 electrons encircling the nucleus. Near the other extreme of the list of elements is curium (not shown in the figure), an element discovered in the 1940's, which has 96 protons and 96 electrons in each atom.

The *Periodic Table of the Elements* is an orderly arrangement of the elements in ascending atomic number (number of planetary electrons) and also in atomic weight (number of protons and neutrons in the nucleus). The various kinds of atoms have distinct masses or

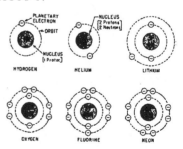

Figure 1-2.—Atomic structure of elements.

weights with respect to each other. The element most closely approaching unity (meaning 1) is hydrogen whose atomic weight is 1.008 as compared with oxygen whose atomic weight is 16. Helium has an atomic weight of approximately 4, lithium 7, fluorine 19, and neon 20, as shown in figure 1-2.

Figure 1-3 is a pictorial summation of the discussion that has just been presented. Visible matter, at the left of the figure, is broken down first to one of its basic molecules, then to one of the molecule's atoms. The atom is then further reduced to its subatomic particlesthe protons, neutrons, and electrons. Subatomic particles are electric in nature. That is, they are the particles of matter most affected by an electric force. Whereas the whole molecule or a whole atom is electrically neutral, most subatomic particles are not neutral (with the exception of the neutron). Protons are inherently positive, and electrons are inherently negative. It is these inherent characteristics which make subatomic particles sensitive to electric force.

When an electric force is applied to a conducting medium, such as copper wire, electrons in the outer orbits of the copper atoms are forced out of orbit and impelled along the wire. The direction of electron movement is determined by the direction of the impelling force. The protons do not move, mainly because they are extremely heavy. The proton of the lightest element, hydrogen, is approximately 1,850 times as heavy as an electron. Thus, it is the relatively light electron that is most readily moved by electricity.

When an orbital electron is removed from an atom it is called a FREE ELECTRON. Some of the electrons of certain metallic atoms are so loosely bound to the nucleus that they are comparatively free to move from atom to atom. Thus, a very small force or amount of energy will cause such electrons to be removed from the atom and become free electrons. It is these free electrons that constitute the flow of an electric current in electrical conductors.

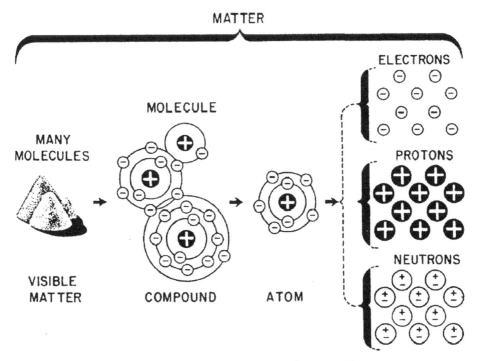

Figure 1-3.—Breakdown of visible matter to electric particles.

If the internal energy of an atom is raised above its normal state, the atom is said to be EXCITED. Excitation may be produced by causing the atoms to collide with particles that are impelled by an electric force. In this way, energy is transferred from the electric source to the atom. The excess energy absorbed by an atom may become sufficient to cause loosely bound outer electrons to leave the atom against the force that acts to hold them within. An atom that has thus lost or gained one or more electrons is said to be IONIZED. If the atom loses electrons it becomes positively charged and is referred to as a POSITIVE ION. Conversely, if the atom gains electrons, it becomes negatively charged and is referred to as a NEGATIVE ION. Actually then, an ion is a small particle of matter having a positive or negative charge.

Conductors and Insulators

Substances that permit the free motion of a large number of electrons are called CONDUCTORS. Copper wire is considered a good conductor because it has many free electrons. Electrical energy is transferred through conductors by means of the movement of free electrons that migrate from atom to atom inside the conductor. Each electron moves a very short distance to the neighboring atom where it replaces one or more electrons by forcing them out of their orbits. The replaced electrons repeat the process in other nearby atoms until the movement is transmitted throughout the entire length of the conductor. The greater the number of electrons that can be made to move in a material under the application of a given force the better are the conductive qualities of that material. A good conductor is said to have a low opposition or low resistance to the current (electron) flow.

In contrast to good conductors, some substances such as rubber, glass, and dry wood have very few free electrons. In these materials large amounts of energy must be expended in order to break the electrons loose from the influence of the nucleus. Substances containing very few free electrons are called POOR CONDUCTORS, NON-CONDUCTORS, or INSULATORS. Actually, there is no sharp dividing line between conductors and insulators, since electron motion is known to exist to some extent in all matter. Electricians simply use the best conductors as wires to carry current and the poorest conductors as insulators to prevent the current from being diverted from the wires.

Listed below are some of the best conductors and best insulators arranged in accordance with their respective abilities to conduct or to resist the flow of electrons.

Conductors	Insulators
Silver	Dry air
Copper	Glass
Aluminum	Mica
Zinc	Rubber
Brass	Asbestos
Iron	Bakelite

Static Electricity

In a natural, or neutral state, each atom in a body of matter will have the proper number of electrons in orbit around it. Consequently, the whole body of matter comprised of the neutral atoms will also be electrically neutral. In this state, it is said to have a "zero charge," and will neither attract nor repel other matter in its vicinity. Electrons will neither leave nor enter the neutrally charged body should it come in contact with other neutral bodies. If, however, any number of electrons are removed from the atoms of a body of matter, there will remain more protons than electrons, and the whole body of matter will become electrically positive. Should the positively charged body come in contact with another body having a normal charge, or having a negative (too many electrons) charge, an electric current will flow between them. Electrons will leave the more negative body and enter the positive body. This electron flow will continue until both bodies have equal charges.

When two bodies of matter have unequal charges, and are near one another, an electric force is exerted between them because of their unequal charges. However, since they are not in contact, their charges cannot equalize. The existence of such an electric force, where current cannot flow, is referred to as static electricity. "Static" means "not moving." This is also referred to as an ELECTROSTATIC FORCE.

One of the easiest ways to create a static charge is by the friction method. With the friction method, two pieces of matter are rubbed together and electrons are "wiped off" one onto the other. If materials that are good conductors are used, it is quite difficult to obtain a detectable charge on either. The reason for this is that equalizing currents will flow easily in and between the conducting materials. These currents equalize the charges almost as fast as they are created. A static charge is easier to obtain by rubbing a hard nonconducting material against a soft, or fluffy, nonconductor. Electrons are rubbed off one material and onto the other material. This is illustrated in figure 1-4.

When the hard rubber rod is rubbed in the fur, the rod accumulates electrons. Since both fur and rubber are poor conductors, little equalizing current can flow, and an electrostatic charge is built up. When the charge is great enough, equalizing currents will flow in spite of the material's poor conductivity. These currents will cause visible sparks, if viewed in darkness, and will produce a crackling sound.

CHARGED BODIES

One of the fundamental laws of electricity is that LIKE CHARGES REPEL EACH OTHER and UNLIKE CHARGES ATTRACT EACH OTHER. A positive charge and negative charge, being unlike, tend to move toward each other. In the atom the negative electrons are drawn toward the positive protons in the nucleus. This attractive force is balanced by the electron's centrifugal force caused by its rotation about the nucleus. As a result, the electrons remain in orbit and are not drawn into the nucleus. Electrons repel each other because of their like negative charges, and protons repel each other because of their like positive charges.

The law of charged bodies may be demonstrated by a simple experiment. Two pith (paper pulp) balls are suspended near one another by threads, as shown in figure 1-5.

If the hard rubber rod is rubbed to give it a negative charge, and then held against the right-hand ball in part (A), the rod will impart a negative charge to the ball. The right-hand ball will be charged negative with respect to the left-hand ball. When released, the two balls will be drawn together, as shown in figure 1-5 (A). They will touch and remain in contact until the left-hand ball acquires a portion of the negative charge of the right-hand ball, at which time they will swing apart as shown in figure 1-5 (C). If positive charges are placed on both balls (fig. 1-5 (B)), the balls will also be repelled from each other.

COULOMB'S LAW OF CHARGES

The amount of attracting or repelling force which acts between two electrically charged bodies in free space depends on two things(1) their charges, and (2) the distance between them. The relationship of charge and distance to electrostatic force was first discovered and written by a French scientist named Charles A. Coulomb. Coulomb's Law states that CHARGED BODIES ATTRACT OR REPEL EACH OTHER WITH A FORCE THAT IS DIRECTLY PROPORTIONAL TO THE PRODUCT OF THEIR CHARGES, AND IS INVERSELY PROPORTIONAL TO THE SQUARE OF THE DISTANCE BETWEEN THEM.

ELECTRIC FIELDS

The space between and around charged bodies in which their influence is felt is called an ELECTRIC FIELD OF FORCE. The electric field is always terminated on material objects and extends between positive and negative charges. It can exist in air, glass, paper, or a vacuum. ELECTROSTATIC FIELDS and DIELECTRIC FIELDS are other names used to refer to this region of force.

Fields of force spread out in the space surrounding their point of origin and, in general, DIMINISH IN PROPORTION TO THE SQUARE OF THE DISTANCE FROM THEIR SOURCE.

The field about a charged body is generally represented by lines which are

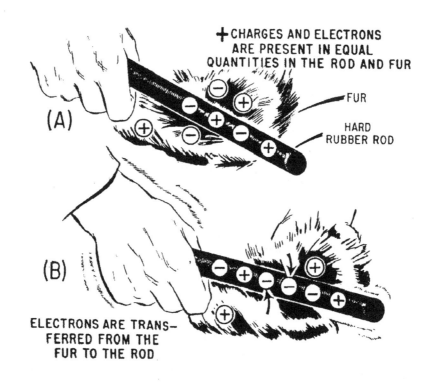

Figure 1-4.—Producing static electricity by friction.

7

referred to as ELECTROSTATIC LINES OF FORCE. These lines are imaginary and are used merely to represent the direction and strength of the field. To avoid confusion, the lines of force exerted by a positive charge are always shown leaving the charge, and for a negative charge they are shown as entering. Figure 1-6 illustrates the use of

lines to represent the field about charged bodies.

Figure 1-6 (A) represents the repulsion of like-charged bodies and their associated fields. Part (B) represents the attraction between unlike-charged bodies and their associated fields.

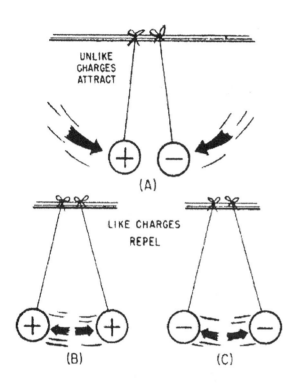

Figure 1-5.—Reaction between charged bodies.

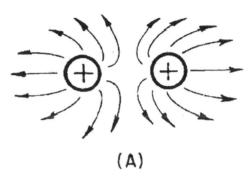

(A)

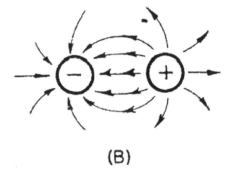

(B)

Figure 1-6.—Electrostatic lines of force.

201

Magnetism

A substance is said to be a magnet if it has the property of magnetism-that is, if it has the power to attract such substances as iron, steel, nickel, or cobalt, which are known as MAGNETIC MATERIALS. A steel knitting needle, magnetized by a method to be described later, exhibits two points of maximum attraction (one at each end) and no attraction at its center. The points of maximum attraction are called MAGNETIC POLES. All magnets have at least two poles. If the needle is suspended by its middle so that it rotates freely in a horizontal plane about its center, the needle comes to rest in an approximately north-south line of direction. The same pole will always point to the north, and the other will always point toward the south. The magnetic pole that points northward is called the NORTH POLE, and the other the SOUTH POLE.

A MAGNETIC FIELD exists around a simple bar magnet. The field consists of imaginary lines along which a MAGNETIC FORCE acts. These lines emanate from the north pole of the magnet, and enter the south pole, returning to the north pole through the magnet itself, thus forming closed loops.

A MAGNETIC CIRCUIT is a complete path through which magnetic lines of force may be established under the influence of a magnetizing force. Most magnetic circuits are composed largely of magnetic materials in order to contain the magnetic flux. These circuits are similar to the ELECTRIC CIRCUIT, which is a complete path through which current is caused to flow under the influence of an electromotive force.

Magnets may be conveniently divided into three groups.

1. NATURAL MAGNETS, found in the natural state in the form of a mineral called magnetite.

2. PERMANENT MAGNETS, bars of hardened steel (or some form of alloy such as alnico) that have been permanently magnetized.

3. ELECTROMAGNETS, composed of soft-iron cores around which are wound coils of insulated wire. When an electric current flows through the coil, the core becomes magnetized. When the current ceases to flow, the core loses most of its magnetism.

Permanent magnets and electromagnets are sometimes called ARTIFICIAL MAGNETS to further distinguish them from natural magnets.

NATURAL MAGNETS

For many centuries it has been known that certain stones (magnetite, Fe_3O_4) have the ability to attract small pieces of iron. Because many of the best of these stones (natural magnets) were found near Magnesia in Asia Minor, the Greeks called the substance MAGNETITE, or MAGNETIC.

Before this, ancient Chinese observed that when similar stones were suspended freely, or floated on a light substance in a container of water, they tended to assume a nearly north-and-south position. Probably Chinese navigators used bits of magnetite floating on wood in a liquid-filled vessel as crude compasses. At that time it was not known that the earth itself acts like a magnet, and these stones were regarded with considerable superstitious awe. Because bits of this substance were used as compasses they were called LOADSTONES (or lodestones), which means "leading stones."

Natural magnets are also found in the United States, Norway, and Sweden. A natural magnet, demonstrating the attractive force at the poles, is shown in figure 1-7 (A).

ARTIFICIAL MAGNETS

Natural magnets no longer have any practical value because more powerful and more conveniently shaped permanent magnets can be produced artificially. Commercial magnets are made from special steels and alloysfor example, alnico, made principally of aluminum, nickel, and cobalt. The name is derived from the first two letters of the three principal elements of which it is composed. An artificial magnet is shown in figure 1-7 (B).

An iron, steel, or alloy bar can be magnetized by inserting the bar into a coil of insulated wire and passing a heavy direct current through the coil, as shown in figure 1-8 (A). This aspect of magnetism is

Artificial magnets may be classified as "permanent" or "temporary" depending on their ability to retain their magnetic strength after the magnetizing force has been removed. Hardened steel and certain alloys are relatively difficult to magnetize and are said to have a LOW PERMEABILITY because the magnetic lines of force do not easily permeate, or distribute themselves readily through the steel. Once magnetized, however, these materials retain a large part of their magnetic strength and are called PERMANENT MAGNETS. Permanent magnets are used extensively in electric instruments, meters, telephone receivers, permanent-magnet loudspeakers, andmagnetos. Conversely, substances

(A)
NATURAL

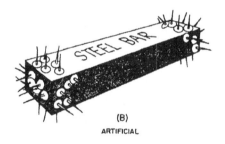

(B)
ARTIFICIAL

Figure 1-7.–(A) Natural magnet; (B) artificial magnet.

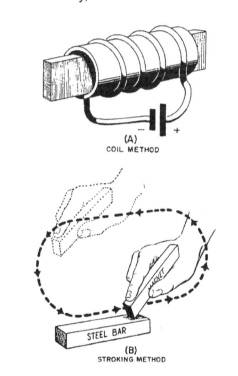

Figure 1-8.Methods of producing artificial magnets.

treated later in the chapter. The same bar may also be magnetized if it is stroked with a bar magnet, as shown in figure 1-8 (B). It will then have the same magnetic property that the magnet used to induce the magnetism-has namely, there will be two poles of attraction, one at either end. This process produces a permanent magnet by INDUCTION-that is, the magnetism is induced in the bar by the influence of the stroking magnet.

that are relatively easy to magnetizesuch as soft iron and annealed silicon steelare said to have a HIGH PERMEABILITY. Such substances retain only a small part of their magnetism after the magnetizing force is removed and are called TEMPORARY MAGNETS. Silicon steel and similar materials are used in transformers where the magnetism is constantly changing and in generators and motors where the strengths of the fields can be readily changed.

The magnetism that remains in a temporary magnet after the magnetizing force is removed is called RESIDUAL MAGNETISM. The fact that temporary magnets retain even a small amount of magnetism is an important factor in the buildup of voltage in self-excited d-c generators.

NATURE OF MAGNETISM

Weber's theory of the nature of magnetism is based on the assumption that each of the molecules of a magnet is itself a tiny magnet. The molecular magnets that compose an unmagne-tized bar of iron or steel are arranged at random, as shown by the simplified diagram of figure 1-9 (A). With this arrangement, the magnetism of each of the molecules is neutralized by that of adjacent molecules, and no external magnetic effect is produced. When a magnetizing force is applied to an unmagnetized iron or steel bar, the molecules become alined so that the north poles point one way and the south poles point the other way, as shown in figure 1-9 (B).

same. If this breaking process could be continued, smaller and smaller pieces would retain their magnetism until each part was reduced to a molecule. It is therefore logical to assume that each of these molecules is a magnet.

A further justification for this assumption results from the fact that when a bar magnet is held out of alinement with the earth's field and is repeatedly jarred, heated, or exposed to a powerful alternating field, the molecular alinement is disarranged and the magnet becomes demagnetized. For example, electric measuring instruments become inaccurate if their permanent magnets lose some of their magnetism because of severe jarring or exposure to opposing magnetic fields.

A theory of magnetism that is perhaps more adequate than the MOLECULAR theory is the DOMAIN theory. Much simplified, this theory may be stated as follows:

In magnetic substances the "atomic" magnets, produced by the movement of the planetary electrons around the nucleus, have a strong tendency to line up together in groups of from 10^{14} to 10^{15} atoms. This occurs without the influence of any external magnetic field. These groups of atoms having their poles orientated in the same direction are called DOMAINS. Therefore,

 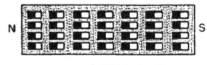

UNMAGNETIZED STEEL (A)   MAGNETIZED STEEL (B)

Figure 1-9.—Molecular theory of magnetism.

If a bar magnet is broken into several parts, as in figure 1-10, each part constitutes a magnet. The north and south poles of these small magnets are in the same respective directions as those of the original magnet. If each of these parts is again broken, the resulting parts are likewise magnets, and the magnetic orientation is the

throughout each domain an intense magnetic field is produced. These fields are normally in a miscellaneous arrangement so that no external field is apparent when the substance as a whole is unmagnetized. Each tiny domain (10^6 of them may be contained in 1 cubic millimeter) is always magnetized to saturation, and the addition of an external magnetic field does not increase the inherent magnetism of the individual domains.

However, if an external field that is gradually increased in strength is applied to the magnetic substance the domains will line up one by one (or perhaps several at a time) with the external field.

MAGNETIC FIELDS AND LINES OF FORCE

If a bar magnet is dipped into iron filings, many of the filings are attracted to the ends of the magnet, but none are attracted to the center of the magnet. As mentioned previously, the ends of the magnet where the attractive force is the greatest are called the POLES of the magnet. By using a compass, the line of direction of the magnetic force at various points near the magnet may be observed. The compass needle itself is a magnet. The north end of the compass needle always points toward the south pole, S, as shown in figure 1-11 (A), and thus the sense of direction (with respect to the polarity of the bar magnet) is also indicated. At the center, the compass needle points in a direction that is parallel to the bar magnet.

When the compass is placed successively at several points in the vicinity of the bar magnet the compass needle alines itself with the field at each position. The direction of the field is indicated by the arrows and represents the direction in which the north pole of the compass needle will point when the compass is placed in this field. Such a line along which a compass needle alines itself is called a MAGNETIC LINE OF FORCE. As mentioned previously, the magnetic lines of force are assumed to emanate from the north pole of a magnet, pass through the surrounding space, and enter

the south pole. The lines of force then pass from the south pole to the north pole inside the magnet to form a closed loop. Each line of force forms an independent closed loop and does not merge with or cross other lines of force. The lines of force between the poles of a horseshoe magnet are shown in figure 1-11 (B).

The space surrounding a magnet, in which the magnetic force acts, is called a MAGNETIC FIELD. Michael Faraday was the first scientist to visualize the magnet field as being in a state of stress and consisting of uniformly distributed lines of force. The entire quantity of magnetic lines surrounding a magnet is called MAGNETIC FLUX. Flux in a magnetic circuit corresponds to current in an electric circuit.

The number of lines of force per unit area is called FLUX DENSITY and is measured in lines per square inch or lines per square centimeter. Flux density is expressed by the equation

$$B = \frac{\phi}{A}$$

where B is the flux density, ϕ (Greek phi) is the total number of lines of flux, and A is the cross-sectional area of the magnetic circuit. If A is in square centimeters, B is in lines per square centimeter, or GAUSS. The terms FLUX and FLOW of magnetism are frequently used in textbooks. However, magnetism itself is not thought to be a stream of particles in motion, but is simply a field of force exerted in space. A visual representation pf the magnetic field around a magnet can be obtained by placing a plate of glass over a magnet and sprinkling iron filings onto

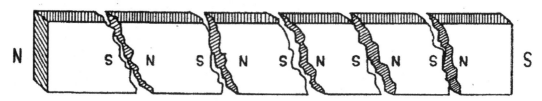

Figure 1-10.—Magnetic poles of a broken magnet.

the glass. The filings arrange themselves in definite paths between the poles.

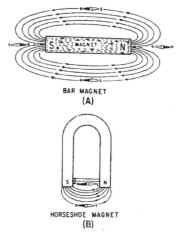

BAR MAGNET
(A)

HORSESHOE MAGNET
(B)

Figure 1-11.—Magnetic lines of force.

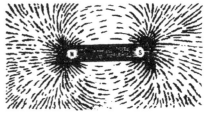

Figure 1-12.—Magnetic field pattern around a magnet.

This arrangement of the filings shows the pattern of the magnetic field around the magnet, as in figure 1-12.

The magnetic field surrounding a symmetrically shaped magnet has the following properties:

1. The field is symmetrical unless disturbed by another magnetic substance.

2. The lines of force have direction and are represented as emanating from the north pole and entering the south pole.

LAWS OF ATTRACTION AND REPULSION

If a magnetized needle is suspended near a bar magnet, as in figure 1-13, it will be seen that a north pole repels a north pole and a south pole repels a south pole. Opposite poles, however, will attract each other.

Thus, the first two laws of magnetic attraction and repulsion are:

1. LIKE magnetic poles REPEL each other.

2. UNLIKE magnetic poles ATTRACT each other.

The flux patterns between adjacent UNLIKE poles of bar magnets, as indicated by lines, are shown in figure 1-14 (A). Similar patterns for adjacent LIKE poles are shown in figure 1-14 (B). The lines do not cross at any point and they act as if they repel each other.

Figure 1-15 shows the flux pattern (indicated by lines) around two bar magnets placed close together and parallel with each other. Figure 1-15 (A) shows the flux pattern when opposite poles are adjacent; and figure 1-15 (B) shows the flux pattern when like poles are adjacent.

The THIRD LAW of magnetic attraction and repulsion states in effect that the force of attraction or repulsion existing between two magnetic poles decreases rapidly as the poles are separated from each other. Actually, the force of attraction or repulsion varies directly as the product of the separate pole strengths and inversely as the square of the distance separating the magnetic poles, provided the poles are small enough to be considered as points. For example, if the distance between two north poles is increased from 2 feet to 4 feet, the force of

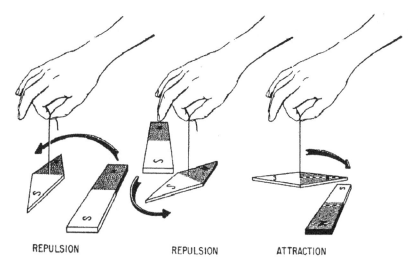

REPULSION   REPULSION   ATTRACTION

Figure 1-13.—Laws of attraction and repulsion.

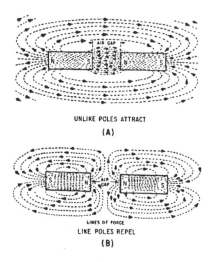

UNLIKE POLES ATTRACT
(A)

LINES OF FORCE
LIKE POLES REPEL
(B)

Figure 1-14.—Lines of force between unlike and like poles.

end of the axis of rotation of the earth. The magnetic axis does not coincide with the geographic axis, and therefore the magnetic and geographic poles are not at the same place on the surface of the earth.

The early users of the compass regarded the end of the compass needle that points in a northerly direction as being a north pole. The other end was regarded as a south pole. On some maps the magnetic pole of the earth towards which the north pole of the compass pointed was designated a north magnetic pole. This magnetic pole was obviously called a north pole because of its proximity to the north geographic pole.

repulsion between them is decreased to one-fourth of its original value. If either pole strength is doubled, the distance remaining the same, the force between the poles will be doubled.

THE EARTH'S MAGNETISM

As has been stated, the earth is a huge magnet; and surrounding the earth is the magnetic field produced by the earth's magnetism. The magnetic polarities of the earth are as indicated in figure 1-16. The geographic poles are also shown at each

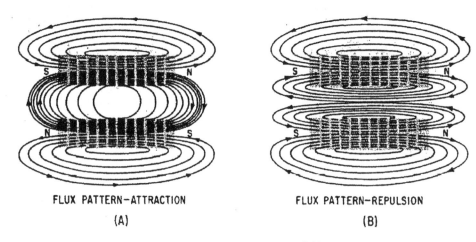

FLUX PATTERN—ATTRACTION
(A)

FLUX PATTERN—REPULSION
(B)

Figure 1-15.—Flux patterns of adjacent parallel bar magnets.

When it was learned that the earth is a magnet and that opposite poles attract, it was necessary to call the magnetic pole located in the northern hemisphere a SOUTH MAGNETIC POLE and the magnetic pole located in the southern hemisphere a NORTH MAGNETIC POLE. The matter of naming the poles was arbitrary. Obviously, the polarity of the compass needle that points toward the north must be opposite to the polarity of the earth's magnetic pole located there.

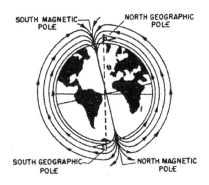

Figure 1-16.—Earth's magnetic poles.

As has been stated, magnetic lines of force are assumed to emanate from the north pole of a magnet and to enter the south pole as closed loops. Because the earth is a magnet, lines of force emanate

from its north magnetic pole and enter the south magnetic pole as closed loops. The compass needle alines itself in such a way that the earth's lines of force enter at its south pole and leave at its north pole. Because the north pole of the needle is defined as the end that points in a northerly direction it follows that the magnetic pole in the vicinity of the north geographic pole is in reality a south magnetic pole, and vice versa.

Because the magnetic poles and the geographic poles do not coincide, a compass will not (except at certain positions on the earth) point in a true (geographic) north-south direction-that is, it will not point in a line of direction that passes through the north and south geographic poles, but in a line of direction that makes an angle with it. This angle is called the angle of VARIATION OR DECLINATION.

MAGNETIC SHIELDING

There is not a known INSULATOR for magnetic flux. If a nonmagnetic material is placed in a magnetic field, there is no appreciable change in flux-that is, the flux penetrates the nonmagnetic material. For example, a glass plate placed between the poles of a horseshoe magnet will have no appreciable effect on the field although glass itself is a good insulator in an electric circuit. If a magnetic material (for example, soft iron) is placed in a magnetic field, the flux may be redirected to take advantage of the greater permeability of the magnetic material as shown in figure 1-17. Permeability is the quality of a substance which determines the ease with which it can be magnetized.

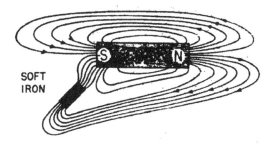

Figure 1-17.—Effects of a magnetic substance in a magnetic field.

The sensitive mechanism of electric instruments and meters can be influenced by stray magnetic fields which will cause errors in their readings. Because instrument mechanisms cannot be insulated against magnetic flux, it is necessary to employ some means of directing the flux around the instrument. This is accomplished by placing a soft-iron case, called a MAGNETIC SCREEN OR SHIELD, about the instrument. Because the flux *is* established more readily through the iron (even though the path is longer) than through the air inside the case, the instrument is effectively shielded, as shown by the watch and soft-iron shield in figure 1-18.

The study of electricity and magnetism, and how they affect each other, is given more thorough coverage in later chapters of this course.

The discussion of magnetism up to this point has been mainly intended to clarify terms and meanings, such as "polarity," "fields," "lines of force," and so forth. Only one fundamental relationship between magnetism and electricity is discussed in this chapter. This relationship pertains to magnetism as used to generate a voltage and it is discussed under the headings that follows.

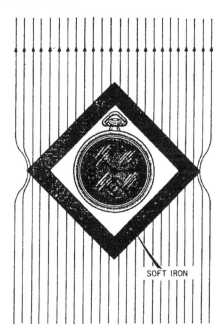

Figure 1-18.—Magnetic shield.

Difference in Potential

The force that causes free electrons to move in a conductor as an electric current is called (1) an electromotive force (e.m.f.), (2) a voltage, or (3) a difference in potential. When a difference in potential exists between two charged bodies that are connected by a conductor, electrons will flow along the conductor. This flow will be from the negatively charged body to the positively

charged body until the two charges are equalized and the potential difference no longer exists.

An analogy of this action is shown in the two water tanks connected by a pipe and valve in figure 1-19. At first the valve is closed and all the water is in tank A. Thus, the water pressure across the valve is at maximum. When the valve is opened, the water flows through the pipe from A to B until the water level becomes the same in both tanks. The water then stops flowing in the pipe, because there is no longer a difference in water pressure between the two tanks.

Current flow through an electric circuit is directly proportional to the difference in potential across the circuit, just as the flow of water through the pipe in figure 1-19 is directly proportional to the difference in water level in the two tanks.

A fundamental law of current electricity is that the CURRENT IS DIRECTLY PROPORTIONAL TO THE APPLIED VOLT-AGE.

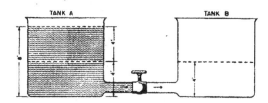

Figure 1-19.—Water analogy of electric difference in potential.

Primary Methods of Producing a Voltage

Presently, there are six commonly used methods of producing a voltage. Some of these methods are much more widely used than others. The methods of utilizing each source will be discussed, and their most common applications will be included. The following is a list of the six most common methods of producing a voltage.

1. FRICTION.-Voltage produced by rubbing two materials together.

2. PRESSURE (Piezoelectricity).- Voltage produced by squeezing crystals of certain substances.

3. HEAT (Thermoelectricity).-Voltage produced by heating the joint (junction) where two unlike metals are joined.

4. LIGHT (Photoelectricity).-Voltage produced by light striking photosensitive (light sensitive) substances.

5. CHEMICAL ACTION.-Voltage produced by chemical reaction in a battery cell.

6. MAGNETISM.-Voltage produced in a conductor when the conductor moves through a magnetic field, or a magnetic field moves through the conductor in such a manner as to cut the magnetic lines of force of the field.

VOLTAGE PRODUCED BY FRICTION

This is the least used of the six methods of producing voltages. Its main application is in Van de Graf generators, used by some laboratories to produce high voltages. As a rule, friction electricity (often referred to as static electricity) is a nuisance. For instance, a flying aircraft accumulates electric charges from the friction between its skin and the passing air.

These charges often interfere with radio communication, and under some circumstances can even cause physical damage to the aircraft. You have probably received unpleasant shocks from friction electricity upon sliding across dry seat covers or walking across dry carpets, and then coming in contact with some other object.

VOLTAGE PRODUCED BY PRESSURE

This action is referred to as piezoelectricity. It is produced by compressing or decompressing crystals of certain substances. To study this form of electricity, you must first understand the meaning of the word "crystal." In a crystal, the molecules are arranged in an orderly and uniform manner. A substance in its crystallized state and in its noncrystallized state is shown in figure 1-20.

For the sake of simplicity, assume that the molecules of this particular substance are spherical (ball-shaped). In the noncrystallized state, in part (A), note that the molecules are arranged irregularly. In the crystallized state, part (B), the molecules are arranged in a regular and uniform manner. This illustrates the major physical difference between crystal and noncrystal forms of matter. Natural crystalline matter is rare; an example of matter that is crystalline in its natural form is diamond, which is crystalline carbon. Most crystals are manufactured.

Crystals of certain substances, such as Rochelle salt or quartz, exhibit peculiar electrical characteristics. These characteristics, or effects, are referred to as "piezoelectric." For instance, when a crystal of quartz is compressed, as in figure 1-20 (C), electrons tend

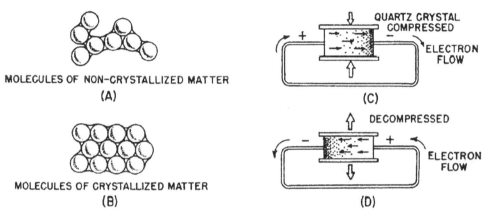

Figure 1-20.—(A) Noncrystallized structure, (B) crystallized structure, (C) compression of a crystal, (D) decompression of a crystal.

to move through the crystal as shown. This tendency creates an electric difference of potential between the two opposite faces of the crystal. (The fundamental reasons for this action are not known. However, the action is predictable, and therefore useful.) If an external wire is connected while the pressure and e.m.f. are present, electrons will flow. If the pressure is held constant, the electron flow will continue until the charges are equalized. When the force is removed, the crystal is decompressed, and immediately causes an electric force in the opposite direction, as shown in part (D). Thus, the crystal is able to convert mechanical force, either pressure or tension, to electrical force.

The power capacity of a crystal is extremely small. However, they are useful because of their extreme sensitivity to changes of mechanical force or changes in temperature. Due to other characteristics not mentioned here, crystals are most widely used in radio communication equipment. The more complicated study of crystals, as they are used for practical applications, is left for those courses that pertain to the special ratings concerned with them.

VOLTAGE PRODUCED BY HEAT

When a length of metal, such as copper, is heated at one end, electrons tend to move away from the hot end toward the cooler end. This is true of most metals. However, in some metals, such as iron, the opposite takes place and electrons tend to move TOWARD the hot end. These characteristics are illustrated in figure 1-21. The negative charges (electrons) are moving through the copper away from the heat and through the iron toward the heat. They cross from the iron to the copper at the hot junction, and from the copper through the current meter to the iron at the cold junction. This device is generally referred to as a thermocouple.

Thermocouples have somewhat greater power capacities than crystals, but their capacity is still very small if compared to some other sources. The thermoelectric voltage in a thermocouple depends mainly on the difference in temperature between the hot and cold junctions. Consequently, they are widely used to measure temperature, and as heat-sensing devices in automatic temperature control equipment. Thermocouples generally can be subjected to much greater temperatures than ordinary thermometers, such as the mercury or alcohol types.

VOLTAGE PRODUCED BY LIGHT

When light strikes the surface of a substance, it may dislodge electrons from their orbits around the surface atoms of the substance. This occurs because light has energy, the same as any moving force.

Some substances, mostly metallic ones, are far more sensitive to light than others. That is, more electrons will be dislodged and emitted from the surface of a highly sensitive metal, with a given amount of light, than will be emitted from a less sensitive

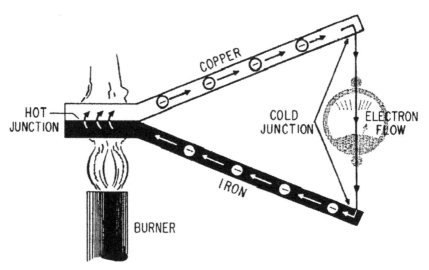

Figure 1-21.—Voltage produced by heat.

substance. Upon losing electrons, the photosensitive (light sensitive) metal becomes positively charged, and an electric force is created. Voltage produced in this manner is referred to as "a photoelectric voltage."

The photosensitive materials most commonly used to produce a photoelectric voltage are various compounds of silver oxide or copper oxide. A complete device which operates on the photoelectric principle is referred to as a "photoelectric cell." There are many sizes and types of photoelectric cells in use, each of which serves the special purpose for which it was designed. Nearly all, however, have some of the basic

features of the photoelectric cells shown in figure 1-22.

The cell shown in part (A) has a curved light-sensitive surface focused on the central anode. When light from the direction shown strikes the sensitive surface, it emits electrons toward the anode. The more intense the light, the greater is the number of electrons emitted. When a wire is connected between the filament and the back, or dark side, the accumulated electrons will flow to the dark side. These electrons will eventually

19

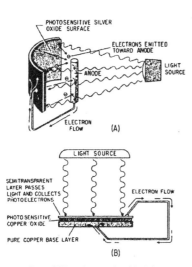

Figure 1-22.—Voltage produced by light.

pass through the metal of the reflector and replace the electrons leaving the light-sensitive surface. Thus, light energy is converted to a flow of electrons, and a usable current is developed.

The cell shown in part (B) is constructed in layers. A base plate of pure copper is coated with light-sensitive copper oxide. An additional layer of metal is put over

the copper oxide. This additional layer serves two purposes:

1. It is EXTREMELY thin to permit the penetration of light to the copper oxide.

2. It also accumulates the electrons emitted by the copper oxide.

An externally connected wire completes the electron path, the same as in the reflector type cell. The photocell's voltage is utilized as needed by connecting the external wires to some other device, which amplifies (enlarges) it to a usable level.

A photocell's power capacity is very small. However, it reacts to light-intensity variations in an extremely short time. This characteristic makes the photocell very useful in detecting or accurately controlling a great number of processes or operations. For instance, the photoelectric cell, or some form of the photoelectric principle, is used in television cameras, automatic manufacturing process controls, door openers, burglar alarms, and so forth.

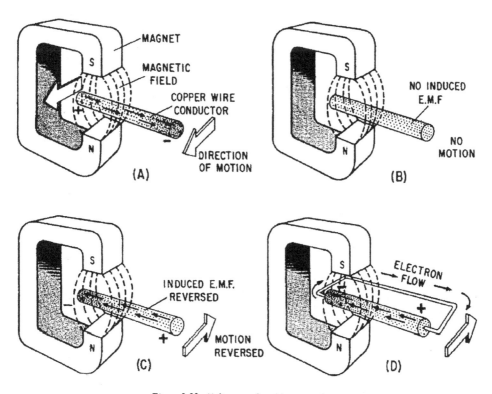

Figure 1-23.—Voltage produced by magnetism.

VOLTAGE PRODUCED BY CHEMICAL ACTION

Up to this point, it has been shown that electrons may be removed from their parent atoms and set in motion by energy derived from a source of friction, pressure, heat, or light. In general, these forms of energy do not alter the molecules of the substances being acted upon. That is, molecules are not usually added, taken away, or split-up when subjected to these four forms of energy. Only electrons are involved. When the molecules of a substance are altered, the action is referred to as CHEMICAL. For instance, if the molecules of a substance combines with atoms of another substance, or gives up atoms of its own, the action is chemical in nature. Such action always changes the , chemical name and characteristics of the substance affected. For instance, when atoms of oxygen from the air come in contact with bare iron, they merge with the molecules of iron. This iron is "oxidized." It has changed chemically from iron to iron oxide, or "rust." Its molecules have been altered by chemical action.

In some cases, when atoms are added to or taken away from the molecules of a substance, the chemical change will cause the substance to take on an electric charge. The process of producing a voltage by chemical action is used in batteries and is explained in chapter 2.

VOLTAGE PRODUCED BY MAGNETISM

Magnets or magnetic devices are used for thousands of different jobs. One of the most useful and widely employed applications of magnets is in the production of vast quantities of electric power from mechanical sources. The mechanical power may be provided by a number of different sources, such as gasoline or diesel engines, and water or steam turbines. However, the final conversion of these source energies to electricity is done by generators employing the principle of electromagnetic induction. These generators, of many types and sizes, are discussed in later chapters of this course. The important subject to be discussed here is the fundamental operating principle of ALL such electromagnetic-induction generators.

To begin with, there are three fundamental conditions which must exist before a voltage can be produced by magnetism. You should learn them well, because they will be encountered again and again. They are:

1. There must be a CONDUCTOR, in which the voltage will be produced.

2. There must be a MAGNETIC FIELD in the conductor's vicinity.

3. There must be relative motion between the field and the conductor. The conductor must be moved so as to cut across the magnetic lines of force, or the field must be moved so that the lines of force are cut by the conductor.

In accordance with these conditions, when a conductor or conductors MOVE ACROSS a magnetic field so as to cut the lines of force, electrons WITHIN THE CONDUCTOR are impelled in one direction or another. Thus, an electric force, or voltage, is created.

In figure 1-23, note the presence of the three conditions needed for creating an induced voltage:

1. A magnetic field exists between the poles of the C-shaped magnet.

2. There is a conductor (copper wire).

3. There is relative motion. The wire is moved back and forth ACROSS the magnetic field.

In part (A) the conductor is moving TOWARD you. This occurs because of the magnetically induced electromotive force (e.m.f.) acting on the electrons in the copper. The right-hand end becomes negative, and the left-hand end positive. In part (B) the conductor is stopped. This eliminates motion, one of the three required conditions, and there is no longer an induced e.m.f. Consequently, there is no longer any difference in potential between the two ends of the wire. In part (C) the conductor is moving AWAY from you. An induced e.m.f. is again created. However, note carefully that the REVERSAL OF MOTION has caused a REVERSAL OF DIRECTION in the induced e.m.f.

If a path for electron flow is provided between the ends of the conductor, elec-

trons will leave the negative end and flow to the positive end. This condition is shown in part (D). Electron flow will continue as long as the e.m.f. exists. In studying figure 1-23, it should be noted that the induced e.m.f. could also have been created by holding the conductor stationary and moving the magnetic field back and forth.

In later chapters of this course, under the heading "Generators," you will study the more complex aspects of power generation by use of mechanical motion and magnetism.

Electric Current

The drift or flow of electrons through a conductor is called ELECTRIC CURRENT. In order to determine the amount (number) of electrons flowing in a given conductor, it is necessary to adopt a unit of measurement of current flow. The term AMPERE is used to define the unit of measurement of the rate at which current flows (electron flow). The symbol for the ampere is I. One ampere may be defined as the fow of 6.28×10^{18} electrons per second past a fixed point in a conductor

A unit quantity of electricity is moved through an electric circuit when one ampere of current flows for one second of time. This unit is equivalent to 6.28×10^{18} electrons, and is called the COULOMB. The coulomb is to electricity as the gallon is to water. The symbol for the coulomb is Q. The rate of flow of current in amperes and the quantity of electricity moved through a circuit are related by the common factor of time. Thus,

the quantity of electric charge, in coulombs, electricity moved through a circuit are is equal to the product of the current in amperes, I, and the duration of flow in seconds, t. Expressed as an equation, $Q = It$.

For example, if a current of 2 amperes flows through a circuit for 10 seconds the quantity of electricity moved through the circuit is 2 x 10, or 20 coulombs. Conversely, current flow may be expressed in terms of coulombs and time in seconds. Thus, if 20 coulombs are moved through a circuit in 10 seconds, the average current flow is 20/10, or 2 amperes. Note that the current flow in amperes implies the rate of flow of coulombs per second without indicating either coulombs or seconds. Thus a current flow of 2 amperes is equivalent to a rate of flow of 2 coulombs per second.

Resistance

Every material offers some resistance, or opposition, to the flow of electric cur rent through it. Good conductors, such as copper, silver, and aluminum, offer very little resistance. Poor conductors, or insulators, such as glass, wood, and paper, offer a high resistance to current flow.

The size and type of material of the wires in an electric circuit are chosen so as to keep the electrical resistance as low as possible. In this way, current can flow easily through the conductors, just as water flows through the pipe between the tanks in figure 1-19. If the water pressure remains constant the flow of water in the pipe will depend on how far the valve is opened. The smaller the opening, the greater the opposition to the flow, and the smaller will be the rate of flow in gallons per second.

In the electric circuit, the larger the diameter of the wires, the lower will be their electrical resistance (opposition) to the flow of current through them. In the water analogy, pipe friction opposes the flow of water between the tanks. This friction is similar to electrical resistance. The resistance of the pipe to the flow of water through it depends upon (1) the length of the pipe, (2) the diameter of the pipe, and (3) the nature of the inside walls (rough or smooth). Similarly, the electrical resistance of the conductors depends upon (1) the length of the wires, (2) the diameter of the wires, and (3) the material of the wires (copper, aluminum, etc.).

Temperature also affects the resistance of electrical conductors to some extent. In most conductors (copper, aluminum, iron, etc.) the resistance increases with temperature. Carbon is an exception. In carbon the resistance decreases as temperature increases. Certain alloys of metals (manganin and constantan) have resistance that does not change appreciably with temperature.

The relative resistance of several conductors of the same length and cross section is given in the following list with silver as a standard of 1 and the remaining metals arranged in an order of ascending resistance:

Silver...............	1.0
Copper.............	1.08
Gold...............	1.4
Aluminum............	1.8
Platinum.............	7.0
Lead..............	13.5

The resistance in an electrical circuit is expressed by the symbol R. Manufactured circuit parts containing definite amounts of resistance are called RESISTORS. Resistance (R) is measured in OHMS. One ohm is the resistance of a circuit element, or circuit, that permits a steady current of 1 ampere (1 coulomb per second) to flow when a steady e.m.f. of 1 volt is applied to the circuit.

ELECTRICAL TERMS AND FORMULAS

CONTENTS

217

ELECTRICAL TERMS AND FORMULAS

Terms

AGONIC.—An imaginary line of the earth's surface passing through points where the magnetic declination is 0°; that is, points where the compass points to true north.

AMMETER.—An instrument for measuring the amount of electron flow in amperes.

AMPERE.—The basic unit of electrical current.

AMPERE-TURN.—The magnetizing force produced by a current of one ampere flowing through a coil of one turn.

AMPLIDYNE.—A rotary magnetic or dynamo-electric amplifier used in servomechanism and control applications.

AMPLIFICATION.—The process of increasing the strength (current, power, or voltage) of a signal.

AMPLIFIER.—A device used to increase the signal voltage, current, or power, generally composed of a vacuum tube and associated circuit called a stage. It may contain several stages in order to obtain a desired gain.

AMPLITUDE.—The maximum instantaneous value of an alternating voltage or current, measured in either the positive or negative direction.

ARC.—A flash caused by an electric current ionizing a gas or vapor.

ARMATURE.—The rotating part of an electric motor or generator. The moving part of a relay or vibrator.

ATTENUATOR.—A network of resistors used to reduce voltage, current, or power delivered to a load.

AUTOTRANSFORMER.—A transformer in which the primary and secondary are connected together in one winding.

BATTERY.—Two or more primary or secondary cells connected together electrically. The term does not apply to a single cell.

BREAKER POINTS.—Metal contacts that open and close a circuit at timed intervals.

BRIDGE CIRCUIT.—The electrical bridge circuit is a term referring to any one of a variety of electric circuit networks, one branch of which, the "bridge" proper, connects two points of equal potential and hence carries no current when the circuit is properly adjusted or balanced.

BRUSH.—The conducting material, usually a block of carbon, bearing against the commutator or sliprings through which the current flows in or out.

BUS BAR.—A primary power distribution point connected to the main power source.

CAPACITOR.—Two electrodes or sets of electrodes in the form of plates, separated from each other by an insulating material called the dielectric.

CHOKE COIL.—A coil of low ohmic resistance and high impedance to alternating current.

CIRCUIT.—The complete path of an electric current.

CIRCUIT BREAKER.—An electromagnetic or thermal device that opens a circuit when the current in the circuit exceeds a predetermined amount. Circuit breakers can be reset.

CIRCULAR MIL.—An area equal to that of a circle with a diameter of 0.001 inch. It is used for measuring the cross section of wires.

COAXIAL CABLE.—A transmission line consisting of two conductors concentric with and insulated from each other.

COMMUTATOR.—The copper segments on the armature of a motor or generator. It is cylindrical in shape and is used to pass power into or from the brushes. It is a switching device.

CONDUCTANCE.—The ability of a material to conduct or carry an electric current. It is the reciprocal of the resistance of the material, and is expressed in mhos.

CONDUCTIVITY.—The ease with which a substance transmits electricity.

CONDUCTOR.—Any material suitable for carrying electric current.

CORE.—A magnetic material that affords an easy path for magnetic flux lines in a coil.

COUNTER E.M.F.—Counter electromotive force; an e.m.f. induced in a coil or armature that opposes the applied voltage.

CURRENT LIMITER.—A protective device similar to a fuse, usually used in high amperage circuits.

CYCLE.—One complete positive and one complete negative alternation of a current or voltage.

DIELECTRIC.—An insulator; a term that refers to the insulating material between the plates of a capacitor.

DIODE.--Vacuum tube--a two element tube that contains a cathode and plate; semiconductor --a material of either germanium or silicon that is manufactured to allow current to flow in only one direction. Diodes are used as rectifiers and detectors.

DIRECT CURRENT.--An electric current that flows in one direction only.

EDDY CURRENT.--Induced circulating currents in a conducting material that are caused by a varying magnetic field.

EFFICIENCY.--The ratio of output power to input power, generally expressed as a percentage.

ELECTROLYTE.--A solution of a substance which is capable of conducting electricity. An electrolyte may be in the form of either a liquid or a paste.

ELECTROMAGNET.--A magnet made by passing current through a coil of wire wound on a soft iron core.

ELECTROMOTIVE FORCE (e.m.f.).--The force that produces an electric current in a circuit.

ELECTRON.--A negatively charged particle of matter.

ENERGY.--The ability or capacity to do work.

FARAD.--The unit of capacitance.

FEEDBACK.--A transfer of energy from the output circuit of a device back to its input.

FIELD.--The space containing electric or magnetic lines of force.

FIELD WINDING.--The coil used to provide the magnetizing force in motors and generators.

FLUX FIELD.--All electric or magnetic lines of force in a given region.

FREE ELECTRONS.--Electrons which are loosely held and consequently tend to move at random among the atoms of the material.

FREQUENCY.--The number of complete cycles per second existing in any form of wave motion; such as the number of cycles per second of an alternating current.

FULL-WAVE RECTIFIER CIRCUIT.--A circuit which utilizes both the positive and the negative alternations of an alternating current to produce a direct current.

FUSE.--A protective device inserted in series with a circuit. It contains a metal that will melt or break when current is increased beyond a specific value for a definite period of time.

GAIN.--The ratio of the output power, voltage, or current to the input power, voltage, or current, respectively.

GALVANOMETER.--An instrument used to measure small d-c currents.

GENERATOR.--A machine that converts mechanical energy into electrical energy.

GROUND.--A metallic connection with the earth to establish ground potential. Also, a common return to a point of zero potential. The chassis of a receiver or a transmitter is sometimes the common return, and therefore the ground of the unit.

HENRY.--The basic unit of inductance.

HORSEPOWER.--The English unit of power, equal to work done at the rate of 550 foot-pounds per second. Equal to 746 watts of electrical power.

HYSTERESIS.--A lagging of the magnetic flux in a magnetic material behind the magnetizing force which is producing it.

IMPEDANCE.--The total opposition offered to the flow of an alternating current. It may consist of any combination of resistance, inductive reactance, and capacitive reactance.

INDUCTANCE.--The property of a circuit which tends to oppose a change in the existing current.

INDUCTION.--The act or process of producing voltage by the relative motion of a magnetic field across a conductor.

INDUCTIVE REACTANCE.--The opposition to the flow of alternating or pulsating current caused by the inductance of a circuit. It is measured in ohms.

INPHASE.--Applied to the condition that exists when two waves of the same frequency pass through their maximum and minimum values of like polarity at the same instant.

INVERSELY.--Inverted or reversed in position or relationship.

ISOGONIC LINE.--An imaginary line drawn through points on the earth's surface where the magnetic deviation is equal.

JOULE.--A unit of energy or work. A joule of energy is liberated by one ampere flowing for one second through a resistance of one ohm.

KILO.--A prefix meaning 1,000.

LAG.--The amount one wave is behind another in time; expressed in electrical degrees.

LAMINATED CORE.--A core built up from thin sheets of metal and used in transformers and relays.

LEAD.--The opposite of LAG. Also, a wire or connection.

ELECTRICAL TERMS AND FORMULAS

LINE OF FORCE.—A line in an electric or magnetic field that shows the direction of the force.

LOAD.—The power that is being delivered by any power producing device. The equipment that uses the power from the power producing device.

MAGNETIC AMPLIFIER.—A saturable reactor type device that is used in a circuit to amplify or control.

MAGNETIC CIRCUIT.—The complete path of magnetic lines of force.

MAGNETIC FIELD.—The space in which a magnetic force exists.

MAGNETIC FLUX.—The total number of lines of force issuing from a pole of a magnet.

MAGNETIZE.—To convert a material into a magnet by causing the molecules to rearrange.

MAGNETO.—A generator which produces alternating current and has a permanent magnet as its field.

MEGGER.—A test instrument used to measure insulation resistance and other high resistances. It is a portable hand operated d-c generator used as an ohmmeter.

MEGOHM.—A million ohms.

MICRO.—A prefix meaning one-millionth.

MILLI.—A prefix meaning one-thousandth.

MILLIAMMETER.—An ammeter that measures current in thousandths of an ampere.

MOTOR-GENERATOR.—A motor and a generator with a common shaft used to convert line voltages to other voltages or frequencies.

MUTUAL INDUCTANCE.—A circuit property existing when the relative position of two inductors causes the magnetic lines of force from one to link with the turns of the other.

NEGATIVE CHARGE.—The electrical charge carried by a body which has an excess of electrons.

NEUTRON.—A particle having the weight of a proton but carrying no electric charge. It is located in the nucleus of an atom.

NUCLEUS.—The central part of an atom that is mainly comprised of protons and neutrons. It is the part of the atom that has the most mass.

NULL.—Zero.

OHM.—The unit of electrical resistance.

OHMMETER.—An instrument for directly measuring resistance in ohms.

OVERLOAD.—A load greater than the rated load of an electrical device.

PERMALLOY.—An alloy of nickel and iron having an abnormally high magnetic permeability.

PERMEABILITY.—A measure of the ease with which magnetic lines of force can flow through a material as compared to air.

PHASE DIFFERENCE.—The time in electrical degrees by which one wave leads or lags another.

POLARITY.—The character of having magnetic poles, or electric charges.

POLE.—The section of a magnet where the flux lines are concentrated; also where they enter and leave the magnet. An electrode of a battery.

POLYPHASE.—A circuit that utilizes more than one phase of alternating current.

POSITIVE CHARGE.—The electrical charge carried by a body which has become deficient in electrons.

POTENTIAL.—The amount of charge held by a body as compared to another point or body. Usually measured in volts.

POTENTIOMETER.—A variable voltage divider; a resistor which has a variable contact arm so that any portion of the potential applied between its ends may be selected.

POWER.—The rate of doing work or the rate of expending energy. The unit of electrical power is the watt.

POWER FACTOR.—The ratio of the actual power of an alternating or pulsating current, as measured by a wattmeter, to the apparent power, as indicated by ammeter and voltmeter readings. The power factor of an inductor, capacitor, or insulator is an expression of their losses.

PRIME MOVER.—The source of mechanical power used to drive the rotor of a generator.

PROTON.—A positively charged particle in the nucleus of an atom.

RATIO.—The value obtained by dividing one number by another, indicating their relative proportions.

REACTANCE.—The opposition offered to the flow of an alternating current by the inductance, capacitance, or both, in any circuit.

RECTIFIERS.—Devices used to change alternating current to unidirectional current. These may be vacuum tubes, semiconductors such as germanium and silicon, and dry-disk rectifiers such as selenium and copper-oxide.

RELAY.—An electromechanical switching device that can be used as a remote control.

RELUCTANCE.—A measure of the opposition that a material offers to magnetic lines of force.

RESISTANCE.—The opposition to the flow of current caused by the nature and physical dimensions of a conductor.

RESISTOR.—A circuit element whose chief characteristic is resistance; used to oppose the flow of current.

4

RETENTIVITY.—The measure of the ability of a material to hold its magnetism.

RHEOSTAT.—A variable resistor.

SATURABLE REACTOR.—A control device that uses a small d-c current to control a large a-c current by controlling core flux density.

SATURATION.—The condition existing in any circuit when an increase in the driving signal produces no further change in the resultant effect.

SELF-INDUCTION.—The process by which a circuit induces an e.m.f. into itself by its own magnetic field.

SERIES-WOUND.—A motor or generator in which the armature is wired in series with the field winding.

SERVO.—A device used to convert a small movement into one of greater movement or force.

SERVOMECHANISM.—A closed-loop system that produces a force to position an object in accordance with the information that originates at the input.

SOLENOID.—An electromagnetic coil that contains a movable plunger.

SPACE CHARGE.—The cloud of electrons existing in the space between the cathode and plate in a vacuum tube, formed by the electrons emitted from the cathode in excess of those immediately attracted to the plate.

SPECIFIC GRAVITY—The ratio between the density of a substance and that of pure water, at a given temperature.

SYNCHROSCOPE—An instrument used to indicate a difference in frequency between two a-c sources.

SYNCHRO SYSTEM.—An electrical system that gives remote indications or control by means of self-synchronizing motors.

TACHOMETER.—An instrument for indicating revolutions per minute.

TERTIARY WINDING.—A third winding on a transformer or magnetic amplifier that is used as a second control winding.

THERMISTOR.—A resistor that is used to compensate for temperature variations in a circuit.

THERMOCOUPLE.—A junction of two dissimilar metals that produces a voltage when heated.

TORQUE.—The turning effort or twist which a shaft sustains when transmitting power.

TRANSFORMER.—A device composed of two or more coils, linked by magnetic lines of force, used to transfer energy from one circuit to another.

TRANSMISSION LINES.—Any conductor or system of conductors used to carry electrical energy from its source to a load.

VARS.—Abbreviation for volt-ampere, reactive.

VECTOR.—A line used to represent both direction and magnitude.

VOLT.—The unit of electrical potential.

VOLTMETER.—An instrument designed to measure a difference in electrical potential, in volts.

WATT.—The unit of electrical power.

WATTMETER.—An instrument for measuring electrical power in watts.

Formulas

Ohm's Law for d-c Circuits

$$I = \frac{E}{R} = \frac{P}{E} = \sqrt{\frac{P}{R}}$$

$$R = \frac{E}{I} = \frac{P}{I^2} = \frac{E^2}{P}$$

$$E = IR = \frac{P}{I} = \sqrt{PR}$$

$$P = EI = \frac{E^2}{R} = I^2R$$

Resistors in Series

$$R_T = R_1 + R_2 \cdots$$

Resistors in Parallel
Two resistors

$$R_T = \frac{R_1 R_2}{R_1 + R_2}$$

More than two

$$\frac{1}{R_T} = \frac{1}{R_1} + \frac{1}{R_2} + \frac{1}{R_3}$$

ELECTRICAL TERMS AND FORMULAS

R-L Circuit Time Constant equals

$$\frac{L \text{ (in henrys)}}{R \text{ (in ohms)}} = t \text{ (in seconds), or}$$

$$\frac{L \text{ (in microhenrys)}}{R \text{ (in ohms)}} = t \text{ (in microseconds)}$$

R-C Circuit Time Constant equals

R (ohms) X C (farads) $= t$ (seconds)

R (megohms) x C (microfarads) $= t$ (seconds)

R (ohms) x C (microfarads) $= t$ (microseconds)

R (megohms) x C (micromicrofrads $= t$ (microseconds)

Comparison of Units in Electric and Magnetic Circuits.

	Electric circuit	Magnetic circuit
Force	Volt, E or e.m.f.	Gilberts, F, or m.m.f.
Flow	Ampere, I	Flux, Φ, in maxwells
Opposition	Ohms, R	Reluctance, R
Law	Ohm's law, $I = \dfrac{E}{R}$	Rowland's law $\Phi = \dfrac{F}{R}$
Intensity of force	Volts per cm. of length	$H = \dfrac{1.257IN}{L}$, gilberts per centimeter of length
Density	Current density— for example, amperes per cm^2.	Flux density—for example, lines per cm^2., or gausses

Capacitors in Series
Two capacitors

$$C_T = \frac{C_1 C_2}{C_1 + C_2}$$

More than two

$$\frac{1}{C_T} = \frac{1}{C_1} + \frac{1}{C_2} + \frac{1}{C_3}\cdots$$

Capacitors in Parallel

$$C_T = C_1 + C_2 \cdots$$

Capacitive Reactance

$$X_c = \frac{1}{2\pi f C}$$

Impedance in an R-C Circuit (Series)

$$Z = \sqrt{R^2 + X_c^2}$$

Inductors in Series

$$L_T = L_1 + L_2 \ldots \text{ (No coupling between coils)}$$

Inductors in Parallel
Two inductors

$$L_T = \frac{L_1 L_2}{L_1 + L_2} \text{ (No coupling between coils)}$$

More than two

$$\frac{1}{L_T} = \frac{1}{L_1} + \frac{1}{L_2} + \frac{1}{L_3} \ldots \text{ (No coupling between coils)}$$

Inductive Reactance

$$X_L = 2\pi f L$$

Q of a Coil

$$Q = \frac{X_L}{R}$$

Impedance of an R-L Circuit (series)

$$Z = \sqrt{R^2 + X_L^2}$$

Impedance with R, C, and L in Series

$$Z = \sqrt{R^2 + (X_L - X_C)^2}$$

Parallel Circuit Impedance

$$Z = \frac{Z_1 Z_2}{Z_1 + Z_2}$$

Sine-Wave Voltage Relationships
Average value

$$E_{ave} = \frac{2}{\pi} \times E_{max} = 0.637 E_{max}$$

ELECTRICAL TERMS AND FORMULAS

Effective or r.m.s. value

$$E_{eff} = \frac{E_{max}}{\sqrt{2}} = \frac{E_{max}}{1.414} = 0.707 E_{max} = 1.11 E_{ave}$$

Maximum value

$$E_{max} = \sqrt{2} E_{eff} = 1.414 E_{eff} = 1.57 E_{ave}$$

Voltage in an a-c circuit

$$E = IZ = \frac{P}{I \times P.F.}$$

Current in an a-c circuit

$$I = \frac{E}{Z} = \frac{P}{E \times P.F.}$$

Power in A-C Circuit
Apparent power $= EI$
True power

$$P = EI \cos \theta = EI \times P.F.$$

Power factor

$$P.F. = \frac{P}{EI} = \cos \theta$$

$$\cos \theta = \frac{true\ power}{apparent\ power}$$

Transformers
Voltage relationship

$$\frac{E}{E} = \frac{N}{N} \text{ or } E = E \times \frac{N}{N}$$

Current relationship

$$\frac{I_p}{I_s} = \frac{N_s}{N_p}$$

Induced voltage

$$E_{eff} = 4.44\, BAfN\, 10^{-8}$$

Turns ratio equals

$$\frac{N_p}{N_s} = \sqrt{\frac{Z_p}{Z_s}}$$

Secondary current

$$I_s = I_p \frac{N_p}{N_s}$$

Secondary voltage

$$E_s = E_p \frac{N_s}{N_p}$$

Three Phase Voltage and Current Relationships
With wye connected windings

$$E_{line} = 1.732 E_{coil} = \sqrt{3} E_{coil}$$

$$I_{line} = I_{coil}$$

With delta connected windings

$$E_{line} = E_{coil}$$

$$I_{line} = 1.732 I_{coil}$$

With wye or delta connected winding

$$P_{coil} = E_{coil} I_{coil}$$

$$P_t = 3 P_{coil}$$

$$P_t = 1.732 E_{line} I_{line}$$

(To convert to true power multiply by $\cos \theta$)

Synchronous Speed of Motor

$$r.p.m. = \frac{120 \times frequency}{number\ of\ poles}$$

GREEK ALPHABET

Name	Capital	Lower Case	Designates
Alpha	A	α	Angles.
Beta	B	β	Angles, flux density.
Gamma . . .	Γ	γ	Conductivity.
Delta	Δ	δ	Variation of a quantity, increment.
Epsilon . . .	E	ε	Base of natural logarithms (2.71828).
Zeta	Z	ζ	Impedance, coefficients, coordinates.
Eta	H	η	Hysteresis coefficient, efficiency, magnetizing force.
Theta	Θ	θ	Phase angle.
Iota	I	ι	
Kappa	K	κ	Dielectric constant, coupling coefficient, susceptibility.
Lambda . . .	Λ	λ	Wavelength.
Mu	M	μ	Permeability, micro, amplification factor.
Nu	N	ν	Reluctivity.
Xi	Ξ	ξ	
Omicron . . .	O	ο	
Pi	Π	π	3.1416
Rho	P	ρ	Resistivity.
Sigma	Σ	σ	
Tau	T	τ	Time constant, time-phase displacement.
Upsilon . . .	Υ	υ	
Phi	Φ	φ	Angles, magnetic flux.
Chi	X	χ	
Psi	Ψ	ψ	Dielectric flux, phase difference.
Omega	Ω	ω	Ohms (capital), angular velocity (2 π f).

COMMON ABBREVIATIONS AND LETTER SYMBOLS

Term	Abbreviation or Symbol
alternating current (noun)	a.c.
alternating-current (adj.)	a-c
ampere	a.
area	A
audiofrequency (noun)	AF
audiofrequency (adj.)	A-F
capacitance	C
capacitive reactance	X_C
centimeter	cm.
conductance	G
coulomb	Q
counterelectromotive force	c.e.m.f.
current (d-c or r.m.s. value)	I
current (instantaneous value)	i
cycles per second	c.p.s.
dielectric constant	K,k
difference in potential (d-c or r.m.s. value)	E
difference in potential (instantaneous value)	e
direct current (noun)	d.c.
direct-current (adj.)	d-c
electromotive force	e.m.f.
frequency	f
henry	h.
horsepower	hp.
impedance	Z
inductance	L
inductive reactance	X_L
kilovolt	kv.
kilovolt-ampere	kv.-a.
kilowatt	kw.
kilowatt-hour	kw.-hr.
magnetic field intensity	H
magnetomotive force	m.m.f.
megohm	M
microampere	μ a.
microfarad	μ f.
microhenry	μ h.
micromicrofarad	$\mu\mu$ f.
microvolt	μ v.
milliampere	ma.
millihenry	mh.
milliwatt	mw.
mutual inductance	M
power	P
resistance	R
revolutions per minute	r.p.m.
root mean square	r.m.s.
time	t
torque	T
volt	v.
watt	w.

Made in the USA
Las Vegas, NV
04 May 2023

71527070R00142